Frontiersmen

Warfare and History

General Editor
Jeremy Black
Professor of History, University of Exeter

Published

Forthcoming titles include:

Frontiersmen:
Warfare in Africa since 1950

Anthony Clayton

De Montfort University

First published in 1999 by UCL Press

UCL Press Limited
1 Gunpowder Square
London EC4A 3DE
UK

and

325 Chestnut Street
8th Floor
Philadelphia
PA 19106
USA

The name of University College London (UCL) is a registered trade
mark used by UCL Press with the consent of the owner.

British Library Cataloguing-in-Publication Data
A CIP catalogue record for this book is available from the British Library.

Library of Congress Cataloging-in-Publication Data are available

ISBN: 1-85728-524-7 HB
1-85728-525-5 PB

Typeset by Best-set Typesetter Ltd., Hong Kong.
Printed by T.J. International, Padstow, UK.

For the fundamental question, the root of all politics, all arts is what do men live by? What makes them tick and keep ticking, and if you answer love and hate, curiosity, ambition, duty and pride, you are already deep, whether you like it or not, in metaphysics . . . It is a revelation of character to see how angrily good-natured men, who regard themselves as completely reasonable beings, will fight about some question of politics (the materialist dialectic) or science (just now it has been once more evolution) upon premises which ignore the ground of the whole discussion — in politics, human nature, or in evolution the will to live.

The attraction of Africa is that it shows these wars of belief, and the powerful often subconscious motives which underlie them, in the greatest variety, and also in very simple forms. Basic obsessions, which in Europe hide themselves under all sorts of decorous scientific or theological or political uniforms, are there seen naked in bold and dramatic action.

Joyce Cary, *The African Witch*
(London: Michael Joseph, 1951 edition), p. 10.

For my father-in-law, Peter, and Nan

Contents

Maps

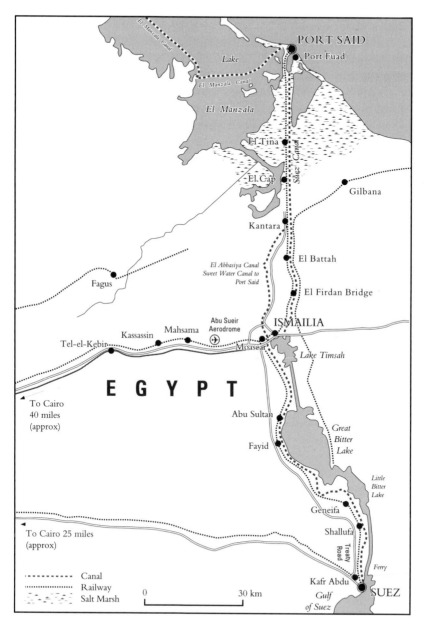

1 Egypt: the Suez Canal Zone

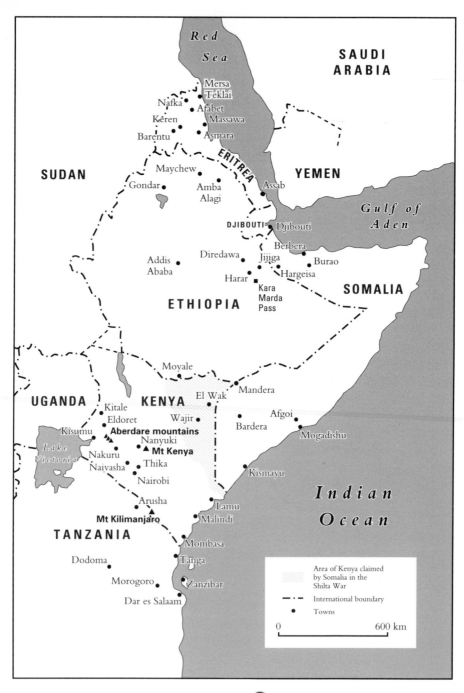

2 Eastern Africa

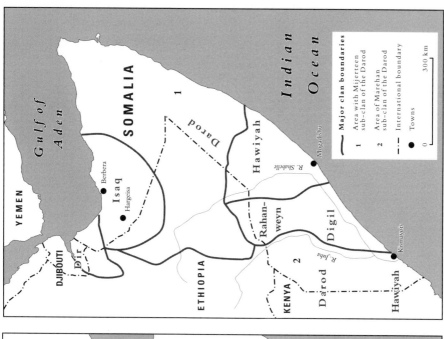

2b Somalia: major clan areas

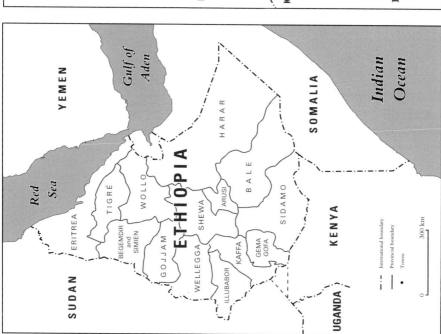

2a Ethiopia: provinces

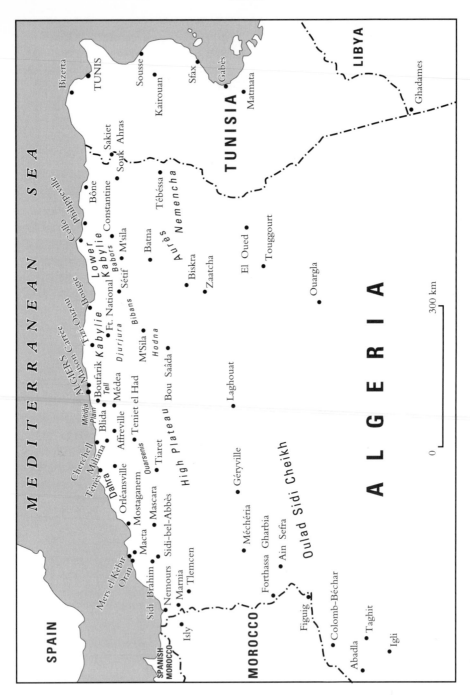

3 Algeria

4 Angola

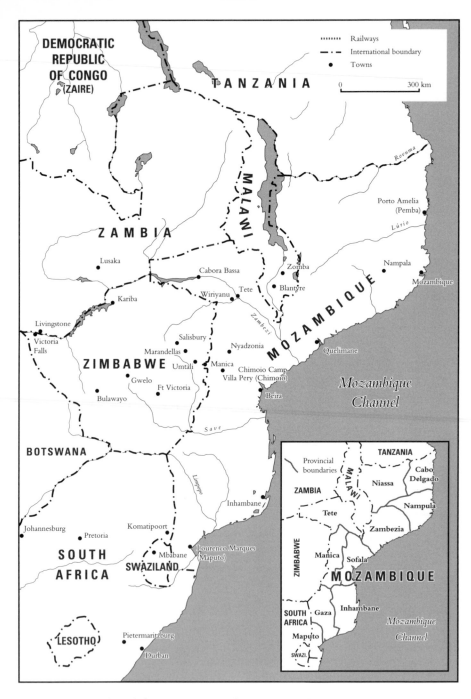

5 Mozambique and Zimbabwe (inset: Mozambique provinces)

6 West Africa: Senegal, Guinea, Sierra Leone and Liberia

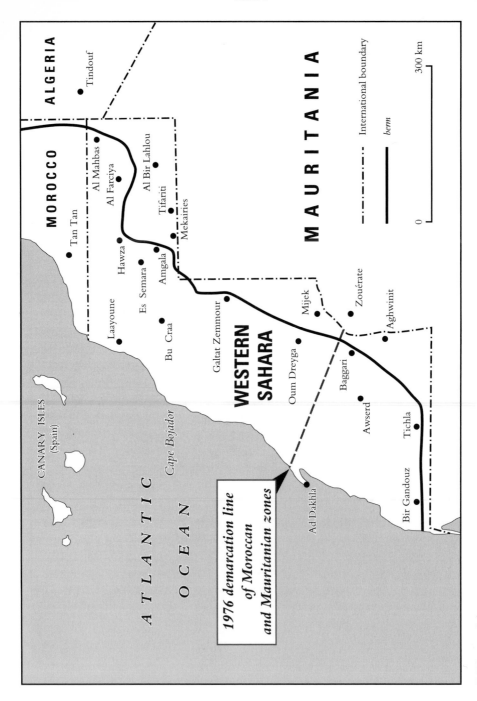

7 Western Sahara

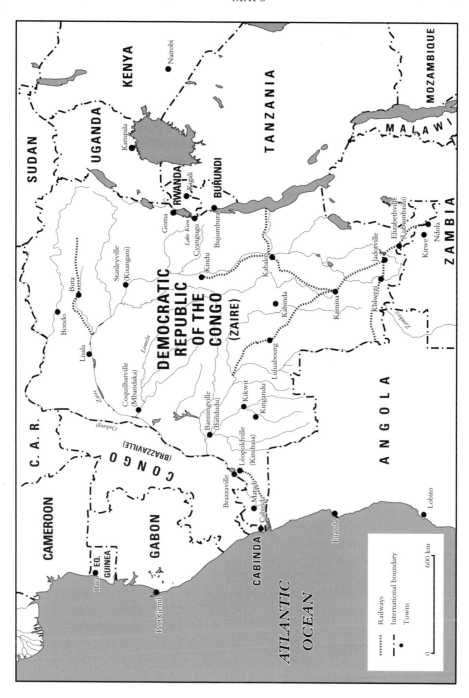

8 Congo (Zaire)

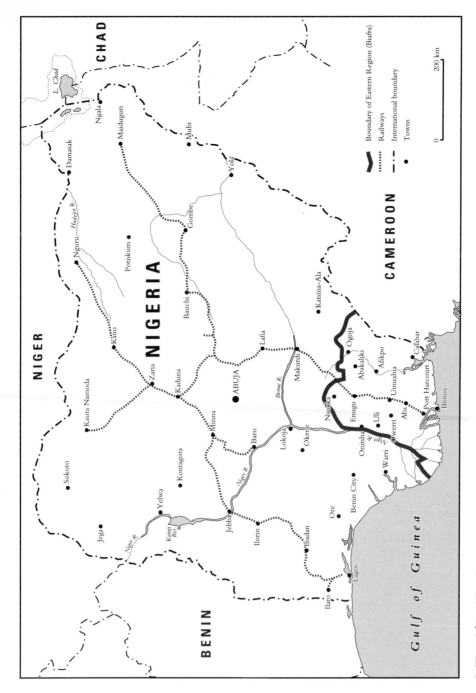

9 West Africa: Nigeria

10 Sudan

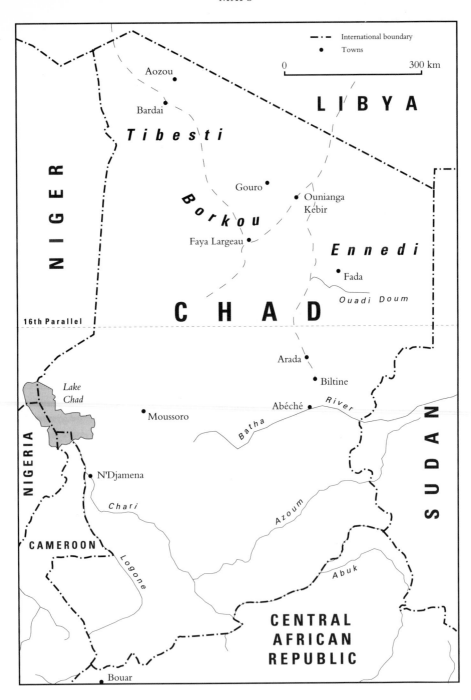

11 Chad

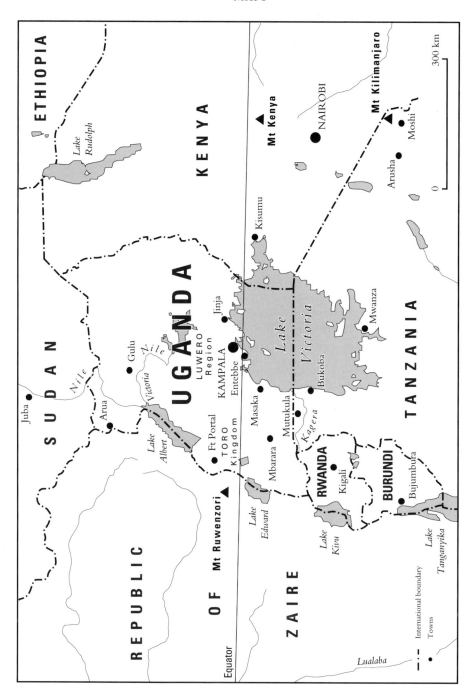

12 Uganda and her neighbours

Preface

A preface provides the author of a book with an opportunity to stand aside from his manuscript for a moment and say what he feels about his work. My feelings about the events that I have had to record are ones of great sadness. As a young man I served in a British colonial government, that of Kenya in the 1950s and early 1960s. After Mau Mau the atmosphere was increasingly one of excitement: we were doing all that we could to facilitate our own departure, train our successors and bring a new nation into being, and we were aware that other British colonial regimes were working with the same ideals. Many of us stayed on against our own career interests to help in the handover period. Except for Southern Africa the early 1960s was perhaps the best period in modern African history, a period of optimism, of much goodwill, in Kenya's one-word national motto, *harambee* – let us all pull together.

I would never have believed that, 45 years on, I would be the author of a work such as this; anyone who has had experience of the real problems of Africa – poverty, disease, ignorance – can only grieve over the colossal waste of life and scarce resources. Historians of warfare, like all good soldiers, hate war.

This work is concerned with the specific subject of the actual warfare itself, its causes, combatants, weapons and methods, victories and defeats – all the proper factual and analytical concerns of a historian. Space does not permit an examination of wider theoretical War Studies subjects such as arms control and disarmament, peacekeeping or conflict resolution, which are in any case more the concern of the international political scientist. Also, difficulties of discovering source material for a number of the conflicts has necessitated a "best reliable source" approach, cross-checking not being feasible.

I owe an especial debt of gratitude to Judith Hudson of the South African Community Agency for Social Enquiry for so freely providing me with so much material on South Africa, and as well as the material on her own thoughts and assessment of the events in Natal.

I also owe very real debts of gratitude to Diane Hillier and Sarah Oliver in the library of the Royal Military Academy Sandhurst, to the Librarian and staff of the School of Oriental and African Studies, and to Mark Bullock, Simon Combes, Lieutenant-Colonel R. S. Corkran, Major R. C. Goldsmith, Dennis Hall, Lieutenant-Colonel Tim Illingworth, Lieutenant-Colonel Julian James, Colonel Annette Leijenaar, Colonel A. Martin-Siegfried and Nigel Pavitt for providing me with material for various sections of the book. I am also very appreciative of the value of discussions that I have had with fellow members of the Institute for the Study of War and Society of De Montfort University and of the Centre for Conflict Studies at the Royal Military Academy Sandhurst.

Once again Monica Alexander has survived the task of deciphering my manuscripts and producing them into legible typescript, for which I can only offer my warmest thanks. Thanks also to Amazon Systems, who word-processed the typescript.

Finally my thanks are again due to my wife Judith and my son and daughter, Robert and Penelope, for their forbearance when the writing of this work has made me more than usually absent-minded.

Anthony Clayton

Chapter One

Introduction

The African continent has had to undergo more fundamental and dramatic changes in this century than any other area of the world within one century of recorded history. The changes, sweeping in successive waves over the continent, left earlier disputes unresolved and created a large number of new conflict situations. Many of these situations of seemingly irreconcilable end-states, old and new, erupted into violence in the period 1950 to 1998. This violence took the widest variety of forms, ranging from technologically sophisticated counter-insurgency campaigns to limited conventional inter-nation and civil wars, and to low intensity or informal inter-ethnic conflicts fought out with hand-weapons. The combatants similarly included not only uniformed soldiers (and policemen) but irregular guerrillas dressed for bush warfare, juveniles in clothing deliberately bizarre, and young men in ordinary working clothes with a cutlass or matchet to hand. The wide varieties reflect the different stages and levels in the continent's turbulent century of change. The varieties do not appear in chronological sequence, in one part of Africa a guerrilla insurgency may be taking place at the same time as elsewhere a campaign using sophisticated modern military hardware.

Pre-colonial Africa contained 7,000 or more political structures that ranged from a few kingdoms with permanent officials civil and military, to more informal loose polities that only functioned cohesively when the threat of attack led to a mobilization of the warrior age-sets, and lastly to acephalous societies where defence, again based on warrior age-sets, was entirely local. In all societies there was a general idea of the ground and resources claimed by that society, but nowhere were frontiers clearly demarcated. In John Illiffe's words, the warrior was essentially a "frontiersman" securing or advancing "innumerable local frontiers" in a search for space *lebensraum*.[1] A traditional ruler, powerful in natural resources and often with the aid of firearms acquired from Europe, could assert domination over large areas and differing

1

ethnicities, in some cases with a standing army. At other levels the nature of conflict was very varied; almost all societies were militarized at a low level. The warriors of pastoral peoples attacked agricultural ethnicities, or a clan of one ethnicity would attack another clan of the same people. The conflicts were generally brutal, with genocidal killings of captives and seizure of women. The struggle was endemic. The scene at the time of the arrival of the colonial powers, therefore, was one of widespread regionalized or localized low intensity conflict in which one polity or ethnicity would often be the ascendant – thereby frequently attracting either destruction or a privileged subimperial status within the incoming colonial system. In some areas the effect, direct or ripple, of the arrival of Europeans had been an erosion of traditional societies and social orders leading to the appearance of armed robber bands, the *ruga ruga* in East Central Africa being a notable example. The frontiers of these bands were the areas, fiefdoms, that they could terrorize. In this pre-colonial era, then, the warriors had an especial status. This status and the warrior tradition need outlining because they were to have some effect on colonial forces, post-independence state forces and irregulars alike, a continuity of a culture of low-level militarization.[2] The role and concept of the warrior emerged from groups of kinsmen banded together for economic survival, usually for hunting, in turn leading to banding for specific military purposes. In many pre-colonial societies, widely differing though these were, a common fact was the warrior band, organized for local or regional defence, raiding or campaigns of conquest. In the more developed polities the warrior hierarchy would advise and on occasions make or unmake the ruler; in less organized or acephalous societies, warriors or retired warriors of proven ability would dominate village councils. Command structures, procedures for mobilization and training, and tactics appropriate for the nature of the society and organization would evolve – some, as for example in Shaka's Zulu forces, of remarkable complexity and ingenuity. In some societies the warrior even became a hero figure, an ideal of community pride or patriotism – although he might be skilfully manipulated so as to present this image. The culture was in a few areas further enhanced by legend built around the primary resistance to colonial rule put up by warriors.

Warriors attained their status through initiation rites. These might include some form of oathing to ensure bonding, cohesion and commitment, a ritual to prove manhood involving a killing or the appearance of a killing, with generally an animal substituting for a human, and dance. Dance was of particular significance as it mixed a measure of male sexual display and physical and mental preparation for combat with music and song to ensure religious and political conformity. Some rituals were so frightening that more timorous young men were thereby revealed as unsuitable for warrior status, a simple selection system. Some features of this warrior culture, often debased, have reappeared in post-1950s conflicts.

The colonial order imposed on almost all of Africa in the last years of the nineteenth century carried with it, in embryo, the Western European concept of the nation state. A new polity, first that of the colonial state, later a new nation, was to be built within frontiers drawn largely but not invariably to meet the diplomatic needs of rival Western European nations. These frontiers created territories, some so large as to present their later post-independence rulers with immense political and administrative problems, others so small as to be doubtfully viable, either politically or economically. Frontiers in several cases artificially divided ethnicities into two or more of the new territories. The larger territories encapsulated many peoples of totally different cultures and religions, bound together by the "colonial glue". The new polity, and later the new nation, began to make allegiance demands on people's livelihood and lives. The colonial economic structures created large new areas of economic activity, involving cities, key transport routes and port facilities, and large-scale movements of peoples to meet labour requirements. In the Maghreb and in East and Central Africa plantation and mining economies came to be run by white settlers who sought to control colonial administrations; in South Africa land and minerals were already under total white control. Traditional trading patterns collapsed and new ones requiring different linkages and dependencies, reflecting the uneven spread of development within a territory, were created, some to engender friction and conflict. The clearest examples to play the lead part in subsequent tragedies were first the change effected by Britain on the economy of north Nigeria, away from trans-Saharan trade – of slaves, leather and ivory – to one dependent on access to the sea, the growing and export of cotton and groundnuts, and second the development by the Belgians of the Shaba (Katanga) province of their Congo colony to a level far superior to the rest of the territory.

The title of the Nigerian writer Chinua Achebe's famous novel *Things Fall Apart* well summarizes the ongoing social effects of the political and economic upheavals following the imposition of colonial rule. Traditional authorities were either destroyed by the new colonial regimes or distorted to serve the regimes' purposes, so losing credibility. In some areas, the colonial powers created new "traditional authorities" of their own. In white settled territories subsistence farming land areas were pressured by taxation and other measures to despatch a large percentage of their menfolk to work for the settler economy, on farms or down mines, in conditions at best barrack but more often shanty in unhealthy urban slums. Territories where colonial economies were developed on the base of the peasant grower – of cocoa, cotton, coffee, oil palm or other products – were more fortunate, but even in these lands subsistence farmers had to adjust to the market and its operators, as yeoman

3

producers. Traditional family life patterns found it increasingly hard to survive under all the stresses of the new commercial economy – the need to earn wages or to produce for survival or profit, the need for labour to migrate, the cost of new facilities such as education sought by all for their children, the struggle for advancement within the colonial societies, wars, the temptations of the possession of material goods that could lead to corruption. Western European school systems gave children new and different ideas about the importance and role of the individual in society, generation gaps and communication difficulties appeared, in some areas compounded by misunderstandings of the words and language of the colonial power. In addition there were new religious and later political ideologies. Christianity appeared to offer liberation from the tyranny of spirit worlds but also appeared to legitimize the colonial order in its position of privilege and to demand an end to polygamy. Christianity was divided, in some areas, notably Uganda, so sharply as to create political conflict; in other territories it coexisted uneasily with large Moslem communities. Colonial administrations divided their territories into districts based on ethnicities, a measure generally intended to protect local customs but one that aroused passive African opposition and in practice heightened local ethnic consciousness, sharpening it for future political or more violent conflict within the new national arenas. Political nationalism appeared led by leaders of a variety of views – Moslem, bourgeois nationalist, radical nationalist, revolutionary – with spin-doctors to replace witch-doctors.

The tensions created by the all-embracing nature of the colonial hegemony, requiring new states of mind, purposes and patterns of reasoning and consciousness, at times revealed themselves in dissonance – an absence of norms of conduct in public life, bizarre breakaway religions, distortions of traditional ethnic practices and rites, abilities within an individual to hold two totally contradictory sets of beliefs and patterns of conduct at the same time, or other excesses of personal behaviour. Colonial administrations, often benign and paternal, particularly in the case of British colonial governments, did much to alleviate some of these traumatic changes, but could not cure them.

The colonial powers established their own military forces, not only for the purposes of wider imperial or local defence or local gendarmerie duties, but also with the express object of contributing to the legitimizing of imperial rule through an association with local arms bearers, an inverted form of warrior tradition. The forces of the two major colonial powers, however, were different in two important respects. Those of Britain were, in peacetime, all volunteers while those of the French empire were drafted by quotas imposed on districts, and the British African units so formed were based on men from one home territory while those of France's "La Coloniale" were all (with the exception of Madagascar) mixed under the traditional but confusingly inaccurate title of *Tirailleurs Sénégalais*. The British voluntary recruitment system was generally targeted on the poorer, less articulate ethnicities within a colony, perceived as producing "martial races", with significant consequences to follow as armies tended to become players, with guns, on the political stage rather than be a national asset. The system's one-territory base served to disseminate some idea of a new national identity with the soldiers themselves retaining certain elements of the warrior tradition set in the new context of the territory, acceptable under colonial control but later to distort into praetorianism. In their day-to-day life, in barracks or in the field, features of the pre-colonial warrior tradition became grafted onto the metropolitan power's prescribed structures of regiment, battalion, company and platoon – praise songs for the hierarchy, songs believed to endow the singer with invincibility, games and dance providing "affective readying" for battle.[3]

At the mid-point of the twentieth century, 1950, there were already clear visible signs that the colonial system, in trouble even before the experience of the Second World War, the formation of the United Nations and the independence of the Indian subcontinent, was coming to an end. The French had had to suppress uprisings in Algeria in 1945 and in Madagascar in 1947; the British had experienced serious unrest in the Gold Coast in 1948, with less serious unrest in Nigeria in 1949. The establishment of the state of Israel had inflamed Arab nationalism to explosion point. In many areas of both colonial African empires there were also indications that the "colonial glue" was beginning to melt at local levels, with a return to inter-ethnic quarrels dating from the pre-colonial eras.

The events that follow represent, in the first instance, rebellion and insur-rectionary or low-intensity guerrilla wars against colonial regimes. Once independence was achieved and with a few exceptions of wars between nations, warfare centred around the problems that arose within the post-colonial state, now the newly independent nation. Many of these in sub-Saharan Africa proved incapable of surmounting a multi-ethnic social and declining economic reality. Late colonial or early post-independence elec-tions, some very questionably conducted, would return leaders from one or a small group of ethnicities on a "winner takes all, loser gets nothing" basis. But minority ethnic sentiment, not to be dismissed as mere "tribalism" when considering the sense of community and identity of peoples perhaps several million strong, became thereby increasingly aroused, and increasingly difficult to disclaim or manage by ethnic majorities even when much larger. Independ-ence, too, brought to the surface economic issues which had been less evident in the colonial era. Dependence on the successful marketing of one crop, balance of payments problems made increasingly difficult by the widening gap between the prices primary products could command against monies needed to purchase modern industrial equipment or consumer goods, issues of loan repayment, imbalance in economic development between regions within a country and between towns and rural areas, corruption in state funds and corporations – such issues affected nearly all African countries. The weakening of Western economies and the increased costs of fuel from 1974 onwards added to almost all of these problems, with the effect of weakening the authority, and often the power to maintain proper law and order, of African governments. In many the difficulties were further compounded by rapid population growth, particularly in towns, and the inabilities of national economies either to absorb or continue the education of frustrated school-leavers. Developments in media communication ensured that political messages, not always edifying and on occasions inflammatory, reached out into bush and bidonville slum. In worst case territories, where dissonance was serious and widespread amounting to "an epidemic of the mind", warfare reverted to anomie, mass murder and genocide; such epidemics could affect hardline white militants as well as black.[4]

Several new sub-Saharan nations, at or shortly after independence in the 1960s, found they also had an immediate frontier defence commitment requiring them to deploy the forces created by the departing colonial power. These forces, it was hoped, would be "modernized men" and acquire a new legitimacy as the authorized lawful arms-bearers of the new nation, a "national army", and where their role was confined to frontier defence they aroused no controversy. In domestic matters, however, with the colonial ethnic structures remaining unchanged or only slightly changed, and the new indigenous officers forming an armed component of the emerging social elites, "national armies" in practice retained strong regional loyalties, often with ethnicities other than those holding the political power; in consequence military actions presented as national were in fact not so.

Armies became factions, one of the players in the power game, another factor contributing to the difficulties and instabilities of many Black African states. These became increasingly unable to meet the military challenges led by internal junior leaders or external faction leaders able to recruit and arm a rival irregular force, or the groups of armed gangs appealing to debased forms of warrior traditions and initiation rites or devising new forms of cruelty and killing. Only a very few regimes managed to cling on to any elements of the concept of the nation's legitimate forces retaining their legitimacy by fighting a civilized war and sparing civilians; more often a maximum use of terror was preferred. Wars of integration or disintegration, on the contrary, generally assumed centrifugal patterns, damaging or destroying a territory's limited economic assets and throwing further thousands of peoples back to refugee life, poverty, ignorance, disease and death.

A final ingredient to several conflicts already sufficiently confused was international interventions. These were generally overtly supportive of nationalist sides in the wars of liberation. In wars of national integration international support for one side or another was frequently but not always related to positions taken by the interested powers in the Cold War, extending to the supply of weaponry and in the case of Angola the deployment of Cuban soldiers as Soviet surrogates. With the exception of the suppression of early post-independence military mutinies in East Africa, some tepid air and naval activity following Rhodesia's unilateral declaration of independence, a covert operation restoring President Jawara in Gambia in 1981 and some minor transport and logistic or humanitarian work, British military activity in post-independence Africa was limited to contributing to the supervising of free elections and the formation of a national army in Zimbabwe and Namibia, and to training and weapon supply. France maintained garrisons in several territories, and intervened, deploying troops in these areas and others, when it appeared French interests or repute were at stake. The United States' bombing of Libya in 1986 constituted an act of war, fortunately not followed up by either side.

After the end of the Cold War, with its consequential withdrawal of interest by the two superpowers, the United States and Russia, intervention by other African countries when it occurred reflected local interests, the support of one side or another suiting a neighbouring territory, or a regional power trying to assert or defend a local hegemony. There were also interventions by United Nations forces, and in Liberia from 1990 by an African force; both these types of intervention have been at times distorted by particular interests.

Clearly any rigid specific definition of warfare of the type used in international law or in conventions would leave anomalies in a study of conflict in late twentieth-century Africa. This study will simply take a working guide: states of armed conflict for political dominance, whether between or within states and involving identifiable organizations or groups by origin national, regional, religious or ascriptive clan or local, such conflicts involving operations of a discernible military pattern and aim within an appropriate brief or lengthy period of time. Such deliberate warfare is distinguishable from coups, temporary popular disorder and purely criminal violence unless they lead to genocidal strife. Warfare also should not include sporadic casual friction arising from disputes such as those of cattle-raiding, the least significant product of very local disputes between neighbours whose societies thereby express another but less significant form of warrior or low-level militarization subculture.

Much of this background will be familiar to students of modern African history; for students of the history of warfare, however, the context of warfare in Africa since 1950 may be unfamiliar and appear very unusual. The purpose of this introduction has, therefore, been that of alerting the non-specialist reader in general terms to some of these special background features to warfare in Africa; they will reappear related to particular conflicts in succeeding chapters.

Chapter Two

Independence wars 1950 to 1962

The first series of anti-colonial liberation campaigns in Africa in the 1950s saw two insurgency movements against the British, one in Egypt on a small scale, the second, the Mau Mau uprising in Kenya, more serious. The French were faced with limited-scale nationalist uprisings in Tunisia and Morocco, and then in 1954 the opening of the largest-scale conflict in Africa in the second half of the century in Algeria. The Portuguese faced the first of the challenges to their African colonial rule in Angola in 1961. The common feature of all six wars was that military advantage lay initially with the insurgent, but when metropolitan security forces had become sufficiently strong and organized their superior technology, small arms, aircraft, bombs and later helicopters ensured that they remained undefeated, and they were able to impose a firm military control on the ground, whatever the political outcome.[1]

Egypt 1951–2

The first of these campaigns broke out in Egypt in 1951. The background needs only a brief introductory summary of Egypt's pent-up resentment against the British presence – harsh exploitation of labour in the First World War; the ongoing British manipulation of Egyptian politics in the interwar and 1939–45 period with its apparent support for the corrupt pasha classes and monarchy; continuous street-level racial insult offered by the masses of British, Australian and New Zealand troops serving in Egypt during the war; Jewish immigration into Palestine and the creation of Israel; and as the final straw the feeble performance of the Egyptian army in the war against Israel in 1948, this performance seen by Egyptians as the result of malign British influence.

Egyptian government requests for the withdrawal of the British garrison, permitted under the 1936 Anglo-Egyptian Treaty, began in late 1945, and were accompanied by rioting and local gun battles. The demands were not accepted by the British government, though the withdrawal of British troops from Cairo for concentration in the Canal Zone was undertaken. Two events were to lead to insurrection. The first was the accession to power of the militant *Wafd* Party nationalist leader Nahas Pasha in 1950, and the second the successful example of defiance of Britain set in the following year by the Iranian government's seizure of the Anglo-Iranian Oil Company's installations. On 8 October 1951 Nahas abrogated the 1936 Treaty; riots and attacks on British army personnel and their families in the Canal Zone towns followed. The British garrison had been much reduced – at the abrogation it totalled only three infantry battalions, two armoured regiments and a small number of artillery units. It was reinforced, with remarkable speed and resolution, by units shipped and flown in from elsewhere in the Middle East and Britain itself, to total 16 battalions with other supporting units by mid-November.

On the ground the military situation was complex. The British presence in the Canal Zone served to split the Egyptian army, a large part of which was in the Sinai area. In turn the British position was weakened by the intimidation and pressures to withdraw brought on the 66,000 Egyptian civilians who worked for the British army and as essential labourers for the railways and Port Said docks. The pressures were motivated by the Egyptian Interior Minister, Fuad Siraggadin. The British met the first difficulty by seizing the one railway bridge across the Canal after a brief shoot-out so ensuring control of communication, and the second by using troops for a variety of civilian labour purposes and by bringing in pioneer and technical units. Events moved into the dimension of warfare on 17 November when Siraggadin let loose an organized force, his ministry's auxiliary police known as the *Bulak Nizam*, in attacks on the British; the *Bulak Nizam* were assisted by enthusiastic youth groups and students in "youth commandos" or, as they were later called, "Liberation Squads".

These auxiliaries had been given some rudimentary rifle training and wore a simple black uniform; their targets were British military personnel and their families, water supplies, roads, railways and base installations of which the most important and most vulnerable were the ordinance depot at Tel el Kebir with its 17-mile long perimeter, and the vital water filtration plant at Kafr Abdu, a little north of Suez. The youth group members and students would sit on house roofs and sketch target installations and military family houses or tents. Armed *Bulak Nizam* and others would use lorries to drag away sections of the Tel el Kebir perimeter fence to enable a raiding party to enter and steal arms or stores. Elsewhere their operations were based on sniping from roof tops and ambushes, and in several of these incidents British soldiers were killed or wounded.

The British response to these tactics was one of vigorous defence – the clearing of villages, the somewhat unwise demolition of houses to open the route to the water filtration plant, and cordon and search operations using armoured-cars and tanks followed by field-security screening of suspects. The demolition of houses, which could have been averted by the posting of a stronger local force, led to an outpouring of anti-British propaganda in Cairo, newspapers proclaiming individual students as national heroes and offering rewards for the killing of British officers. As the campaign intensified, an Egyptian village was bombarded with three-inch mortar bombs, and in defence against an attack on the Tel el Kebir depot British field artillery, aircraft and mortars were all used, leading to the surrender of 160 *Bulak Nizam*. Finally the British Army commander, General Sir George Erskine, ordered the total disarming and expulsion of the police and *Bulak Nizam* in Ismailia, an operation involving in all three battalions of infantry, tanks and armoured cars in a pitched battle around the police barracks; in this action 46 *Bulak Nizam* were killed and 65 wounded.

This action was followed on the next day, 26 January 1952, by infuriated Egyptian crowds burning British clubs, hotels, shops and offices in Cairo, and a number of people were killed. The British army made preparations for a return to Cairo, in the face of which King Farouk first ordered Egyptian soldiers to restore order in the capital and then dismissed the Nahas cabinet. Military operations in the Canal Zone declined to the level of thieving, but some 40 British soldiers had been killed with over 70 wounded in the two-month campaign. The Egyptian dead must have totalled at least 150.

For the British, time was gained. During this time the British government was able to adjust itself to the necessity of military withdrawal from the Canal Zone, the American development of the hydrogen bomb and Yugoslavia's quarrel with Moscow being seen as reducing the Soviet threat. An agreement for withdrawal was reached in July 1954, though subsequent events were to reopen the issue.

Kenya 1952–6

The Mau Mau revolt in Kenya was primarily a result of the pressure on the land of the rising population, in particular within Kenya's largest ethnic group, the Kikuyu, resulting in peasant overcrowding in Kikuyuland together with the enforced removal of surplus labour, mostly Kikuyu, from white settlers' farms. The Kikuyu saw themselves constricted by the colonial demarcation of settled areas and tribal reserves; Mau Mau, or, as it styled itself, the Kenya Land Freedom Army, was concerned with new Kikuyu frontiers. Discontent was fuelled also by the low, bare subsistence-level wages paid to urban labour, a high proportion being Kikuyu in the case of Nairobi. Another dimension concerned an internal Kikuyu conflict, between the immiserised and those with land, property or status; at an ideological level a conflict existed between cultural renewal and anti-colonial rebellion. No educated or Christian Kikuyu were active insurgents despite their general sympathy for the Kikuyu cause, but at the same time Kikuyu traditional beliefs were not, in the minds of the masses, harnessed by the Mau Mau cause. The colonial government, paternal but weak, had neglected danger signals and was taken by surprise when the uprising broke out in September–October 1952.[2]

The insurgents from the start were handicapped by lack of military experience, only a few having served during the Second World War, paucity of firearms and the absence of any trans-frontier safe area where they could rest, regroup, plan and train. At the outset of the uprising they numbered at least 12,000 active insurgents, almost all Kikuyu or Kikuyu-related peoples, with a large "passive wing" of city dwellers, petty traders, communication workers and others who supplied those in the field with food, medical supplies and intelligence. A few Mau Mau possessed stolen sporting guns or pistols, and during the campaign more of these were stolen and others improvised, but the majority of Mau Mau insurgents fought with spears or *pangas* (local matchets). Terror was used deliberately through the mutilation and torture of victims, and also to impose cohesion on coerced and frightened followers by means of barbaric and binding oathing rituals. The oaths served to set a man apart, changing his nature to one of almost anomic violence often targeted among farm or domestic servants against trusting employers. This change was seen and with great success presented by the colonial authorities as an atavistic return to barbarism, so legitimizing its own operations against Mau Mau.

Mau Mau was largely pre-literate; it had no ideological motivation or revolutionary warfare theory to follow. Some believed trees, groves or rocks contained magic powers that could be invoked to help them. At the outset the insurgents called themselves the Land Freedom Army or the Freedom Struggle Association. The precise origin of the term Mau Mau is unclear. The rebellion was essentially an insurgency of various local groups of guerrillas, each led by a strong personality or personalities, fighting in ways most suitable to its local area of operations. Attempts were made to create some co-ordinating organizational framework and in August 1953, although already too late, a Kenya Defence Council was set up following a clandestine meeting of group leaders. But this body, and its later successor, the Kenya

Parliament, never gained control of or even acceptance by all the forest leaders. These frequently quarrelled among themselves; there was friction between the groups in the Aberdares and those on Mt Kenya, and friction between the totally illiterate and the semi-literate. Discipline in the group was ferocious.

Mau Mau men lacked any kind of uniform; they were often dressed in rags with hair and clothes daubed in red murram. They came increasingly to live off roots and animals they could hunt. A small number of women accompanied the groups. Mau Mau's chief assets were their own remarkable personal bravery and ability to move, often undetected, to harass, surprise and ambush. Insurgent groups communicated by "letter boxes", places of concealment in trees or under stones, or by arrows made from bent bamboo or other branches or incisions made on trees to indicate direction. They covered their tracks by walking on the side of their feet, running often for miles on their toes, or by wearing animal hooves. All these signs and indicators were, sooner or later, recognized by British intelligence staffs.

The initiative lay with Mau Mau at the outset, with attacks on settler farm buildings and livestock and killings of Kikuyu loyalists in September 1952, the assassination of a senior Kikuyu chief in October and the killing of white settlers, including in one instance a wife and children in January 1953. The arrest in October 1952 of Jomo Kenyatta, who was charged with and later convicted of managing Mau Mau in a protracted trial in which colonial prejudices grossly distorted justice, served as a great recruiting incentive for the insurgents. Scores of young men moved into central Kenya's two mountain ranges, the Aberdares and Mt Kenya, to join one group or another. On 26 March 1953 Mau Mau mounted its two most spectacular attacks, the first an 80-strong gang raid on the police station at Naivasha in the Rift Valley in which two constables were killed, the remainder put to flight, prisoners released and a few rifles seized, and the second a massacre of some 84 men, women, children and babies at Lari on the Valley's escarpment. The massacre was the result of a long-standing local land feud with its origins going back to the period of the alienation of land for white settlement.

Up to September 1952 Kenya's military garrison had consisted of but two battalions of the King's African Rifles (KAR), African troops with British officers; the Kenya Police was a force also quite inadequate to meet the Mau Mau challenge. With the declaration of a State of Emergency three other KAR battalions were brought in, with initially one indifferent British Army infantry battalion in late October 1952; two more very efficient battalions were flown in from Britain in April 1953, with a further two in September 1953. With other small local units the military force available amounted to three brigades in the field by the end of 1953. In 1954 an engineer regiment arrived to construct a necessary road across the Aberdare range. The military command system was changed from its quiet backwater style of 1952 with the arrival first of an effective if tactlessly outspoken Director of Operations, Major-General Robert Hinde, in February 1953 and later in June with the arrival of Erskine, now a senior general with authority over all military and police operations. He was not given the gubernatorial powers that General Sir Gerald Templer had been given in Malaya as it was held that the Mau Mau uprising affected only one area of the territory, not the whole. He was, however, given a letter of authority, which he kept in his spectacle case, to assume these powers if he thought it necessary, a contingency thought possible from the militant anti-government views of local white settlers.

The Kenya police force was also greatly expanded by the hurried recruitment of 700 young British officers on contracts, not all of whom proved suitable, together with the mobilization of the police reserve whose members were local white residents.

The Hinde–Erskine strategy followed closely that developed by the British under Templer in Malaya. The main features of this strategy were the "trinity" system of command, of the administration, military and police; the development and co-ordination of intelligence gathering, which in Kenya included the use of counter-gangs of former insurgents; the pushing of insurgents into "prohibited areas" or free-fire zones with consequential food denial; the concentration of local populations into protected villages; and the formation in March 1953 through a local levy of a "Kikuyu Guard" force to defend the villages. This force, later amalgamated with the former colonial "tribal police" retainers of the administration and totalling 25,000, was to prove all important, both in the bravery of its weakly-armed members and in the provision of security for the Kikuyu people. With the provision of security came a change of conviction, away from some 90 per cent general Kikuyu support for Mau Mau's methods (though not necessarily its aims) to support for the government.

The British Royal Air Force was also committed. A squadron of Lincoln heavy bombers was used, with little effect, to bomb forest areas. Mau Mau soon learnt to light fires as dummy targets and then move on elsewhere. More useful were American Harvard T-6 training aircraft adapted for precision dive-bombing, the noise of the machines adding to the effect. The most valuable air assistance to the Army, however, were the reconnaissance, supply and liaison flights of the light civilian aircraft flown by the Police Reserve Air Wing. Air photography was also useful, especially when using infra-red techniques to locate insurgent camp fires.

The early military operations were limited to flag marches, patrol visits to farms and the remote police stations and the military cordoning of an area being searched by the police.

With the arrival of more troops farms would be given a small garrison, and the best British troops used to start the eradication of Mau Mau control in the Kikuyu heartlands, effected by the ambushing of parties moving after curfew. With this largely attained, and security in some measure assured by the village concentrations and the Kikuyu Guard, offensive patrolling into the higher areas of the Aberdare range – cold, dark, dank forest from 2,135 to 2,745 metres with dense bamboo from 2,745 metres – could begin. Successful patrolling in the Aberdares and Mt Kenya required good junior leadership, usually but not always available in what was still an army of conscripts, along with jungle-craft, navigation, map-reading and ambush skills. Forest patrols would sometimes spend between two and five days out. British regiment patrols were generally accompanied by personnel from the local settler Territorial reserve regiment. Rhinoceros, elephant and buffalo could add to the dangers; the noise of non-dangerous animals, monkeys, hyena and others added to the overall eerie atmosphere. Infantrymen, still equipped with old bolt-loading rifles, found heavier weapons such as Vickers machine-guns of little value in the bamboo; only submachine-guns and mortars proved useful additions. Insurgent groups avoided open battles from choice, but they occasionally resulted from deliberate patrol work, ambushes on Mau Mau supply routes, the flushing out of insurgent hide-outs or successful pursuit. The police were equipped either with revolvers, Greener pellet guns or rifles.

The towns and cities, particularly Nairobi, where the African population was terrorized by Mau Mau intimidation, secret "courts" and executions, posed particular problems for which day-to-day police raids following tip-offs and small-scale identification parades of suspects were inadequate. In April 1954 Erskine mounted a large 12-day operation involving one KAR and four British infantry battalions, and 26 police combat platoons in and around Nairobi. The city was encircled by an outer cordon, and sectors by turn were close-cordoned and searched with over 16,000 suspects taken away for questioning and in most cases detention. The success of this operation enabled more troops to be deployed in finally securing the Kikuyu heartlands and in new large-scale sweep operations involving several battalions using the newly completed road across the Aberdares, all supported by artillery and bombing from RAF aircraft. From early 1955 some of the sweeps were assisted by hundreds of Kikuyu villagers beating the ground to flush out any insurgents in hiding, a measure of the change in attitudes towards the uprising.

By the time that Erskine handed over his command to General Sir Gerald Lathbury in May 1955 the insurgents had been reduced to some 3,000 men, constantly harried by patrols and from the air, and with supplies from Kikuyuland and the towns cut off. One insurgent leader, General China, had given up in April 1954 and tried to arrange a mass surrender of some 2,000 in the Aberdares. His efforts failed as a KAR battalion in an adjoining area encountered and destroyed a large insurgent group, unfortunately leaving the 2,000 with the impression that the surrender negotiations were a ruse. A second surrender offer in early 1955 had only limited success.

Lathbury believed that greater use of the counter-gangs of former insurgents prepared to operate in reconnaissance and penetration missions would strengthen the effectiveness of the big area-sweeps by several battalions in this final stage of the campaign. These counter-gangs would join up with insurgent groups and then, at night, overpower them. Lathbury's strategy brought success with the killing, capture or voluntary surrender of many more insurgents and leaders. By early 1956 the insurgents had been reduced to some 900, and with the tracking down and capture of the most important Mau Mau leader, Dedan Kimathi, in October, the military campaign was virtually over. Kimathi was tried and hanged, but after independence a major Nairobi street was renamed after him. The remaining military units were left guarding the forest edge, with limited patrolling in a few areas.

Mau Mau was estimated to have lost some 11,500 dead. The government's forces lost 590 killed, of which 63 were European, together with civilian losses of 1,800 loyalist Africans, 32 Europeans and 26 Asians. The "state of emergency" lasted until 1960, more to provide for the continued holding of detainees than for any military reason.

The military operations were accompanied by a variety of other measures handled by the administration and the police. All Kikuyu in employment were obliged to carry employment records, some 100,000 Kikuyu were removed, under very rough conditions, from the white settled areas, and in Kikuyuland penalty fines or stock confiscations were levied on individuals or communities believed to be supporting insurgents. Severe penalties were imposed for illegal possession of arms, for oath administration and for aiding or supplying insurgents. The most important administrative measure of all, however, was the process known as "rehabilitation" involving some 78,000 people detained during police raids and army sweeps and identified by hooded loyalists as suspects. The detainees were held first in large detention camps outside central Kenya and after questioning and confession were moved on by stages to camps where they were given a mixture of hard work, discipline and civic teaching, with eventually a few privileges, some pay and finally release if regarded as rehabilitated successfully. The camps were hurriedly prepared, insanitary and with poor food and medical arrangements. Criticism led to improvements, but not before many inmates had died.

All aspects of the campaign attracted considerable and influential attention and criticism locally and, more important, in Britain, where abuses by the security forces were well reported. General Erskine issued firm orders on the proper conduct of operations and the metropolitan British battalions maintained high standards. There were, however, a number of cases of maltreatment of prisoners by locally recruited Europeans in the Kenya Regiment or Police Reserve as well as the institutional violence in the detention camps and prisons. Some of the worst cases were beatings and killings by the Kikuyu Guard. The Commissioner of Police, Arthur Young, wanted to prosecute the offenders, and on being told by the colony's governor that he could not do so, he resigned. In the end, in 1955, an amnesty in respect of past abuses by the Kikuyu Guard was packaged with the second surrender offer to the insurgents, and the Guard was then reorganized under tighter discipline.

The most serious of the cases occurred after the campaign was over, at a prison camp for hardcore detainees at Hola, in Kenya's coastal province. There, in March 1959, 11 detainees who refused to work were clubbed to death by prison guards. The Kenya government unwisely stated that they had died from drinking from a poisoned water cart. The truth, however, emerged, occasioning an angry debate in the British House of Commons. The incident played a significant part in bringing about the change of attitudes within the ruling Conservative Party that culminated in Prime Minister Macmillan's famous "Wind of Change" speech in Capetown in February 1960.

The apparent success of the British counter-insurgency campaign and the restoration of order needs to be set in context. The military operations were only one part of an overall strategy which included land reform, massive investment in the opening up of new land areas for small-holder, particularly Kikuyu, agriculture, improved wages and conditions of employment, developed social services, the gradual breaking-down of social colour bars, and political progress presented initially as a move to "multi-racialism". The broad-front strategy served to convince first peoples other than the Kikuyu and later the Kikuyu themselves that the old "White Man's Country" order was being dismantled. The dismantling represented the wishes and assertion of London – which had to bear most of the costs of the campaign – and the Conservative Party's realization that future British interests in Kenya were not going to be served by the military defence of white colonists but by partnership in peripheral trading capitalism with an emerging local Kenyan elite.

Mau Mau's success was that the uprising was the catalyst for these changes leading surprisingly quickly to Kenya's independence in 1963. But it was from the new elite, Kenya's nascent bourgeoisie, rather than the forest fighters that, after his release from detention, Kenyatta was to choose his ministers and civil servants. A British garrison remained in Kenya until 1964. In two other British African territories the road to independence required the presence of British troops to preserve law and order – Zanzibar in 1961 and again in 1963, and Swaziland in 1963. The latter commitment is described in a later chapter.

France and North Africa I: Tunisia and Morocco 1952–6

The root causes of France's opposition to colonial nationalism and the prodigious military efforts committed to try to retain French control lay deep in French history. The French national tradition, that of the Roman Church, Roman Law, Bonapartism, even revolutionary Jacobinism, was one of centralism. Both the political right and left believed in a French *mission civilisatrice* in an indivisible union; colonial nationalists were seen as *dissidents* or heretics. The French military, with few exceptions, perceived that the reservoir of formidable soldiers provided by the three North African territories, Morocco, Algeria and Tunisia, had played the lead role in France's post-1942 military renaissance in Italy and the Liberation campaign, and that they remained essential to maintain national prestige and assertion in a world dominated by *les anglo-saxons*, America and Britain. Most French generals had North African or colonial experience, and many further argued that loss of French control of the Mediterranean's southern shores endangered all Europe. This view was, of course, shared by the large settler communities: 150,000 in Tunisia, 300,000 in Morocco, 975,000 in Algeria in 1945, all with powerful political allies in Paris.

French thinking was further constrained by the political structure of the 1946 Fourth Republic. As in the Third Republic of 1875 to 1940, power lay in the legislature, particularly the *Chambre des Députés*, the lower house, only the elected *Assemblée Nationale* being thought to carry sufficient legitimacy to bridge the political divide between conservatives and radicals opened by the 1789 revolution. The post-1946 *Chambre* suffered, however, from fatal political weaknesses. The Communist Party regularly polled between a fifth and a quarter of the votes; it was after 1947 perceived to be the tool of Moscow, and therefore impossible to have in any government or political alliance. The Socialists, some of whom in any case held centralist views on French overseas possessions, could not form any alliance for colonial emancipation with the Communists for fear of being labelled as fellow-travellers, and, if they were to join in any government at all, they had to do so in coalition with the several right, centre-right or centre parties opposed to colonial emancipation. Coalitions with these were unstable and governments often had to draw on different majorities for different aspects of their policy. There were 14 different governments between 1950 and 1958. In terms of political direction of the military the usual compromise recourse was that of military restoration of law and order before any political discussion, a recourse that simply extended the conflict.

This flawed system, compounded by the mediocre abilities of most of its players, was leading France to disaster in Indochina. By the 1950s middle-ranking and a few senior officers were saying that counter-insurgency campaigning must be pursued with ruthlessness, using free-fire zones, wide powers of arrest, cordoning and searching, the movement of whole communities when necessary, harsh interrogation of suspects, the despatch of conscripts (these were not sent to Indochina unless they so volunteered), psychological warfare and above all the priority of the military and its needs over feeble-minded civilian political reservations. This school of thought was to be brought from the ideological conflict in Indochina to North Africa, adding to the already rigid mind-set with which France responded to insurgency there, in particular in Algeria with its very different circumstances. This mind-set led to the constitutional crisis caused by the collapse of the Fourth Republic in 1958 and the accession to power of Charles de Gaulle, after which political direction of the military was very firm, even when challenged.

Before the Algerian war, however, France had already had to engage in two, much smaller-scale, campaigns in the Maghreb.[3] The first was in the French protectorate of Tunisia where heavy-handed French administrations were attempting to resist the urban bourgeois nationalist party *Neo-Destour*, led by Habib Bourguiba. The first serious military clash occurred in January 1952 when the French banned a *Neo-Destour* conference, placed Bourguiba under house arrest and conducted cordon and search operations, mostly in the Cap Bon area, for others suspected of subversion. Bourguiba's arrest led to riots and clashes with the police and gendarmerie and the killing of a French officer and a loyalist *khalifa*, several hundred acts of sabotage and large numbers of arrests. Spasmodic violence and the killing of French *colons* and pro-French Tunisians continued throughout the summer, worsening sharply in October with a fresh series of killings, including some by the newly formed French *colon* vigilante groups.

The next year, 1953, saw some moderation of French policies until December when Ferhat Hashed, a popular militant trade union leader, was murdered, probably by vigilantes. This killing sparked off a new series of attacks upon French military personnel and loyalists in early 1959, with in response further vigilante killings of nationalists. France quickly strengthened the small garrison and brought in reinforcements from elsewhere in North Africa and from West Africa, to a total of 40,000. The Army commander, General Boyer de Latour du Moulin, also favoured a traditional French Maghreb military technique, the use in Tunisia's highlands of *goums*, small units of 120 men, mostly irregulars, on foot together with 60 more on ponies all supported by a small mule-mounted supply detail. The troops were used to effect, achieving a high kill rate and the recovery of much weaponry. An amnesty was offered to insurgents willing to give themselves up, initially achieving some success.

May 1954 was, however, to see the catastrophic French Indochina defeat at Dien Bien Phu, with the subsequent accession to power in Paris of Pierre

Mendès-France, the ablest of the Fourth Republic's premiers. Mendès-France conceded the offer of an autonomy status to the protectorate. This status was not sufficient to appease the nationalists, and a further eruption of violence broke out in October. Boyer, now holding civil authority as Resident-General in addition to military command, offered a new and more generous amnesty sending joint Franco-Tunisian teams into the highlands to explain the terms. The result was a considerable success, some 90 per cent of the contemporary insurgents surrendering themselves and their weapons.

The more extreme militant nationalists, encouraged by President Nasser of Egypt, rejected autonomy, their passions heightened by the outbreak of the Algerian war in November 1954. Some 20 groups of insurgents took to the field in January 1954, with one of the most active groups, led by a veteran insurgent leader, Tahar Lassoued, styling itself the "National Tunisian Army of Liberation". Fighting, mostly now between rival Tunisian factions rather than against the French, occurred chiefly in the highland areas, particularly around Matmata. The French deployed aircraft and artillery; these together with counter-gangs and *colon* vigilantes, killed some 200 members of the different groups in their reassertion of control.

The French government, now heavily involved in Algeria, conceded full independence to Tunisia in March 1956, so ending the purpose of ongoing insurgency. The Tunisian government then made a final once-and-for-all amnesty offer and purely local Tunisian insurgency came to an end.

In Morocco the French inability to come to terms with post-war nationalism was also to lead to armed conflict. The Sultan, Mohammed V, had from 1947 onwards advanced the nationalist cause partly from his own personal convictions but also to secure himself against criticism from nationalist politicians. The French riposte directed by two successive old-school *Armée d'Afrique* Resident-Generals, Generals Juin and Guillaume, was to try to use the chieftains from the Atlas mountains, the *grands caids*, and their Berber followers as a counter to the Sultan and the urban Arab politicians. At the time of a political crisis in 1951 over 200,000 horsed Berber retainers of El Glaoui, the Pasha of Marrakesh and other *caids* swarmed into the streets of the Moroccan cities to enable the French to appear as holding a balance. Later, serious rioting, the consequence of Hashed's murder in Tunisia, followed in December 1952 requiring the French to deploy 2,000 police and 3,000 troops. Prompted by the French, in 1953 Glaoui demanded the abdication of the Sultan and in August Guillaume arbitrarily deposed Mohammed V and replaced him with an elderly and ineffective member of the royal family, Ben Arafa, as Sultan.

Ben Arafa commanded neither respect nor authority and the exiled Mohammed became the focus of a now angered nationalism uniting Arab and Berber. The last months of 1953 saw terrorism, sabotage and attacks upon

French farms, factories, shops and homes, to worsen in 1954 when a powerful *colon* counter-terrorist organization, mainly middle- and artisan-class white, appeared. This group called itself the *Organisation de Défence Anti-Terroriste* (ODA-T) and was financed by *colon* industry and trade. It was to carry out a number of brutal killings. This brutality was matched by the cruelty and excesses of the French Moroccan police, many of whom were Corsican.

Violence increased in 1955 with clashes and bloodshed in Casablanca and Marrakesh becoming widespread throughout Morocco in August, including a massacre of 49 *colons*, including women and children. In October a full-scale insurgency campaign opened in the Rif and Middle Atlas, the active insurgents, probably some 700, initially proclaiming themselves as the "Moroccan Liberation Army" (MLA); at the same time rioting and terrorism returned to the Moroccan cities.

The French military strength had by this time been brought up to 105,000, on paper. Soldiers in the Moroccan units, a small number of *Tirailleurs* and much larger numbers of the irregular *goums*, of especial importance in mountain warfare, were, however, deserting, some joining the MLA. Glaoui dealt the crumbling French policy a fatal blow by switching sides and joining the demands for the return of Mohammed V. The return was conceded amid violent political controversy in Paris, the Sultan arriving home in triumph on 19 November. Formal independence followed in 1956, but not before more bloodshed in the remaining months of French rule.

Fighting took two forms. The first was that of reprisals against the Berber chieftains and *caids* who had earlier opposed the Sultan. Numbers were killed or mutilated, many while on their way to make submission to the Sultan. French forces were ordered not to intervene and an order by the Sultan to end terrorism was not fully obeyed in the major cities for some time.

In the Rif the Sultan's return did not end the insurgency. Insurgent groups, now several thousand strong and drawn from clans hitherto supportive of the French, linked with their Algerian counterparts. In an effort to break this link the French military evacuated all inhabitants from a zone 30 km deep along 150 km of the border. The insurgents also attacked one particular Berber clan, the Beni Snassen, whose political activities they resented. The difficulties facing the French commander, General Agostini, were heightened by the ongoing desertions of Moroccans from his 15,000 troops deployed in the Rif; others who did not desert but refused to fight had to be disarmed and withdrawn by lorry, for which process Agostini had to fall back on the Foreign Legion. Large areas within the Rif passed out of French control.

Only in February 1956 did the situation begin to improve. In 1955 the Spanish Moroccan commander, who disliked France, had allowed insurgent groups to take refuge in the Spanish area – into which on occasions the

French had launched "hot pursuit" raids. In the New Year a Franco–Spanish agreement ended this hostility; also a number of hardline insurgent militants were killed, whether by French or Moroccan hands remains unclear. France agreed not to use Morocco as a base for operations in Algeria, and in return Morocco permitted the remaining French forces to prevent Moroccans from joining the Algerian insurgents. A measure of peace returned to the border areas, though the presence of Algerian insurgents fleeing from the French across the border brought occasional violence.

France and North Africa II: Algeria 1954–62

France's war in Algeria was of an altogether different order, both in scale and time. Algeria was deemed part of metropolitan France, the Paris ministry responsible being that of the Interior. By 1954 the *colon* population had risen to over a million. The constitutional arrangements set out in the 1947 *Statut de l'Algérie* left real power in the hands of the administration and the *colons*, while the eight and a half million indigenous Moslems had no effective voice. Elections were in any case distorted – tax, land and social service arrangements all discriminated heavily against the Moslem indigenous population, many of whom were treated daily with rudeness in the streets and workplaces. The indigenous population was rising fast; at the same time the French had destroyed local chieftaincies that might in times of stress have provided *interlocateurs valables,* and the most effective nationalist political leaders were exiled to France and others were arrested and detained. The French had failed to heed the warning provided by an uprising in the Constantine area in 1945. At the same time, exponentially, the post-war French loss of Syria and Lebanon, military reverses in Indochina and events in Tunisia and Morocco all prepared the ground for rebellion.

The social circumstances outlined above determined the nature of the war to follow. Plans for the uprising were made by a small secret group of nine, the *neuf historiques,* who called themselves the *Comité Révolutionnaire d'Unité et d'Action* (CRUA). None were educated *évolués,* seven were Arab, two were Kabyle Berbers. The *neuf historiques* were Mohammed Boudiaf, Ahmed Ben Bella (a former French Army warrant officer), Mohammed Khider, Hocine Ait Ahmed, Mostafa Ben Boulaid, Larbi Ben Mhidi, Rabah Bitat, Mourad Didouche and Belkacem Krim. The plans provided for insurrection to begin on the night of 31 October 1954, All Saints, a religious festival of significance to the *colons,* for a political front, the *Front de Libération Nationale* (FLN) and an *Armée de Libération Nationale* (ALN), and for an external mission based in Cairo to secure international support.

The limited number of attacks and killings that started on 31 October led the French for some time to underestimate the rapidly expanding scale of the rebellion. At first the insurgents operated in small groups, avoiding pitched battles with the French military. They emulated the Vietminh, but never enjoyed the Vietminh's greatest asset, an area they could control and in which they could hide up and remain secure. Their targets – attacked by a quick strike and a quick withdrawal – were *colon* estates, French military posts and Algerian loyalists, their aim being as much political to attract attention as military. The chain of scrub-covered mountain ranges across northern Algeria was a great asset for the FLN, being ideal for raids and ambushes and a serious difficulty for the French in view of the very limited number of roads. At the outset weaponry was mostly sporting guns, with a few more military firearms acquired from a variety of sources, together with home-made bombs. From the start cruelty and terror, both in the manner of castration, throat-slitting or disembowelling and in the numbers killed or mutilated, formed a vital part of FLN operations. The terror was designed deliberately not only to terrify *colons*, loyalists and small French outposts, but also to set French *colons* against the indigenous population and undermine the whole French-dominated economy. Recruitment, generally by word of mouth, was greatly assisted by the FLN's six-member cell structure, a system gradually extended over all of northern Algeria. The structure provided supplies and intelligence and also distributed propaganda.

The French were caught ill-prepared, their intelligence organizations correctly forecasting rebellion but ignorant of the scale and the identities of most of the leaders. The garrison was 65,000 strong but were mostly in non-combatant units, only some 3,500 being fit for field operations; the French were also heavily dependent on lorries for transport. The Army's unimaginative commander, General Cherrière, was directed to fight on a policy of *repression limitée* with no aircraft bombing, a reflection of the fragility of the Paris political scene. Several sweeps were launched, in which numbers of people were arrested and held in wretched conditions, but the French found real intelligence hard to acquire. Among their few successes were the arrest of the FLN chief in Algiers, the killing of Mourad Didouche, and the capture of Mostafa Ben Boulaid and Rabah Bitat, three of the *neuf historiques*, but overall the first winter of the war was a miserable experience for both the FLN and the French. (Ben Boulaid later escaped, only to be killed in battle with the French.)

Both sides used the relatively low scale of operations to build up their strength. French reinforcements included an airborne division from Indochina and a number of other units bringing the garrison up to some 110,000 by the spring of 1955. As important were the arrival of the first small helicopters, and on the command and staff side, some of the ablest officers in the French Army, notably General André Beaufre. A new and at the outset liberal-minded governor-general, Jacques Soustelle, also initiated a programme of involving the military in direct administration of troubled areas in the *Sections Administratives Specialisées* (SAS), with a wide range of rural and social development, educational, medical and propaganda commitments. These proved popular and successful – until a ruthless military sweep or search undid months of work, with recriminations at command level to follow.

As 1955 passed, the military situation worsened for the French. The insurgents could now field groups of 50 or more; in riposte the French began to disregard the *limitée* directives, using bombs, rockets and collective punishments, including reprisal executions. An event in August marked a turning point in the war, a massacre in unimaginably bloody circumstances and encouraged by the local indigenous population of 71 Europeans and 61 Algerians, many being women and children, in Phillippeville. The massacre was followed by reprisals by *colon* groups equally murderous, in which at least 2,500 perished. The massacre encouraged the FLN to further efforts, destroyed the liberalism of Soustelle and led in practice to an abandonment of *limitée*. To add to French difficulties, some Algerian soldiers deserted, and Moroccans still serving refused to fight.

The French reply was nevertheless a massive build-up of troops, for which the period of conscription was lengthened from 18 to as much as 30 months so as to provide a full two years' service in Algeria, together with the recall of time-expired conscripts. By August 1956 the Army's strength had reached 390,000, to rise to over 410,000 in the following year. The 390,000 total included substantial numbers of North and black Africans, and the figure does not include some 18,000 gendarmes and *garde-mobiles*, 30,000 airmen and 6,000 navy personnel. General Henri Lorillot, the new commander, reorganized the military strategy so as to use units of conscripts, black Africans and some 26,000 locally raised auxiliaries known as *harkis* as static garrisons, and committing his best troops from the *Coloniale* regiments, largely regular and professional infantry, together with the Foreign Legion in pursuit groups which would follow up a group of insurgents for days or, if necessary, weeks. From 1956 detachments of these pursuit groups could be lifted by helicopter. The result was soon evident, Colonel Bigeard's 3rd Colonial Parachute Regiment killing 125 FLN in a pursuit operation. Although never admitted, napalm bombing also proved effective. Construction of a stop-line of wire and minefields along the Tunisian border was also begun to prevent insurgents crossing into Algeria or retreating to a safe haven. The static garrisons fitted into Beaufre's *quadrillage* system in which areas were classified into free-fire zones from which the whole population had been evacuated, zones in which inhabitants and their movements were very strictly controlled, and the major population centres. The system proved increasingly successful. The French navy developed an air/sea surveillance system screening all ships sailing towards Algeria, paying especial attention to any that had left Balkan or Middle Eastern ports. Ships were boarded and over the years considerable quantities of weaponry seized.

French military difficulties, however, remained immense despite their vast numerical superiority. Although food and amenities were provided for the conscripts morale was low. The extension of the draft and recall of reservists had led to protest demonstrations in France. An FLN ambush in which 20 recalled *Coloniale* infantry reservists were killed, the discomfort of heat in summer and cold in winter in the new breeze-block forts and watchtowers, and the obvious contempt of soldiers in the elite *Coloniale*, parachute and Foreign Legion units for the *quadrillage* garrison soldiers all dispirited the conscripts, much of whose time had to be spent in open road-building for later use by elite units in armoured vehicles.

The FLN was also succeeding in building up its strength. By 1956 its attacks extended to the Moroccan border area. The internal military wing, the ALN, now totalled some 8,000 full-time, uniformed and paid insurgent *moujahidines*, supported by approximately 20,000 part-time auxiliaries, intelligence gatherers and food and medical suppliers. Loosely formed groups were being replaced by a structured organization of battalions – *failek* – of 350, companies – *katiba* – of 100 which were the usual field battle unit, and sections – *ferka* – of 35. Money and rifles, grenades and mines were arriving from a variety of sources, and an ALN unit destroyed a small rival insurgent group, the *Mouvement Nationaliste Algérien* (MNA), led by Mohammed Bellounis. In the first two years of fighting, the insurgents had killed more than 500 members of the French security forces at the cost to themselves of some 3,000. In great secrecy the movement had held a major conference of its internal and external leaders in Algeria in the Soummam Valley in August 1956. This gathering established a collective political leadership structure and a military general staff with Belkacem Krim, one of the Kabyle *neuf historiques* with a formidable insurgency reputation, as its head. The ALN was given a rank structure of NCOs and officer ranks to colonel. The *wilaya*, or regions of Algeria, were each to be controlled by a joint political and military committee. Within them some powerful new field commanders appeared, notably Amar Oumrane and Ramdane Abane in the Algiers *wilaya* 4 with the local city commander Saadi Yasef, and in the mountains Ait Hamouda Amirouche, notable for his extreme cruelty. It was generally agreed that the French could not be defeated in battle, and future military operations should be planned to influence world opinion.

The conference also agreed war aims – the ending of French control of Algeria and its land, and the creation of a socialist republic; there was to be no compromise or *bourguibisme*. The event marked an ascendancy of the FLN fighting internally over the external group based in Cairo, and also to some extent an ascendancy of the Kabyles over the Arabs. The externals were further weakened by the interception by the local French command in Algeria of an aircraft flying leaders of the externals, including four of the *neuf historiques*, Ahmed Ben Bella, Hocine Ait Ahmed, Mohammed Khider and Mohammed Boudiaf, from Cairo to Morocco. All were detained in France.

The Suez conflict of November 1956, a product of the Arab–Israeli hostility, lies largely outside the scope of this work. It only needs mention here in that the French belief that President Nasser's support for the FLN was intolerable and must be ended was the leading reason for the decision by the French to intervene. In warfare terms the interesting innovatory feature was that the commander of the French troops involved, General Jean Gilles, directed operations from an aircraft. The lack of success of the intervention further increased the beliefs of the officers of the counter-revolutionary warfare school elite regiments that the Algerian campaign must be won.

This belief greatly influenced the major event of the following year, 1957, known as the Battle of Algiers, an event which was to have a variety of consequences.

In late 1956, held in check by *quadrillage*, the FLN decided to switch its main thrust from the rural areas to the city of Algiers for propaganda and purely military and terror reasons. Ben M'hidi was given the command. Assassinations and bombings (including some set up by attractive fair-skinned Algerian girls presenting themselves as Europeans) secured FLN control of the Moslem part of the city, the Casbah, with its 80,000 inhabitants, despite counter-killings and bombs from *colon* counter-terrorist groups. Law and order collapsed, and the newly arrived commander-in-chief, the enigmatic General Raoul Salan, narrowly survived an assassination attempt. FLN activist strength was estimated at 1,400. The FLN called for the closure of shops and a general strike and the French authorities called in the 8,000-strong 10th Parachute Division, commanded by the redoubtable General Jacques Massu and composed of the most professional but ruthlessly efficient regiments in the French army. The division's soldiers first broke the shop closure by forcibly opening the shops and then, by equally firm methods (detainees replacing strikers), both the strike and the school boycott. Parachute troops then moved into the city operating an urban variation of *quadrillage* known as the *îlot* system of street headmen, street checkpoints and the reporting of all movement in the Casbah; areas were cordoned off and carefully searched, on occasions raids and sometimes helicopter lifts being mounted.

Some 24,000 men, women and girls were arrested, hundreds being subjected to torture, to the French the atrocities of the FLN against the *colon* civilian population justifying such measures. The corpses of approximately

3,000 who died in prison were either immured or weighted, lifted out to sea by helicopter and dumped. Bigeard's 3rd Colonial Parachute Regiment unearthed the bomb factory, and Ben M'hidi was caught but later died in prison. In an attempt to ease the pressure on the FLN in the city, attacks, some of which were very successful, including one killing 70 soldiers, were mounted by the insurgents in the *wilaya 4* Algiers hinterland. Massu's reaction was devastating. Three parachute regiments were temporarily withdrawn from Algiers to reassert control with one, Bigeard's regiment, killing 96 insurgents for the loss of eight in a spirited engagement. The FLN attempted to take advantage of the temporary absence with a wave of killings, met in turn by a *colon* pogrom of indigenous Moslems. Massu's troops were brought back to the city where in a final purge Yasef's lieutenants and other leading insurgents were killed. Yasef himself was arrested and the conduits for weapons supply to the FLN exposed and closed down. Excesses continued: in May as a reprisal for the killing of two parachute soldiers 80 of the indigenous population were slaughtered by special forces.

The Battle of Algiers had two results. In military terms it was a tactical victory for the French. The FLN organization in the city was destroyed, not to revive for three years. The surviving leaders escaped to Cairo and FLN morale suffered accordingly. Far more important, however, were the reactions to the severity and harshness of the French military operation. Many indigenous people, hitherto not wholly hostile to the French cause, were turned from it. Some French in Algeria, including a general who resigned, were also revolted. In France itself church leaders, liberal political leaders and academics opened a barrage of criticism; for the first time there was serious questioning over the propriety of the French campaign and the events contributed to the fall of the Mollet Socialist government in May.

With the Algiers area under French control, fighting for the remainder of 1957 moved to the rural and frontier areas. On the Tunisian border the mine and wire-fence barrier was increased to a formidable obstacle named after the Defence Minister, Morice. The Morice Line was in key areas 20 km in depth, so prohibiting any crossing in one night. It comprised three or four electrified wire entanglements, minefields, and radar and flood-lighting surveillance with strong-points 2 to 3 km apart. To man the line 40,000 men were needed. Behind the line was a road to facilitate the speedy movement of elite pursuit units. On the Moroccan border a less complex but still formidable barrier, the Pedron Line, stretching 150 km inland from the coast, was built.

The lines proved very effective. On occasions a few FLN groups equipped with Bangalore torpedoes, high-tension wire-cutters or tunnelling equipment succeeded in breaking through but most groups, including several large bands, were exposed and annihilated. On one occasion only two insurgents from a group 1,200 strong crossed all the obstacles. The pressures on the FLN led to some defections and internal quarrelling among the leaders. In the quarrelling and vendettas Abane was murdered. Bellounis's MNA briefly reappeared but achieved nothing. The killings spread to the Algerian communities in France, the FLN and other groups killing over 770 of each other in 1957 with greater totals in the years to follow.

Despite these apparent French successes the war in all its cruelty raged on. French forces would fire and destroy villages and move ever increasing numbers of people from their homes. The FLN continued to apply terror, killing over 300 in a massacre in an area suspected of supporting the MNA. The French turned to psychological warfare, partly in projects designed to convert their increasingly hesitant conscript soldiers into supporting the war and partly to try and return the loyalties of the indigenous population to the French cause by courses of reindoctrination, tracts and loudspeakers. Success was limited by the often squalid and overcrowded camp conditions into which now nearly a million indigenous people had been forced to move. Both sides fought an intelligence war, the French using counter-gangs and double agents, the FLN on one occasion controlling an entire 1,000-strong Kabyle unit which the French, until a belated discovery, believed was working for them.

By the end of 1957 the Fourth Republic was strained to the limit. In the field three army corps headquarters at Oran, Algiers and Constantine controlled between them in 300 units one armoured, two motorized infantry, one alpine and eight infantry divisions, with in addition a general reserve of one rapid motorized, one large infantry and two parachute divisions, these latter all including elite *Coloniale* and Foreign Legion units. There was, however, evidence of restiveness and some desertions among the 20,000 Moroccan and Tunisian soldiers and the 20,000 Algerian conscripts. The French met this difficulty by "diluting" the units with Frenchmen, Antilles personnel, *colons* and others. West African units became similarly restructured either formally or by the posting of individuals. The divisions and resentments between the conscript and *quadrillage* units and the elite units worsened, the conscripts simply wanting the war to end and to return home, the elite units, in particular their officers, believing that they alone were patriots in danger of betrayal by politicians, and that all the efforts and deaths of the previous years must not be in vain. They believed that on the ground victory was in sight while at soldier level many young *colons* drafted in to them for their national service were all only too eager to share these views of their officers. The military command failed to appreciate that military successes did not mean the end of the uprising.

At the political level the *colons* were becoming ever more restive and vocal in Algiers, while in Paris successive administrations working within the

Fourth Republic system were unable to devise or impose any political solution. On the international scene France was coming under increasingly vocal criticism at the United Nations and even within NATO. The situation came to a head in the first six months of 1958. In February French aircraft crossed the border and bombed a village in Tunisia, Sakiet, in which, it was claimed, an FLN group had taken refuge. An international outcry followed, resulting in the fall of the Paris government in April and an interregnum. In this interregnum *colon* leaders, most of dubious repute, seized government buildings in Algiers and with the support of Massu and the acquiescence of Salan set up a Committee of Public Safety of themselves and military officers. This body, after various threats, rejected a government being formed in Paris and demanded that General de Gaulle take power in France. There followed several hectic days of confusion in which parachute units were despatched from Algeria to Corsica with, it seemed, a threat to move on to Paris. In these hysterical conditions the French President, Coty, invited de Gaulle to form a government, an invitation de Gaulle accepted, making it clear that for an interim period all policy was to be on his terms.

De Gaulle held no liking for Algeria's *colons*, whose pro-Vichy record in the Second World War he had not forgotten. Unusually for a French officer he had never served in Africa; above all he could understand the force of nationalism. He believed in the renaissance of a great France and, before long, came to see that this would mean concessions to, and if necessary abandonment of, Algeria. He had been brought to power by political and military forces who felt sure that he, as a soldier, would deal firmly with the insurgents, but at no time did he see himself beholden to these groups, or indeed to anyone.

It seems that at first in 1958 he thought his own personal prestige might bring about a solution to the problem, then after a visit to Algeria and seeing that it alone could not do so, in 1958–9 he prepared plans for an associate status for Algeria, with accelerated economic development. By mid-1960 he had come to accept that talking to the FLN was inescapable. De Gaulle's early contacts with the FLN proved abortive, but by 1961 he was prepared to open serious negotiations.

These then were the ideas and emerging policies, taking full legitimate shape within the frame of the new Fifth Republic constitution of September 1958, a Gaullist victory in a general election in November and de Gaulle's own win in the December presidential election. His authority was now politically unchallengeable. At the same time and in response the FLN created a Provisional Government of the Algerian Republic (GPRA) in Tunis; this body rejected de Gaulle's early contacts, his October *paix des braves* amnesty offer, any form of association status and the economic development plan. To emphasize the GPRA's uncompromising attitude, a campaign of bombings and killings in France was launched. This served only to alienate French public sympathy and attract police attention to the FLN's fund-raisers.

The second half of 1958 saw only minor change in the military situation. Improved training, command, intelligence gathering (including interception of FLN units signalling to bases in Morocco and Tunisia) and the use of disinformation tactics secured the French a further round of small-scale local successes. These included the unearthing of FLN groups in hides and caves in mountains, the final destruction of Bellounis's followers who had supposedly returned to the French side but had in fact turned to mass-killings of their own selection, and the total destruction of an FLN attempt to break through the Morice Line. By the end of the year the FLN were war-weary, heavy casualties had reduced *katibas* to little more than 40, desertions were increasing and the leaders were in dispute, four colonels being executed for plotting to destroy the GPRA. Sabotage and killings nevertheless continued, and the FLN's major asset, the force being prepared externally in Tunisia, grew steadily stronger.

In December de Gaulle, dissatisfied with the wily Salan whom he suspected of having applied undue pressure on Moslems in the November elections, replaced him with an air force general, Maurice Challe, as commander-in-chief. Challe was tasked to mount new offensives. These were clearly to secure the best basis for negotiations but perhaps also in de Gaulle's mind was the spectre of Dien Bien Phu. It had to be shown to the army that whatever was to come, the military ending of the war was not to be one of defeat.

Challe, an exceptionally able officer, accordingly mounted the largest-scale and most sophisticated series of operations in the history of post-1945 decolonization campaigning. He first reduced the numbers of units engaged in *quadrillage*, replacing them by *harkis*, extended the free-fire zone areas and developed new tactics for the general reserve elite units. These had gained a new rapidity and flexibility with the arrival in substantial numbers of big troop-carrying Boeing Vertol H-21 helicopters known as *bananes*. These would fly whole units to a scene of action, which would have received a prior bombing and machine-gunning from three or four aircraft; when the units had reduced the FLN to small groups of five or six insurgents fleeing for their lives, *commandos de chasse*, trained especially to live like insurgents and know their habits, would hunt them down relentlessly, by day and night, guided by *harkis*. Insurgents were thus kept on the run for days or weeks, in extremes of heat or cold, at times not daring to speak above a whisper. Any others not killed in these two phases were harried by machine-gunning, napalm bombs and rockets from the air. As in Kenya, Harvard aircraft proved notably effective. The *bananes* could also lift light artillery to support the general reserve units. Challe himself commanded from a field headquarters equipped with advanced technology communications and intelligence-gathering equipment.

By 1958 the French Air Force strength in Algeria totalled over 600 aircraft and 100 helicopters, to increase eventually to 940 and 175 respectively with on occasions further support from aircraft based in France. The machines included 275 Harvards, 100 Mistral jet fighters, 75 Skyraiders, 40 B-26 bombers and a number of F-47 Thunderchiefs. Targets were almost invariably FLN units, the large aircraft bombing in the free-fire zones so making life impossible with attacks on FLN personnel, camels and stock. Reconnaissance aircraft flying continuously forced the FLN to move by night; if in the dark their movements were spotted illuminating flares would be dropped – with terrifying effect. The FLN later recorded they were most frightened by the reconnaissance aircraft which they felt watched their every movement, the Harvards with their noisy engines, bombs and napalm, the helicopter gunships and the sudden appearance of jet aircraft. They possessed no anti-aircraft missiles and were ordered not to fire at aircraft as ammunition was scarce and not to attack airstrips as these were too securely defended. All they could do was master camouflage and learn to interpret the significance of the approach of each different type of aircraft.

Using these land and air assets and tactics Challe launched a series of massive sweeps, from west to east across north Algeria, to force the FLN back against the Morice Line. The first, Operation *Couronne* in the Oran hinterland, took place in February 1959, with 1,600 insurgents being killed and 460 captured. *Couronne* was followed by *Courvoie* in the Algiers hinterland in April, May and June. A double-pronged *Jumelles* was planned for the Kabyles in July until intelligence reports led to a change of plan, carried out with great flexibility and efficiency, for a sweep called *Etincelles* in the Hodna. This area cleared, Challe returned to the Kabyles in October, killing 3,746 insurgents, with a final *Pierres Précieuses* operation in the North Constantine in November. For these large sweeps Challe would commit up to or over 25,000 troops in addition to those already present. For the numerous smaller operations taking place at the same time up to ten battalions might be sent out for two or more weeks at a time. Once an area was cleared SAS detachments arrived for administration, social services and road construction. A negative aspect was, however, the increased number of people who had to be moved for the extended free-fire zones, a further half million, for whom camps and facilities were again inadequately prepared, resulting in numerous deaths from malnutrition and disease. Only towards the end of the year was Challe able to limit the free-fire zones following the use of *harkis* to control terrain.

Some individual successes merit mention. An intercepted signal led to the capture of a *wilaya* leader; French intelligence then for some time controlled a substitute so capturing arms and ammunition. In March 1959 Amirouche, whose ferocious cruelty was applied to any of his own followers suspected of disloyalty – a suspicion on occasions planted by the French – was tracked down, and 73 of his followers were killed. A week later following a tip off and pursuit by a French force of eight-wheeled EBR armoured cars and half-track troop-carriers, Amirouche was himself killed. This success for the French was followed a little later by the death, perhaps at the hands of his own men, of another particularly ruthless *wilaya* leader, Si M'hmed.

By the autumn of 1959 the internal FLN had been smashed and its capabilities limited to occasional attacks on loyalists or small-scale sabotage, its only ray of hope appearing to be the beginning of mortar and light artillery fire on the Morice Line from the external FLN force in Tunisia. The French army had won the purely military campaign inside Algeria, but with the following consequence: the belief in the minds of French officers and elite units that the military victory equated to political victory had been strengthened to a point of fanaticism. Few saw the fallacy, but among them was de Gaulle who saw that if necessary, however victorious the army might be, it had to be broken by the French state to ensure the state's primacy. In Algeria de Gaulle's ideas had progressed to the point of proposing "self-determination" in September 1959. His policy, however, became viewed with increased suspicion by the *colons* who formed their own territorial defence force and established sympathetic contacts with the hardline counter-revolutionary warfare military officers. A crisis broke in January 1960 when the *colon* leaders and their followers tried to seize power in the streets of Algiers, the parachute units standing idly by. De Gaulle ignored his alarmed military and civilian advisers and stood firm. "Barricades Week", as the event was called, collapsed. One victim, however, was Challe, whom de Gaulle regarded as having been too sympathetic to the *colons*. Challe's successor, Crépin, a loyal Gaullist, was not authorized to proceed with the final stage of Challe's strategy, a sweep into the Aurès.

Barricades Week contributed to de Gaulle's decision that serious negotiation with the FLN was unavoidable. Other factors included the near civil war situation that the passionate divisions over Algeria had aroused within French society, Algerian violence in France on one occasion leading to a police massacre of several scores of Algerians, the enormous cost of the military operations, his own age and possible staying power, and the success of the GPRA in attracting international backing. A particular disappointment for him was the failure of secret negotiations with a breakaway group of FLN leaders who were betrayed and executed. In November 1960 he proposed a national referendum in both France and Algeria on self-determination for Algeria, to be held in January 1961. Despite *colon* opposition and a GPRA call to Moslems for a boycott, this referendum produced a substantial "Yes" majority in both Algeria and France. De Gaulle announced that he would open talks with the FLN and ordered a military truce.

The hardline military viewed this development as betrayal. A new terror organization, the *Organisation Armée Secrète* (OAS), was formed in secret, seeking to "eliminate" de Gaulle, against whom there had already been several assassination attempts. A conspiracy to seize power in Algiers was hatched by four generals, including Salan and Challe, the latter motivated by his deep concern over the fate of the *harkis* in an FLN Algeria. The attempt, launched in April 1961, failed with only a few officers and units participating. De Gaulle appealed for loyalty to himself directly to his troops, over the heads of the generals, in a profoundly emotional broadcast. Challe gave himself up, the other three were eventually caught and all were imprisoned. The political effect, however, was to divide the army, so weakening de Gaulle's hand in the negotiations with the FLN.

The military result of the abortive coup was that warfare in Algeria became three-sided. The OAS recruited large numbers of adherents from the *colons* and those military who had sided with the plotters, and its "Delta Commandos" opened their own campaign of killings and terror. The targets included French personnel loyal to de Gaulle, moderate *colons* and hundreds of Moslems. OAS activities spread to France with attacks on liberals and Moslems, de Gaulle again narrowly escaping assassination. In early 1962 the OAS epidemic of the mind extended their activities to the destruction of public utilities and the economic infrastructure in Algeria. The French countered with special police personnel, *les barbouzes*.

July 1961 had seen short but sharp fighting in Tunisia. Under the independence agreement France had retained the use of the naval port of Bizerta. Following frontier clashes President Bourguiba demanded that the French withdraw and harassment of the French installations, including light artillery fire, began. To demonstrate vigour in negotiations with the FLN, France despatched troops, some being dropped by parachute, and at least 350 Tunisians were killed.

A final round of ferociously cruel OAS and FLN killings and torturings formed a backcloth to the last stages of the negotiations. In March 1962, following the OAS killing of French conscript soldiers, 20,000 French troops under the new commander, General Charles Ailleret, and supported by air-to-ground rocket fire cleared the *colon* Bab el Oued area of Algiers in a bloody cordon and search operation. Elsewhere French soldiers stood by while loyal Moslems and on occasions *colons* were massacred. The FLN and OAS then concluded a truce, in practice to implement ethnic cleansing, to enable the *colon* population faced with a coffin or suitcase option to choose the latter. Some 1,450,000 people, the majority *colons* but including some Moslems, were shipped away mostly to France in conditions of misery and ruin. An even worse fate befell the *harkis*. French orders directed that they be abandoned to their fate. Some were massacred under the eyes of their former French sponsor units, others were put to work with no protection clearing mines on the Morice Line. A few were fortunate enough to find French military sponsors prepared to disobey orders and smuggle them to France.

Independence for Algeria came on 3 July 1962. The French agreements with the FLN had provided for civic rights, political representation and security for the *colons*, under the protection of a French garrison for three years. The provisions, together with others in the agreement, notably those supposedly securing French use of the Mers el Kebir naval base, Saharan testing facilities for nuclear weapons and joint exploitation of Saharan oil, proved short-lived.

The total casualties of the war will never be known for certain. French military casualties, including Foreign Legion, Maghreb African troops and deaths from disease or suicide, amounted to some 35,000. Civilian casualties totalled over 3,500 Europeans and 30,000 indigenous population, with an estimate of a further 150,000 in revenge killing. The French estimated the FLN lost 141,000 killed in action, 12,000 more killed by Amirouche and others, and 4,000 killed in France. Deaths in resettlement camps, disease and despair can be estimated conservatively at a further 300,000.

For France the end of the conflict soon brought reward. France had no further need to be defensive in her international relations, and with a sound economy founded on the Monnet plan and new atomic weaponry, de Gaulle became a dominant figure in European and world affairs, with a return to obedience if not loyalty by most of his army before long. OAS activity in France continued for some time but gradually died down with the passing of time. Salan, the last of the 1961 generals still in prison, was released after the 1968 student worker riots when de Gaulle felt it necessary to fall back upon the army; the others had been released earlier.

For Algeria the end of French rule was not to mark the end of violence. Recriminations were exchanged even before independence. Colonel Boumedienne, at the head of the external FLN, formed a temporary alliance with Ben Bella. There ensued a struggle between the various factions, the interim executive of Ben Khedda and the GPRA, Ben Bella and Boumedienne, and a number of *wilaya* leaders, notably the Kabyles leaders Belkacem Krim and Mohammed Boudiaf, two of the *neuf historiques*. Armed groups of the different factions engaged in shooting in the cities and mountains. Eventually in September 1962 Mohammed Khider, another surviving *neuf historique*, arranged a ceasefire. Boumedienne's external FLN units entered Algiers to celebrate and to loot, and following endorsement by a newly elected Constituent Assembly a government headed by Ben Bella but including Boumedienne was formed. Subsequent events are considered later.

France and West Africa: Cameroun

The strain of the Algerian campaign left France with neither the will nor the resources for any further large-scale military resistance to nationalist demands in Africa. The process of decolonization for France's West and Equatorial African colonies, and for Madagascar, was therefore smooth with but two local exceptions: Mauritania, which saw very minor military operations, and Cameroun.[4]

Cameroun had been mandated to France after the First World War and then after 1945 had become a United Nations Trust Territory. The special status led to the appearance of a militant nationalist movement, the *Union des Populations du Cameroun* (UPC), in the mid-1950s. Its leader, Um Nyobe, was a militant, riots broke out in 1955 and the UPC was banned. Some 2,000 of its members, operating underground, launched a maquis-style sabotage campaign in late 1956, targeting railway lines, bridges and telephone wires together with houses in the southern Sanaga-Maritime province. A number of political assassinations of figures alleged to be loyal to the French also took place. In 1957 violence spread to the Bamileke region, with attacks on missions, traditional chiefs and Europeans. Local faction in-fighting was as much a cause as opposition to the French.

The French deployed local *Tirailleurs Sénégalais* detachments and a rein-forced *gendarmerie garde camerounaise;* the campaign's most spectacular event was a parachute drop by two companies of *Coloniale* parachute infantry on Eseka airport, an operation necessary to secure communications between Douala and Yaoundé. In September 1958 Um Nyobe was killed by French security forces. His death brought violence to an end in the Sanaga-Maritime province, though sabotage and killings continued in Bamileke until independ-ence in 1960 and for a brief while afterwards.

Figures of insurgent strengths and people killed were exaggerated by nationalists. Several hundred Africans were certainly killed either by the security forces or the UPC, although nationalists allege several thousand. A few Europeans were killed by the UPC.

Angola 1961

If France had been in no mood for decolonization in the early 1950s, Portugal as late as January 1961 still appeared to believe that any such political development would never apply to the Portuguese territories at all. Portugal's long presence in Africa, "civilizing mission" rhetoric and a belief that national survival depended on empire all fostered a national self-delusion. Revolt when it struck came as a total surprise.[5]

The short-lived uprisings in Angola in 1961, which the Portuguese were able to suppress, nevertheless showed the characteristics that were to prove too much for Portuguese military power 12 years later and caused a domestic Portuguese political crisis even more profound than that in France in 1958. The uprisings reflected not only an internal Angolan African bid for freedom, but also substantial external support for the uprisings and, as important, the mounting internal Portuguese crisis caused by the fissures within the Portuguese corporate – neo-fascist – state of Prime Minister Salazar.

Created in the early 1930s, Salazar's *Estado Novo* was an authoritarian regime backed by the *Policia Internacional de Defesa do Estado* (PIDE), an exceedingly effective secret police permitting no effective political opposition. In the Second World War Salazar had achieved respectability by a timely joining of the Allied cause. This respectability enabled Portugal to become a founder member of NATO, have influential friends in the West – and access at reduced cost to military hardware.

The colonies, "overseas provinces" from 1951, were oppressively administered. Angola had a Portuguese settler population of over 300,000 including thousands of urban working class or inland yeoman farmers besides the big estate and mine owners. Mozambique had a smaller total, some 220,000. The African population was subjected to severe obligatory labour compulsion, petty administrative tyranny, low wages and either a simple literacy education or none at all. The uprising represented the threefold frustration of plantation labour, forced cotton-growing and urban slums. In Angola formal education was virtually limited to the Portuguese and *mesticos*, people of mixed ancestry; only a very few Africans qualified for *assimilado* status. Opposition groups, *mestico* and African, appeared in the 1950s but remained ineffective, their leaders under arrest.

The Portuguese army had lived comfortably, with very limited combat experience since 1918. There was little effective centralized control and the practice of appointing politically reliable colonels as ministers created friction with senior generals. In the "overseas provinces" there were no effective staffs, and logistics and training had both been neglected. The army was in no state to respond quickly to a sudden emergency in a remote province.

The first of the 1961 uprisings broke out in January. The insurgents were members of a dissident Christian sect (a frequent form of African protest in pre-literate communities) that set out to destroy European property and crops on the central plateau of Angola in anger against compulsory labour. The rising, named the *Guerro de Maria* after its leader Antonio Mariano, was quickly and savagely suppressed by the Portuguese military. In February the *Santa Maria,* a Portuguese cruise liner, was hijacked at sea, the hijackers initially planning to sail the vessel to Luanda in Angola and from there mount a challenge to the whole *Estado Novo.* They were deflected from this (the ship sailed to Brazil), but in Luanda, possibly in anticipation of the ship's arrival, a crowd of several hundred Africans attacked a prison in which nationalist leaders were being held, and police headquarters. The attacks were almost certainly organised by the *Movimento Popular de Libertção de Angola* (MPLA), a largely *mestico* Marxist party based in Luanda; the attackers used rifles and machetes. They were suppressed with severity by the police and white vigilante groups, 36 Africans and eight police and prison officers being killed. Rioting and further casualties followed the next day.

The third uprising, backed from across Angola's frontiers, led to a military campaign. The insurgents came principally from the Bakongo peoples of northern Angola, who had their own additional reasons for rebellion – land grievances, resentment over Portuguese nomination of a Bakongo king who was a Catholic, and incitement from the large and mostly Protestant Bakongo population in the former Belgian Congo. The leader of the *União das Populações de Angola* (UPA), Holden Roberto, had been educated by Baptist Protestants and was related to the Congo army commander and later president, Mobutu. Small numbers of UPA activists had been crossing over into Angola to prepare the revolt. A few were deserters from the Portuguese army. The uprising also had some support from another ethnic group, the Kimbundu, but it did not spread throughout the territory. Nor did the MPLA, in difficulties after the suppression of the Luanda riots, make any move in support. Overall the uprising's effect was weakened by the Bakongo predominance and the limited political preparation. Few insurgents at the outset had firearms. As the uprising progressed insurgent weaponry became more effective, including mines and grenades as well as rifles and machineguns. Some had been stolen from contingents, in particular Ghanaian, serving in the Congo or sympathizers in the Congo's *Force Publique*; some were home-made and unreliable. The majority of the insurgents, however, still carried only matchets or cutlasses and weapon supply from the Congo dried up after the fall from power of Lumumba in September 1960.

The revolt broke out on 15 March with a series of attacks by bands of insurgents, in all totalling between 4,000 and 5,000, in the coffee plantation areas of the north. Two areas were particularly affected, the San Salvador-Canda area adjoining the Congo and the Dembos mountains, but the insurgents quickly moved southwards. In the first 24 hours at least 200 Portuguese, including women and children, were killed, most with especial cruelty: flaying alive, torture, blinding, crucifixion or burial alive. Others survived, mutilated. More killings followed. The same ferocity was applied to a much larger number of Africans particularly of the Ovimbundu people regarded as loyal to the Portuguese, *mesticos* and *assimilados*. The first killings were not accompanied by destruction of property, the UPA believing the Portuguese would go, leaving all to them. The later attacks, however, aimed at the destruction of the coffee crop, farms and buildings.

In this anomic violence, use of terror and in much of its fieldcraft the Bakongo uprising was an old-style peasant uprising resembling Mau Mau. Insurgents were initiated, many reluctantly after intimidation, in rituals including oathing, a "sacrament" involving the marking of a cross on the forehead, hymns which assured that any killed would rise again after three days, and invocations to the militant Congolese nationalist leader, Lumumba. Some of the attacking insurgents had taken hemp. Many firmly believed that the Portuguese would leave precipitately, as the Belgians had done. The uprising, however, differed from Mau Mau in its UPA political base and its clearer political aims which provided an effective voice to the outside world, especially the United States. Admitting the use of terror, Roberto argued that it was necessary to force the Portuguese to see reason. The UPA announced the creation of an Angolan National Liberation Army (ANLA) in June 1961 with Roberto as commander-in-chief and two deserters from the Portuguese Army as chief of staff and director of operations, but neither then nor previously did the insurgents have any operational plan linking the various bands.

Caught unprepared the Portuguese reaction was slow but the early killings, a tactical error on the part of the insurgents, did provide time and a warning which served to save the larger settlements and towns. The province's military garrison totalled some 3,000 in two regiments, both in Luanda. In each regiment only one battalion was trained – the other two were training units. All the soldiers were Africans. There were a small number of military aircraft and others from private flying clubs, but at first farmers and loyal Africans had to improvise the defence of stockaded farms and townships themselves. They then began to organize armed reprisal groups of citizen militia; these came to exact cruelty of equal ferocity upon any insurgents they caught. The rainy season had made many roads impassable, delaying military reinforcement. The Portuguese air force, however, was able to offer some limited support in this early stage. The insurgents' greatest success was the occupation of the town of Bembe and the encirclement, a virtual siege, of the district capital town, Carmona, and other smaller towns and areas in the north.

Villages known to have supported insurgents were burnt and the inhabitants killed. The decapitated heads of insurgents were stuck on poles around stockades. Men from other ethnic groups not involved in the uprising were massacred in these reprisals, notably Mbundu in the Cuanga valley and others even further away. By May Portuguese military reinforcements totalling some

50,000 men were belatedly arriving. The reinforcements included parachute troops and special force units. They made the reopening of communications and the recapture of the 100 or more northern administrative posts their first priority, together with the defence of plantations. Bembe was reoccupied in June. By October the army had largely succeeded in restoring order and excesses by settlers and others were stopped. The Army's own methods, however, were often drastic, including air strikes using napalm; the authorities also embarked on a village concentration, or *aldeamento*, policy. The insurgents now turned to a new priority, that of inflicting casualties on the Portuguese troops by means of ambushes, mines, booby traps and concealed road obstacles that turned lorries over. When pursued by the Portuguese, insurgents were able to cross back into the safety of the Congo, but they remained handicapped by poor training, limited weaponry and quarrels among themselves.

As in Kenya, villageization denied insurgents food, rest and medical supplies. Increasing numbers of Portuguese troops kept them continually on the move by harassing sweeps and patrolling. The issue was eventually decided by the destruction and occupation of the three main insurgent strongholds, all after heavy fighting: Nambuagonso on 9 August, the Serra de Canda hill range on 24 August and the Pedra Verde mountain group defended by several thousand well armed insurgents in September. Field artillery, bombing and napalm were all used. Approximately 50,000 Bakongo were killed or died of hardship or disease as a result of the suppressions, while thousands more, including many visibly suffering from napalm burns, streamed across the border into the Congo. Some retreated to the Dembos mountains in the hope that they could be maintained as a fighting force by means of a "Ho Chi Minh" supply trail from the Congo, but this did not occur and from 1962 to 1964 insurgent activity became increasingly limited and ineffective. Total casualties for the year 1961 have been reliably estimated as 2,000 Europeans and 50,000 Africans killed; both the size of the military force committed and the total casualties in the one year greatly exceeded those in the British campaign against Mau Mau.

The Portuguese implemented a few labour and administrative reforms following the uprising and social services were set up in the *aldeamentos*. The Salazar regime signally failed to draw any wider political lesson; the revolt was referred to as the "interruption" of Portugal's historic civilizing mission, further self-delusion setting the stage for the major campaigns to follow. The August 1961 occupation and the burning of the tiny Portuguese fort-enclave of São João de Batista de Ajuda by troops of the newly independent state of Dahomey and the Indian Army's seizure of Goa in the following December were signs of the times.

Chapter Three

Independence wars 1962 to 1980

The second series of anti-colonial liberation campaigns, fought from the mid-1960s to 1980, differed from the earlier conflicts in that governments lost and insurgents secured permanent control over specific areas of the territories affected. Four weapons in particular helped turn the scales in favour of the insurgents in the field: anti-personnel mines, the sturdy Russian-designed Kalashnikov AK-47 self-loading rifle, the Soviet rocket-propelled manual grenade launcher RPG-7 and the Soviet SAM-7 manual anti-aircraft, anti-helicopter missile, the two last giving artillery support to the insurgent (for details of these weapons, see Appendix: Technical Note). The growing strengths and successes of the insurgency movements combined with other external pressures accordingly forced governments to realize that total military defeat, sooner rather than later, was inevitable. Insurgency movements were therefore able to set the pace for political change when circumstances occasioned the opening of negotiations.

The main campaigns were fought in the three Portuguese territories of Angola, Mozambique and Portuguese Guinea, and in Zimbabwe/Southern Rhodesia. In the case of Portugal the pressures of the long drawn-out colonial conflicts were the prime cause of the 1974 revolution in the metropole, as a result of which colonial authority collapsed.[1] The end in Rhodesia was more complex, a result of not only military action but very strong international and economic pressures. Additional reasons for the insurgent military successes were the larger numbers of guerrillas in the field, the foreign training of a number of leaders, a modern weaponry including mortars and field artillery as well as the rifles, missile launchers and mines, the ability to retreat across an international border to a supportive neighbour for recuperation and reorganization, and international interest and support, particularly but not exclusively from Communist countries.[2]

In Portuguese and many Rhodesian eyes this Communist support confirmed their view that the nationalists were simply the tools of a worldwide Kremlin conspiracy. Military doctrine, much influenced by French thinking of the 1950s, accordingly planned counter-revolutionary warfare against a perception, based on the writings of Mao Tse Tung and others, of a carefully staged subversion moving from a preparatory phase creating a politico-military organization, to a phase of agitation and terror, then a guerrilla phase leading to the takeover of a whole area and establishment of a revolutionary government, which in a final phase would field a regular army. Each phase, it was argued, would gather increasing international support and sympathy. The Portuguese saw this support as misguided and prejudiced. The insurgency movements, in differing degrees, followed the Maoist pattern. All of them could claim the moral dignity of fighting an anti-colonial war of liberation but in some, particularly in Angola and Zimbabwe, the leadership had certain additional local territorial aims. The internal strife that followed in Angola, Mozambique and Zimbabwe after independence saw the further pursuit of their aims, and is considered in a later chapter.

Angola 1962–75

The severity of the Portuguese suppression of the 1961 uprising brought a relative peace to Angola for two years, insurgency being limited to the very small UPA groups in Cabinda and the Dembos mountains. The growing divisions and territorial rivalries between the different insurgent groups continued to weaken severely the nationalist challenge. The Marxist MPLA under Agostino Neto continued to draw its support from the Luanda region *mesticos* and the Mbundu. The UPA, after its severe suffering in 1961, was further weakened by the defection in 1964 of part of its purely African Chokwe and Ovimbundu following under Jonas Savimbi. In 1966 this largely southern group formed the *União Nacional para a Independência Total de Angola* (UNITA), with a military wing, FALA. Roberto's UPA linked with another group under the new name *Frente Nacional de Libertação de Angola* (FNLA) in 1962 and shortly afterwards set up a government-in-exile in Leopoldville (now Kinshasa). This government received international support and was given recognition both by the Organization for African Unity (OAU) and the Congo (Leopoldville) government, who then expelled the MPLA. In the small enclave of Cabinda, a detached and oil-rich province of Angola on the north side of the Congo River, two small separatist nationalist movements, the *Front pour la Libération de l'Enclave de Cabinda* and the *Comité Révolutionnaire de Cabinda* appeared. These divisions ensured that the Portuguese were able to maintain a measure of control over some 90 per cent of Angola until the more united and successful uprisings in Mozambique and Portuguese Guinea brought about metropolitan revolution.

The MPLA put together a specific military doctrine in 1963, based on Maoist principles of revolutionary war, the concept of an essential unity of people's militia, active insurgent groups and in due time a regular army. Great stress was laid on political preparation and education, with rural base areas to follow. The military wing became known as the EPLA.

The MPLA first attempted to penetrate the Cabinda enclave by infiltration from Congo-Brazzaville. This attempt failed as the local Bakongo resented the EPLA's Mbundu or *mestico* officers, preferring their own resistance movement, FLEC, despite its ineffectiveness. Under pressure from the Portuguese army the MPLA moved into Zambia and began offensive operations against the Portuguese in the south and east in 1966. An early attempt to cross Angola ran into opposition from the FLNA and was wiped out, and fighting between the two factions continued for some time. Later, EPLA's short-term raids across Moxico province into Bié at first gained some notable successes, some 40 per cent of the territory being under threat. Ambushes, skilful minelaying and light 60 mm mortars supplied from Eastern Europe were all used to good purpose. Small rocket launchers began to arrive in 1970. To prove especially effective in all the campaigns against the Portuguese were the small antivehicle mines which were easy to lay in earth roads and the anti-personnel mines capable of inflicting vicious wounds on, or between, a man's legs. Other weapons supplied to EPLA either direct from Eastern Europe or African nation conduits included Kalashnikov rifles, grenades and light machine guns. Training for a small number of EPLA members was provided in Eastern Europe; more significant for the future was the presence in the Congo of Cuban military instructors. In the late 1960s the MPLA's 2,000-strong EPLA posed the most serious of the military threats to the Portuguese and considerably intensified the scale of the conflict.

By 1970, however, the MPLA was overreaching itself and making the mistake of attempting to spread the conflict over the whole territory, which it did not have the resources to do, rather than peg out and hold specific liberated areas. Some of its methods, enforced recruitment in particular, were arousing resentment. Larger mobile units, organized into columns of 250 subdivided into squadrons of 150 and platoons of 30 moving deep into the centre of Angola, formed vulnerable concentrations easier for the increasingly efficient Portuguese command and intelligence staffs to locate – and destroy. A particular weakness for the MPLA was the logistic difficulties attending an insurgent outward foot march of six weeks or more; detection and harassment were inescapable. The MPLA fared no better in the north, where its small, weakly armed groups were attacked by both the Portuguese and the FNLA, sometimes in co-operation. The FNLA blocked escape into the Congo, destroying groups attempting to do so.

The MPLA's strength at this time was approximately 5,000 men, making it the largest of the three insurgent movements, but only a small percentage could be despatched and maintained in the field in Angola at any one time. A major offensive was made by two groups and ten squadrons at the end of 1971. Its aims included the destruction of UNITA as well as attacks on the Portuguese but it made virtually no headway against either, the Portuguese inflicting heavy casualties. The late 1971 offensive was exceptional and not repeated on the same scale. The greatest numbers were at work in the rainy season when low cloud limited Portuguese aerial reconnaissance. A forward base named Hanoi I had been set up in Angola just across the Zambian border. Another base, Hanoi II, had been destroyed earlier by Portuguese air attack. Operations were supposed to be controlled by a small military political co-ordinating committee headed by the MPLA's president, Agostino Neto, with Henrique Carreira responsible for Cabinda operations and Daniel Chipenda for the eastern front; in practice disputes arose from setbacks and misunder-standings from poor communications. By 1972 large-scale sweeps by the Portuguese had pushed most MPLA insurgents back across the border into Zambia or the Congo.

The FNLA claimed a strength of some 10,000 men in the early 1970s, but 4,000 or even less is more likely. Most of these were based in the Congo, conducting small-scale forays across the border, a very poor use of this safe-haven logistic base. Other 200- to 300-strong groups operated in the Dembos mountains, where they tied down a considerable proportion of the Portu-guese garrison. Their aims were harassing Portuguese forces, kidnapping local loyalists and attacking coffee plantations. The FNLA also maintained a small force of some 300 along the eastern border, largely to assert a presence in the MPLA area. It achieved little, other than impeding the MPLA. FNLA activity was weakened by a mutiny in 1971 in the Congo, which was only suppressed with the help of local troops, and by Roberto's authoritarian personal style and the exclusion of any other than Bakongo from decision-making. Their weaponry came from the Congo – and also China, which was not to be outdone by the Soviet Union; some financial support may also have come from secret United States channels.

UNITA, with a field force of some 500, was the smallest of the insurgent forces, one reason being that it lacked any permanent foreign base refuge. UNITA's strength lay in the eastern Protestant highlands, its leader, Jonas Savimbi, coming from one of the area's royal dynasties. Migrant labourers fleeing from fighting in the north reinforced its numbers. It believed in political indoctrination, Savimbi having studied in Europe and trained in guerrilla warfare in China. It claimed to be a national rather than an ethnic movement, and enjoyed some Chinese support. UNITA opened its military attacks in December 1966 from Zambia, the first on a Portuguese military post at Cassamba being a limited success, the second, an attack on the border town of Teixera de Sousa, a costly failure. UNITA then attempted to cut the Benguela railway, at the time used by Zambia for the exporting of copper; as a consequence UNITA was ordered to move out and Savimbi expelled. UNITA nevertheless remained a guerrilla force in being, notably in the Bié area, even if it was not particularly active.

In 1972, after several earlier attempts, the MPLA and FNLA agreed to set up a joint command but the command never operated satisfactorily and two dissenting factions broke away from the MPLA.

In most of Angola, particularly the south and east, the sparse population and nature of the ground itself – flat sandy soil with little vegetation – assisted the Portuguese. Vehicles were not necessarily bound to move on roads with the attendant risks of mines and ambush. The long frontier borders, which were difficult to control and through which it was difficult to prevent infiltration, were, however, a serious problem. The garrison was increased to some 60,000 by 1970, of which over a third were locally recruited Africans; in addition there were numerous armed local white community and African village protection groups to supplement the military and police. The country was divided into four operational zones, in turn divided into sectors. Priority was given to the north and to Cabinda. Some reports of the time also suggested the presence of South African troops protecting the Cunene hydroelectric scheme in the south or in "hot pursuit" operations across the border with South West Africa other reports note mercenaries from Katanga guarding the northern diamond mines. There was certainly close co-operation with South Africa on intelligence matters, particularly after 1967 when the MPLA appeared to pose a threat to South West Africa. Two frigates and other smaller vessels patrolled the coastline and major rivers.

The Portuguese saw the containment of insurgency as a combination of military intelligence and psychological action, the latter to regain popular support by religious, ideological, social, medical, economic and political measures. Unfortunately for the Portuguese their military units had neither the time nor the trained personnel for an effective psychological campaign even if, within the rigid framework of Portuguese thinking, such a campaign could have been mounted.

The greatest military asset held by the Portuguese was their unchallenged mastery of the air. Air-to-ground strikes were mounted by a variety of aircraft – Italian Fiat G-91s, German Dornier DO-27 trainers especially adapted, American F-84 Thunderjets, Lockheed PV-2s and Harvard T-6 trainers, again adapted. By 1973 the Air Force totalled over 3,000 men with 51 air-to-ground strike aircraft, over 50 light reconnaissance machines, 16 transports and 15 helicopters. Forward units and long-term patrols were supplied from the air, and insurgent woodland food cultivation plots or *kimbos* were destroyed. Perhaps most valuable of all was the arrival in increasing numbers – over 60 by 1971 – of French Alouette III helicopters. These were used for liaison, reconnaissance, casualty evacuation, spraying of defoliants and close support work, each aircraft being capable of carrying four soldiers. In its operations the Portuguese, under the very able General Francisco da Costa Gomes from 1970, followed the French example – a *quadrillage* garrisoning system with mobile reaction groups. Vehicles were strengthened against mines and special vehicles were devised to detonate them safely on roads, while the most important routes were tarred so virtually precluding mine-laying. Dry season sweeps over the flat ground followed the French *commando de chasse* pattern in Algeria, with elite force units either parachuted or flown in to reinforce ground patrols or garrisons, or to clear areas occupied by insurgents already weakened by bombing, napalm and herbicides. A handful of cavalry squadrons also participated in these sweeps and pursuit operations covering the flanks. The kill-rate, estimated by American experts to be 1 to 1, was however very low; the Portuguese claim to have killed over 10,000 insurgents by the end of 1971 appears very exaggerated.

For the population of the east and southeast, the Portuguese campaign involved villageization, the new *aldeamentos* being fortified more effectively than those of 1961. Again following the French strategy in Algeria which had been carefully studied on the ground by visiting Portuguese officers in the 1950s, the Portuguese embarked on the wholesale movement of communities away from the troubled areas, many to the Cunene Basin in the south. Over a million people had been moved by 1973, creating demographic vacuums in the north and elsewhere. The moves, often effected with brutality, were resented by the peoples concerned and provided both propaganda advantage and recruits for the nationalists. The military became concerned with these reactions and urged a slowing down of the transportations. The resentment largely negated the army's extensive psychological social welfare "hearts and minds" programmes. The economic consequences of the transportations were also severe, with heavy losses of production leading to food shortages, only partially offset by the construction of new roads and airfields.

A feature of the campaign was the relative quiet and stability in the cities, particularly Luanda with its numerous MPLA followers. This success was the work of the secret police, the PIDE, now renamed DGS (*Direcção General de Segurança*), who controlled their own force of *Flechas* (Arrows) – non-white barrack gendarmerie.

The last 18 months of the campaign were a period of stalemate. The Portuguese were commanded by several aggressive and able generals, da Costa

Gomes to 1972 and his successor da Luz Cunha from 1972, with Bettencourt-Rodrigues as local commander in the east until 1973. The MPLA's losses – some 2,000 insurgents – in 1971 and 1972 and the withdrawal of Soviet support led to internal divisions and desertions, the surrender of one whole squadron to the Portuguese and to a rift between Neto and Chipenda, the eastern front commander whom Neto blamed for the failures. Chipenda was removed from his command and some of his closest associates murdered. Activity on the eastern border was reduced to very small-scale raids and bombardment of such Portuguese positions as they could reach with their Soviet 120 mm and 82 mm mortars, supplied before the ending of Soviet support. An MPLA attempt to send a force of 150 into Cabinda from the Congo was foiled by the FNLA and other MPLA activity in the north and in the enclave was very limited, DGS *Flechas* contributing to the MPLA's failures in the north.

The FNLA had made some recovery but was still failing to use its Congo base to advantage. Despite the joint command the MPLA was still seen as an enemy, not an ally. Roberto planned a major offensive in 1974, but it never opened. UNITA remained more concerned with the administration of the small area of the southeast that it controlled rather than seeking to extend it; it received a little support from China but lacked the foreign support given to the others. The Portuguese tolerated, and perhaps gave some support to, the UNITA-held area as a check on the MPLA. UNITA never engaged the FNLA, with whom it had an understanding to work against the MPLA.

Although the Portuguese in Angola remained more in control than in the other territories and could claim their operations had exhausted the insurgents, the costs in men and resources were very heavy extra burdens. The garrison's total strength had risen to 65,000 with over a thousand casualties. In this way, and despite the fatal divisions among the nationalists, Angola made its important contributions to the collapse of Portuguese power in 1974.

Mozambique 1963–75

The insurgency campaign against the Portuguese in Mozambique was very much more effective. The nationalist cause was united and received more effective weaponry. The terrain, particularly the forests in the north, was well-suited to infiltration and guerrilla operations and ill-suited to more sophisticated equipment.

The catalyst for revolution occurred in June 1960, when a mass demonstration concerning local issues at Mueda, in the north of Mozambique, was fired upon by police and troops, over 500 people being killed. As a result three protest nationalist groups in exile amalgamated in June 1962 in Dar es Salaam to form *Frenta de Libertação de Mozambique* (FRELIMO), with as its very capable president the liberal, Western-oriented Eduardo Mondlane. Leaders and key personnel travelled abroad, including just under 200 to Algeria with others going to Tanzania, for training and preparation for a guerrilla campaign to start on 25 September 1964. The training included political education; support and funds came from the Organization for African Unity (OAU) and a number of Communist and non-aligned countries.

The Portuguese were aware of these preparations. The PIDE had secured some success through infiltration and had made a number of arrests. They did, however, badly underestimate the strength and the appeal of FRELIMO, believing that the movement might launch raids in the north from across the Rovuma river, the border with Tanzania, but would not at any time be capable of striking elsewhere or of occupying and holding substantial areas of the territory. Their garrison at the outset numbered some 16,000 troops, FRELIMO's initial strike force totalled only 250, who operated in sections of 10 to 15.

The opening attacks were upon administrative and military posts in the northern Cabo Delgado province where the insurgents were well supported by the local ethnic groups, the Makonde. These attacks were moderately successful, but the insurgents found at first that penetration further inland was more difficult as a much larger ethnicity, the Macua, tended to support the Portuguese on account of their dislike of the Makonde. Numbers of Macua, with some Yao and Nyasas, joined the Portuguese-raised home-guard militia. Some early penetration into Niassa followed, together with very small-scale attacks in the third, most westerly, of the three northern provinces, Tete, and in the central Zambezia province. Despite their limited results these attacks imposed upon the Portuguese the necessity to maintain widespread garrisons, which in turn enabled the insurgents to establish and consolidate their authority quite firmly in northern Cabo Delgado and Niassa. Recruitment was continuous and attacking insurgent bands could total 90 to 100 by the end of 1965. Women played a much greater role in FRELIMO than with any of the Angolan groups. Armed women engaged in political educational, clerical and communications work, food cultivation and on occasions in the actual fighting; they were not only important in themselves but in the impact they made on communities in the liberated areas. FRELIMO soldiers when operating in bands wore a ragged uniform, ranks being distinguished by badges. The better training and control to be seen in FRELIMO ensured that attacks were well-planned and less likely to turn to mindless anomic killing. With one possible exception, to be noted later, FRELIMO never mounted any massacres. Rational decisions, even if cold and brutal, were replacing epidemics of the mind. At the same time FRELIMO drew a large part of its strength from areas from which labour had migrated. In areas of successful peasant farming FRELIMO often made little appeal.

As in Angola, Portuguese retaliatory action was vicious and indiscriminate, with the burning of villages, reprisal executions of men suspected of supporting FRELIMO and "hot pursuit" operations across the border into Malawi. Suspects were also made to march ahead of Portuguese troops as human mine-detectors.

By the end of 1966 FRELIMO was fielding some 7,500 men. They had resumed attacks in Niassa and Tete and were beginning to penetrate Manica province; they were now operating from Zambia as well as Tanzania and infiltrating fairly freely across southern Malawi. The Tete region included the site and construction of a vast dam project across the Zambezi river at Cabora Bassa, a project intended directly to supply hydroelectric power to South Africa and at the same time indirectly involve South Africa with the Portuguese cause. From 1968 the dam area became the prime FRELIMO target, though because of its perceived future value in an independent Mozambique the dam itself was not often attacked directly. Dangerous bombardments and effective raids were instead mounted on the construction works, logistic installations and supply routes.

On 3 February 1969 FRELIMO's leader, Mondlane, was assassinated by means of a book parcel-bomb delivered to his home in Dar es Salaam. The murder was almost certainly the work of the Portuguese, though at the time there was considerable internal dissension within the FRELIMO leadership, Mondlane being criticized for his links with the West. His successor, Samora Machel, was a Marxist and from the time of his accession to power FRELIMO looked increasingly to the Soviet Union for support.

The Portuguese were forced steadily to increase their garrison in the face of FRELIMO attacks. By the end of 1967 the garrison had reached over 65,000, of which some 60 per cent were African, and the Portuguese themselves admitted to casualties of 212 soldiers killed, 166 "died" and 3,500 wounded, the large majority of the casualties resulting from mines. As in Angola the Portuguese immediately had recourse to *aldeamento* or villageization – with again the results generally being counter-productive. In accordance with their underestimate of FRELIMO's potential, the bulk of the Portuguese forces were deployed in the north, thus FRELIMO's 1968 attacks on Cabora Bassa came as an unwelcome surprise. The dam area had to be protected by a force of 15,000 men.

In 1970 the vigorous but over-confident General Kaulza de Arriaga was appointed commander-in-chief and, as in Angola, launched a combined military and psychological offensive against the insurgents. The military part took the form of a very large-scale action opening in May 1970 and lasting three months; Operation *Gordian Knot* caught FRELIMO by surprise. They suffered heavy casualties and lost bases and supplies. The Portuguese claimed 651 killed and over 1,800 captured. Many of these, either willingly or under coercion, agreed to return to the forest in Portuguese controlled counter-gangs or in *Flechas*. The Portuguese air force also flew deep into Tanzania in "hot pursuit" operations. The air force strength in Mozambique was smaller than that in Angola, a reflection of the reduced capabilities of aircraft flying over forest areas. It was nevertheless a useful force of a squadron of eight Fiat G-91s, two squadrons of T-6 Harvards and 16 helicopters. Naval launches patrolled the rivers, Lake Malawi and the coast, sometimes carrying naval infantry notorious for their brutality.

The scale of South African support remains unclear; certainly South African mercenaries using private aircraft painted in Portuguese colours were engaged in defoliation. Some reports suggest South African helicopters were used for the quick movement of troops.

Arriaga planned a vast chain of strongly defended *aldeamentos* linked by roads and airstrips in Tete and along the Rovuma as a form of human barrier, together with social service schemes of schools, clinics, model farms and markets within the *aldeamentos,* the merits of which were set out in leaflet raids by the air force. Over a million leaflets were dropped in 1972, but in respect of the development schemes, resources were simply not available for their completion. Arriaga's reoccupation of areas in the north was temporary and unreal and a fatal distraction from the growing threat further south.

Despite his large garrison, Arriaga's forces were inadequate to contain the insurgency. Further, friction between the military and police developed in the general frustration, to weaken both. By 1971–2 the Portuguese were forced back on the defensive in Tete, with Zimbabwe African National Union (ZANU) insurgents moving into northeast Rhodesia adding a new menace to that of the growing FRELIMO threat. Movement in and out of Tete town was so hazardous that in anger and frustration the local Portuguese com-mander ordered his 6th Commando to massacre the inhabitants of three villages, Wiriyamu, Chawola and Juwau on 16 December. Between three and four hundred people were killed. The Portuguese military position worsened further when early in 1972 FRELIMO changed from the harassment of Cabora Bassa to an infiltration southward towards Vila Pery. South Mozam-bique had produced most of the senior FRELIMO leaders and proved immediately supportive. The area also had a historic tradition of successful opposition to the Portuguese in the nineteenth century, a theme developed in FRELIMO political teaching. The Beira railway was attacked, white farmers were targeted, and it appeared that the port of Beira itself was threatened from the south. White settlers rioted in Beira, demanding the transfer of 10,000 troops from Angola, a move completed only three weeks before the revolution in Lisbon.

By 1972, and in the face of the hard and apparently endless campaigning, morale in the Portuguese forces was declining. Patrols would go out and lie up quietly until they could with decency return to their units, or they would make so much noise that they knew FRELIMO would identify them and move away. Arriaga tried to meet this problem with a programme of political education for soldiers, but war-weariness was rife and increased by the growing Portuguese casualty rate as FRELIMO attacks using Russian and Chinese rocket launchers became increasingly effective. Two-thirds of the Portuguese soldiers were black, including many in the elite *Grupos Especiais* and *Grupos Especiais de Paraquedistas* (airborne troops). It is possible that such a unit was used in the massacre of 17 villagers at Nhacombo in Tete province on 6 January 1974, though other factors point to a FRELIMO reprisal for Wiriyamu. The evidence is conflicting and the truth never likely to be known. The Portuguese received or purchased weaponry from America, Britain, France, Italy and West Germany, supplied by them for NATO purposes but redeployed in Africa.

By April 1974 between a quarter and a third of Mozambique was in FRELIMO hands. Even in the north, supposedly regained following *Gordian Knot,* Portuguese bases were surrounded and harassed continuously – a colonel was shot on the runway of the airstrip of one, Mueda. In March 1974 SAM-7 Soviet man-pack size infra-red homing anti-aircraft missiles first appeared and the hitherto unchallenged Portuguese air force sustained its first losses and casualties. The Portuguese were on the edge of defeat. No reliable casualty figures exist for either side, but the death toll for each side will have extended to several thousands.

Portuguese Guinea 1961–74

The campaign in Portuguese Guinea was the most technically advanced of the three insurgencies, and in response produced some exceptionally able Portuguese generalship. Although the territory of Portuguese Guinea was small, in area the size of Belgium, it was to be the stage in miniature of a classic struggle with far-reaching consequences. The insurgents gained from a highly supportive neighbouring territory, Guinea-Conakry, which was itself receiving considerable Soviet support following its rejection of association arrangements with its former colonial master, France. Guinea, and later Senegal, provided base areas from which insurgents had only very short distances – and lines of communication – to cover before being able to strike effectively at the Portuguese. Bush provided cover, and rivers, creeks and inlets offered useful waterways for small groups. The territory, neglected by the Portuguese, had little infrastructure to complicate the insurgency. The insurgents themselves were grouped in a nationalist movement, the *Partido Africano de Independência da Guiné e Cabro Verde* (PAIGC), that despite the lack of development in the territory secured a greater level of mass mobilization than any of the groups in Angola or Mozambique.

The PAIGC had roots going back to 1952 and emerged as a political party in 1956, with as its aim the liberation of both the mainland Portuguese Guinea and the Cape Verde islands. Many of its important figures, including the movement's *mestico* leader, Amilcar Cabral, came from Cape Verde, a factor later to create some friction and one ineffective rival grouping. Initially peaceful in its political aims, the PAIGC turned to violence in 1959 after a strike in which Portuguese troops killed 50 Bissau dockworkers in an event known as the Pidjigusti massacre. Cabral left secretly for Conakry, where he established a headquarters and announced the opening of a military campaign for the summer of 1961.

Using his training and fieldwork experience as an agronomist, Cabral was able to train cadres and devise a very successful homespun mass political philosophy. The main features of this philosophy included firm political control of the military by a *bigrupo* or joint political and military command structure from 1964 onwards, political mobilization aroused by carefully trained cadres that could communicate with and relate to villagers and peasants, and a political creed that, while based on a Marxist analysis and essentially socialist, was not dogmatic or rigid but responsive to local conditions. It was also sufficiently "broad church" to avoid damaging breakaway movements and, despite strains, link together the Cape Verde *mesticos* and the mainland ethnic group, the Balante, which supplied the largest proportion of the insurgents. This evident unity secured the undivided efforts of foreign supporters, the OAU and the Soviet Union as well as Guinea-Conakry and to a lesser extent Senegal.

In areas which it came to control, PAIGC administrations were based on councils in which a majority of the members, although PAIGC approved, were not necessarily PAIGC members. Elections were held in areas liberated from 1963 onwards, and at a national level in 1972 – two years before independence. Attempts by the fighting insurgents to reward themselves, either with political power or property, were put down. Villagers participated actively in both the judicial and social service arrangements, thereby developing a consciousness and sense of unity further fostered from 1972 by PAIGC's own Radio Liberation.

The PAIGC's military strategy was equally well thought-out and in practice generally if not always followed. It aimed at the liberation, after political preparation, of specific areas, starting in the interior rather than in a border area in conformity with Marxist tenets on the essential unity of opposites, front and rear. From these areas insurgency would ripple out to surround towns, though not to attack them. In this way Portuguese control was to be forced back into the towns, with communications between them under continuous attack, thus bringing about the collapse of government. Attacks, small-scale at the outset, usually by groups of 30, were to be made on Portuguese military and administrative posts and economic installations, but there was to be no indiscriminate killing or use of mass terror though Africans supporting the Portuguese were singled out.

For the Portuguese, Guinea's importance was symbolic more than economic. It contributed little to Portugal and there was no settler population, but Lisbon assessed that its loss would predicate the loss of Angola and Mozambique. Portuguese assets included the dislike of the large Moslem Pula (Fulani) population for the Balante and the territory's water network, which they could control by motor-boats and use for transport more safely than the roads. But the weak garrison, still only a few infantry companies as late as 1963, forced them onto the defensive from the start.

The campaign's opening months in 1961 to 1963 saw raids both by the PAIGC and its rival group *Frente para a Libertação e Independência da Guiné Portugesa* (FLING) on military posts and commercial warehouses. FLING, however, soon declined to a few camps in Senegal, producing virtually no military activity. In January 1963 PAIGC operations opened in earnest, with as its new feature the encirclement of three inland towns, Buba, Fulacunda and Tite. Very swiftly the insurgents' ripple strategy secured them substantial gains – 15 per cent of the territory by the end of the year including the island of Como. Initially PAIGC fighting units were small, averaging 20 men, but units grew in size to over 100. By 1971 the strength of the military wing of the PAIGC, *Forces Armadas Revolucionaras da Populace* (FARP), totalled well over 6,000 with increasing numbers of foreign advisers, including some from Cuba, the Soviet Union and Czechoslovakia. The larger units operated by night out of base areas in Guinea or, from 1966, Senegal, with smaller, mobile, often irregular or part-time *tabarca* guerrilla detachments in the liberated areas. These, together with the "militia" local supporters, conformed with the Maoist three-tier principle. Almost all were equipped with the Soviet AK-47 Kalashnikov or its Chinese replica. The PAIGC's command and control provided for three regional commands, north, south and east, with each of the regions divided into sectors. Casualties were treated in field hospitals in the Guinea and Senegal bases; some were sent to Eastern Europe.

The operational art included numerous attacks on barracks, airfields and sea and river ports, with very extensive road mine-laying and ambushes. Mines were also hung from trees. Once again the psychological effect of the anti-personnel mines, requiring perhaps three or four comrades to rush to the aid of a man who had lost his all, was profound. Chinese convex-faced directional fragmentation bombs launched from ambush at targets and projecting some 600 steel fragments had an equally devastating effect. Some attacks were supported by Guinean field artillery firing across the border, others, from 1971 onwards, by the PAIGC's own 122 mm rocket launchers.

The Portuguese response was to build up the strength of their own garrison, to total some 30,000 by 1971. About one half of this total were locally recruited, many coming from among the Pula. Their style, particularly after an unsuccessful attempt to reoccupy Como in 1964, remained essentially defensive, the guarding of strong points protected by obsolete 140 mm howitzers. These would return fire when a post came under mortar attack but the assessments for this return fire were haphazard, rough calculations of direction and range. Other equipment included the NATO 7–62 self-loading rifle, and Daimler and Panhard armoured cars. Among the fixed-wing aircraft were Harvards, Fiat G-91 aircraft with British engines and American PV-2 Harpoon bombers, together with Noratlas transports. Napalm was used, but the use of defoliants was generally limited to work in support of road-building to avoid ambush. General Schulz, commander-in-chief from 1964 to 1968, reasserted a measure of control over major roads and embarked on an *aldeamento* fortified village policy, arousing the same resentment as had appeared in Mozambique. Counter-insurgency equipment was improvised – beer bottles suspended on wire perimeter fences clinked as a warning when insurgents tried to cut the wire and wooden staffs with a strip of metal on one end were used for mine detection. On occasions companies would be dropped by parachute.

From 1968 onwards the conflict entered its last and most dramatic stage. The Portuguese appointed as commander-in-chief a general of exceptional ability, Antonio da Spinola. At first sight an old-fashioned cavalryman with eye-glass and riding crop, Spinola possessed a wider political and humanitarian vision than any of the other Portuguese commanders. He immediately set out a rejuvenated political programme and instilled military operations with his own vigour, immediate priorities being co-ordination of the administration and military and improved intelligence gathering. He was able to draw on the increased number of Portuguese personnel trained by the United States in the light of the Vietnam experience.

On the political side, Spinola planned for a *Guiné Melhor* – Better Guinea. The Army was committed to a massive road-tarring and house, hospital and school building programme. The *aldeamento* policy was extended – but on a voluntary basis. Despite strict orders to exterminate the PAIGC Spinola opened discreet contacts with its leadership, going unarmed to meetings with them and trying to convince them that his new Guinea would accommodate them. To the end greatly respected by his opponents, Spinola would ensure equal treatment for both Portuguese and PAIGC casualties to be evacuated by helicopter.

He nevertheless continued to fight the campaign hard, assisted by the arrival of 12 Alouette III helicopters, of particular value in a territory as small as Guinea since they could reach an incident area very quickly. An area in which insurgents were identified would be strafed by aircraft cannon and machine-gun fire, then bombed, then finally 12 to 16 helicopters would arrive each carrying some five or six soldiers. Earlier in Angola Spinola was frequently to be seen jumping out first from a helicopter under fire or personally leading a bush patrol for several days. In Guinea he contributed the same personal charisma, to the admiration of his regular soldiers but not of his less motivated conscripts. He created his own special force, the *Commandos Africanos,* over 80 per cent African. He also directed an attack by armed exiles in November 1970 against the government of Guinea-Conakry and the PAIGC's headquarters in the city. The attack was a failure, and for a long time the Portuguese denied any complicity. Probably more genuine were the Portuguese denials of involvement in the murder of Cabral in Conakry in 1973. The cause was primarily rivalry between Cape Verde and mainland PAIGC chiefs, but it is possible that there were some secret Portuguese contacts with Cabral's killer, his naval commander. Otherwise in the case of Portuguese Guinea, Portuguese forces were not committed to "hot pursuit" across the borders of Guinea-Conakry or Senegal, nor did they engage in mass food-denial operations.

The PAIGC showed its solidarity in its reaction to Cabral's death by remaining steadfastly united. It received a massive input of new weaponry in 1973 – these included SAM-7 missiles which were first used in March of that year and began to impose a steady toll upon Portuguese aircraft, four in the first half of 1973 alone. Cuban personnel appear to have been at work, either as instructors or actually firing the rockets. Nigeria supplied some Soviet 122 mm field guns which were used to bombard Portuguese posts at ranges beyond those to which the older Portuguese guns could reply. In addition two Portuguese strongpoints suffered very heavy casualties as a result of PAIGC artillery, thereby further eroding the Portuguese ability to continue the campaign. Reports of Portuguese pilots refusing to fly over certain areas and desertions of Portuguese troops began to circulate. Strongpoint garrisons of 120 to 1,000 men were reduced to living under siege conditions, frightened and anxious only to return home, with Portuguese control limited to the capital, a few townships and, on occasions, roads.

As early as 1968 Spinola appreciated that a military victory was unattainable and on successive visits to Lisbon attempted without success to convince the Portuguese government of this. President Senghor of Senegal, apprehensive over the influence the pro-Communist President of Guinea-Conakry, Sekou Touré, might gain from a PAIGC victory, then recommended a ceasefire to be followed by negotiations. This peace process was warmly commended to Lisbon by Spinola, but was again turned down. In September he resigned, giving as his reason "the lack of support by the central government in Lisbon for his policy of increasing participation of the African people in building an enlarged African-Luso-Brazilian community". On his retirement he wrote a book, *Portugal and the Future* (*Portugal e o Futuro*), developing this theme and pointing out the impracticability of purely military solutions in view of the costs, the ability of the insurgents to secure recruits and intimidate those opposed to them, and international reaction likely to follow any severe action such as food denial. His successor, Bettencourt-Rodrigues, continued the unavailing struggle until the Lisbon revolution despite a formal declaration of independence by the PAIGC in September 1973. This declaration was recognized by a majority of UN members and formal admission to the UN followed in December, an equation with the reality within the territory.

No accurate casualty figures for the 11-year campaign exist. The Portuguese admitted 1,875 metropolitan soldiers killed; the loss of some 6–8,000 indigenous soldiers also seems probable. Insurgent casualties will have been higher, probably in the order of 12,000 dead.

Revolution in Portugal and the Aftermath 1974–5

The crises of Mozambique and Guinea brought matters to a head in Portugal, where the strains of the wars had become intolerable for the poorest country in Western Europe, causing the system to collapse.

As early as April 1961 a group of senior defence staff officers had decided that Portugal's policies in Africa could not succeed in the long term and formed a conspiracy to oust Salazar. The conspirators, including notably da Costa Gomes, then a colonel, were betrayed and retired or were transferred. As the wars dragged on, the strains became yet more clear. At least 11,000 metropolitan Portuguese soldiers had been killed and a further 30,000 or more wounded or mutilated. The limbless and blind, the scarred physically and mentally, were everywhere to be seen. The expense of the wars had led to increased taxation, inflation and rising living costs; men, including numbers of skilled workers and professionals, were called up for extended periods of conscription – and many recalled for a second or even third tour. Soldiers deserted, and there was a mass emigration of young men due for call-up. Left-wing Lisbon dockworkers from time to time pushed military equipment destined for Africa into the sea.

Internationally Portugal had become an outcast, South Africa and, on occasions, Israel her only friends. Markets in countries opposed to Portugal's wars had been lost, national economic assets had had to be sold to foreign enterprises. There had been a brief flicker of hope in 1968 when Salazar, disabled by a stroke, was replaced by Marcello Caetano, but it soon became clear that real power remained with the ultra-conservative President, Admiral Tomas, and a group of senior armed service officers determined to pursue the wars. This group did not include Spinola or da Costa Gomes.

Within the army's officer corps the wars had necessitated change and expansion. Opportunities to enter the military academy, before 1961 largely limited to young men of conservative backgrounds, were widened. University graduates were accepted for a shortened course. Many of these had been imbued with the student radicalism of the 1960s, or were avowed communists or extreme left-wing socialists. These saw the colonies in Leninist terms, of capitalist exploitation by companies, or settlers using the Portuguese army to defend their interests. Even a number of the more traditional Portuguese officers underwent a conversion to radicalism. Others saw a future for Portugal in Europe and no longer one in Africa. A Movement of the Armed Forces (*Movimento das Forcas Armadas* – MFA) reflecting various discontented young and middle-level officer groupings, was formed in 1973. It was supposedly non-political and concerned with officers' careers; in practice it was the reverse. By the end of the year its more vocal figures were openly critical of the colonial wars, some even advocating revolution. There was also a general feeling that unless action was taken the army would be made the scapegoat for the failure of the government's policies and for military defeat.

General Spinola's book, published in February 1974, came as the signal for action, particularly when both Spinola and da Costa Gomes refused to attend a meeting specially convened at the presidential palace to reaffirm Portuguese African policy; as a consequence of their refusal both were dismissed. A coup attempt in March failed; on 25 April a better prepared coup succeeded with mechanized units led by MFA officers taking control of key installations in Lisbon without any difficulty or bloodshed. A "Junta of National Salvation" was formed by the MFA who invited Spinola to head a new government. Within the MFA, however, the more radical groups steadily gained ascendancy. They first obliged Spinola to abandon his Lusitanian community dream and to grant full independence to Guinea and Mozambique for 10 September 1974 and for 25 June 1975 respectively. They then forced him to resign amid an outbreak of strikes, occupation of factories and farms, and demonstrations in favour of da Costa Gomes, who believed Portugal should free herself from African commitments, a view in line with the MFA radicals.[3]

The events that ensued in Portugal – a tumultuous period in which government only returned from the extreme left to the centre left with difficulty – are outside the scope of this work. Within each of the African territories events were to follow a different pattern as the Portuguese withdrew. In Guinea, the PAIGC welcomed the coup, though fighting continued in a desultory way until agreements were reached with the new Portuguese military. The PAIGC's insistence on the inclusion in the new state of the Cape Verde islands proved a hitch, but agreement was eventually reached and the Portuguese withdrew all troops in the autumn. It was agreed there would be no reprisals. The military withdrawal was effected smoothly and in the event Cape Verde achieved independence later on its own.

In Mozambique, despite the new regime's release of over 500 FRELIMO captives, the war continued, with the Portuguese soldiers ever less willing to fight and FRELIMO opening a new front in Zambezia in July. When Spinola on 27 July conceded the right to full independence the atmosphere changed. Negotiations opened in Lusaka; these concluded on 7 September with a ceasefire, the agreed June 1975 independence date and a FRELIMO-led transitional government.

This government had then to deal with Portuguese settler reactions. Machel was prepared to allow them to remain and one group specifically sought accommodation with FRELIMO. Another larger body, RICO (Portuguese for "I stay"), was more militant, and from its followers emerged a group who styled themselves the "Dragons of Death". The Dragons moved in on Mozambique's capital, Lourenço Marques, seized key government installations and proclaimed that they would set up their own government. The Portuguese reacted firmly and troops were ordered to reoccupy areas and installations taken by the Dragons, a mission accomplished in five days. The Dragons' action, however, led to an African counter-action of rioting in which over 100 people, almost all African, were killed. Again the Portuguese Army had to intervene to restore order until, on 13 September, FRELIMO troops entered the capital. The year 1974 saw a steady exodus of the Portuguese settler population; this exodus was continued throughout 1975, leaving only very small numbers from the original 220,000 and having a disastrous effect on Mozambique's economy.

In Angola the first 18 months after the Lisbon revolution were even more chaotic. Spinola hoped for a ceasefire and a two-year transition period in which it might be possible to prevent the MPLA taking power, but this project collapsed with his fall from power and the preference of the last extreme left-wing Portuguese governor, Admiral Rosa Coutinho, for the MPLA. The FNLA's mix of links and often rash support from the non-Soviet world, notably the United States, together with a massive delivery of weapons from China fuelled the MPLA's suspicions and ambitions. France gave UNITA and the small Cabinda group FLEC some covert aid and support. The three rival nationalist movements began to struggle for power and resources in the name of ideology and ethnic loyalties, so setting the stage for foreign intervention and the civil war to follow. UNITA agreed to a ceasefire with the Portuguese, but the MPLA and FNLA would not. Negotiations opened, and were complicated by the ongoing fighting, vicious race rioting in July in Luanda in which nearly 200 Africans were killed, and an attempt to declare independence by Portuguese whites in October, a project suppressed by the Portuguese military. In January 1975 the three movements cobbled together an agreement in Nairobi which established a transitional government and agreed an independence date of 11 November. The agreement soon broke down. In February Chipenda's wing of the MPLA revolted against the party and merged with the FNLA, and in March fighting between the MPLA and FNLA broke out, several hundred people being killed. The MPLA with Soviet assistance attacked the FNLA and UNITA in Luanda, while FNLA–MPLA fighting continued in the north and south. In June the MPLA opened an attack on UNITA in Luanda and on FLEC in Cabinda. Despite international attempts at mediation the fighting intensified in July and August. The MPLA succeeded in clearing both of its rivals out of Luanda and expelling UNITA out of most of the coastal and central districts. The Portuguese began to withdraw their troops and people who had been loyal to them, the British Royal Air Force providing some of the transport. By mid-November all Portuguese troops and thousands of settlers had left.

On the day of independence, 11 November, the MPLA proclaimed a government headed by Neto in Luanda, while UNITA and the FNLA proclaimed a rival government headed by Roberto in Ambriz. The MPLA was the better placed, holding the country's capital and chief port. The issue was, however, not to be decided on local strengths and Angola was to become the scene of international great-power politics – the Cold War by proxy.

The two major former Portuguese possessions now both had Marxist governments in their capitals. South Africa's buffer zone of white-controlled territories to the north had been breached in two areas. Subsequent events were to reveal the full wider consequences of the collapse of Portuguese power.

Zimbabwe 1965–80

The British colony of Southern Rhodesia was, in status, a territory of the colonial Empire. From its earliest days it had, however, been ruled by its local

white settler minority which produced its own political leaders and administration, a fact recognized by the British grant of full internal self-government
in 1923. A post-1945 British-created Federation of Rhodesia and Nyasaland,
linking Southern Rhodesia with the two Colonial Office administered territories to the north, Northern Rhodesia and Nyasaland, came to an end in
1963, these northern territories moving towards independence in the following year under African majority rule. The Southern Rhodesian government
under its premier, Ian Smith, refused to accept such political development
and, in defiance of pressure from Britain, unilaterally declared the territory a
fully independent state on 11 November 1965. The 1961 constitution of the
territory provided for a large majority of white members in the legislature
with no prospect of any short or medium-term advance to African majority
rule. White minority rule seemed established for ever. Faction fights and riots
in the African areas of the major towns from the later 1950s onwards were a
forewarning of African resentment.

The 15 years that followed the declaration of independence saw an unfold-
ing series of political, international, economic and military pressures on the
territory that eventually brought about majority African rule, the totality of
these pressures rather than any single one being the catalyst for change. The
narrative that follows concentrates on the military operations, setting these
only briefly in the wider context of other events; these cannot be described
in detail here.[4] The military operations themselves fall into three quite
distinct phases. The first phase, between 1965 and 1972, was one in
which Rhodesian security forces without much expansion maintained a clear
ascendancy, and insurgent activity was limited and well under control. In the
second phase 1972–6 insurgent activity increased sharply, and the situation
became a military stalemate which began to draw seriously upon Rhodesia's
resources. In the third phase, after 1976, the Rhodesian forces were fighting
a losing war.

International reaction to Rhodesia's declaration of independence was
wordy and included economic sanctions and an oil embargo, with British
naval patrols to enforce the blockade and RAF aircraft sent for a few months
to Zambia. These measures were almost entirely ineffective as South Africa
provided a virtually complete loophole. Insurgent activity from the start
suffered from continuous and crippling internal divisions, those between the
Zimbabwe African People's Union (ZAPU) founded in 1961 by Joshua
Nkomo, and its 1963 breakaway rival, the more militant Zimbabwe African
National Union (ZANU) led at the outset by the Revd Ndabaningi Sithole.
ZAPU and ZANU each developed a military wing, the Zimbabwe People's
Revolutionary Army (ZIPRA) backed by the Soviet Union, and the Zimba-
bwe National Liberation Army (ZANLA) respectively. ZIPRA was prepon-
derantly Ndebele with a higher proportion of townsmen than ZANLA which

was predominantly Shona and peasant. Both in these early years were penetrated by the Rhodesian Central Intelligence Organization who were aware of their training and movements. They additionally suffered badly from inexperience, though small numbers from both had received some training in Tanzania, Eastern Europe or China. ZIPRA strategy tended to follow Soviet thinking, with an emphasis on weaponry and the hope of an eventual conventional battle and victory such as that of the Vietminh at Dien Bien Phu. ZANLA placed greater emphasis on politicization of the areas in which they planned to operate.

Rhodesia's forces in 1965 included the police (in practice a gendarmerie, 8,000 strong, of which one-third was white, with a reserve of some 5,000), and an army of two regular infantry battalions, one white, the Rhodesia Light Infantry (RLI), and one of black soldiers and white officers, together with a small Special Air Service (SAS) unit, other smaller army units (including batteries of 25-pounder field artillery, later supplemented by some South African medium guns), and a reserve regiment for conscripts after service. Rhodesia's powerful air force comprised a squadron each of Hawker Hunter fighter-bombers, Canberra bombers and Vampires capable of being used for air-to-ground strikes, together with a number of light aircraft, notably Cessna Lynx which also proved useful in machine-gunning and bombing, and adapted civilian machines. Of especial value were Alouette helicopters, their total number gradually being increased to 50, with more on loan with their crews from South Africa. As in the Portuguese campaigns they served as gunships and troop transports. Also used for troop transporting and for the dropping of parachute troops were a variety of aircraft including Dakotas.

The campaign proper opened in April 1966 when a 14-strong ZANU group crossed into Rhodesia from Zambia. On 28 April seven of this group, all Chinese trained, were surrounded and killed by police at a farm near Chinoyi in the northwest. This action has been commemorated by nationalists since, with 28 April named as Chimurenga Day. Chimurenga is a Shona word originally used to describe the resistance struggle against the arriving white settlers in the 1890s but now re-used to describe the 1965–80 conflict. Other members of the ZANU group went on to kill a white farmer and his wife before their own capture and arrest.

The years 1966–8 saw a limited number of insurgent incursions. In one in August 1967, a 90-strong combined ZAPU and South African National Congress (ANC) force met with disaster, almost all being killed or captured by Rhodesian forces. Other such joint incursions in August 1967 by 80 ZIPRA and ANC in early 1968, by 125 men in early 1968 and in July 1969 by 90 men met similar fates, with heavy insurgent and very light security force casualties. The journey from Zambia and the concentration of Rhodesian forces near the border made such incursions suicidal. In the insurgent camps in Zambia and Tanzania morale slumped and recriminations abounded. The year 1969 was almost without incident. A very small-scale urban bombing campaign mounted by left-wing whites, academics and others scarcely represented even nuisance value.

For the insurgents the lesson was the need for greater care and preparation, in particular intelligence gathering. ZANU criticized ZAPU's links with the ANC and their Soviet confrontational partisan-style action before proper political preparation and the formation of cadres. There was friction and occasional clashes between the two groups over coerced recruiting. ZANU itself turned to China for both doctrine and instructors; they also sought FRELIMO's consent to operate from Mozambique. FRELIMO would have preferred ZAPU, but they were unwilling. Under the guise of being part of FRELIMO, ZANU began a slow but thorough build-up of forces in Tete province, supervised by the ZANU command, *Dare re Chimurenga*. ZANLA's recruiting included the invoking of the spirit of the Shona national prophet of the 1896 resistance period, Chaminuka, by means of a medium claimed to be the reincarnation of Nehanda, a powerful medium of that period. At the same time its technological capabilities were extending to inter-unit radio communication, in turn monitored by Rhodesian army signals intelligence. ZIPRA, with its high percentage of Ndebele personnel, presented the last Ndebele ruler Lobengula as its hero.

These linkages with ancestors were of very great importance. Unlike Kenya's Mau Mau, where traditional religious beliefs played virtually no part in rallying mass support for the nationalist cause, in Zimbabwe, the mediums, through shared systems of rituals, effectively conveyed ideas on the rightful ownership of land and the propriety of moving into sacred groves or caves, giving the insurgents more claim to be a people's uprising.

Overall, despite one small-scale attack on the Victoria Falls airport in January 1970 and other occasional stock thefts, sabotage attempts or landmine traps, Rhodesia appeared to have little cause for anxiety. Police counter-insurgency units, sometimes helicopter lifted, were in use more often than troops; also particularly effective were PATUs (Police Anti-Terrorist Units) – tracking units formed from former members of the Police Reserve. These, and small military patrols, were greatly helped by a locally produced light field radio. The police also developed counter-gangs of captured insurgents turned to loyalism on the Kenya model, and numbers of Africans were arrested and convicted for covert support for the insurgents.

Following the incursion by ANC insurgents, South Africa provided over 2,500 reinforcements, some police and some military personnel purporting to be police, to assist. Their presence was a mixed blessing for the Rhodesia command; the South Africans gained badly needed experience but were later to prove a political liability.

Two attempts to unite ZAPU and ZANU, one in October 1971 leading to a short-lived Front for the Liberation of Zimbabwe and one in March 1972, were brokered by the president of Zambia; both failed. Official Rhodesian figures covering the period to June 1970 claimed that 170 insurgents had been killed since 1966. Twenty whites had been killed by insurgents.

The second phase of the war began in December 1972 when both the military and the political situation began to deteriorate. The collapse of Portuguese authority in Mozambique in 1974 opened the whole of the 800 km Rhodesia/Mozambique border for operations. The South African government, fearful of the arrival of a Cuban force in Mozambique as well as Angola, developed its efforts to act as "honest broker", believing that a moderate African government would be its best protector. The presence of at least 2,000 South African troops in Rhodesia was used as a lever, but most were withdrawn in 1975. Both insurgent movements received further support from the OAU, China, Cuba, the Soviet Union and Algeria.

Opening this renewed phase of activity a ZANLA force under Rex Nhongo crossed the Mozambique border and attacked Altena farm in the north. This attack was quickly followed by a succession of assaults on white farms in the north, occasioning several security force casualties. The success of the attacks and ZANLA's emphasis on politicization denied intelligence to the government and provided recruits for the insurgents. Attacks were also launched against the railway line to Beira. ZANLA co-operation with FRELIMO grew; in both, command was devolved to regional and local levels. By early 1976 some 1,600 insurgents were operating within Rhodesia with at least a further 2,000 under training and many thousands more awaiting the opportunity to train. New weapons reaching the insurgents included the destructive Soviet RPG-7 grenade launcher and mortars.

Not before time the Rhodesian government at the end of 1972 set up a Joint Operational Command for military, air, police and administration in the northeast. The Army's deployment was called *Hurricane,* totalling 20 companies by the end of 1973. The Zambian border was closed in the hope, to prove vain, that the ZIPRA insurgents in the area would be eliminated and the security forces released become available for use against ZANLA in the northeast. February 1973 saw the forced move into protected villages of 50,000 people in the northern Chiweshe area, a move much resented and providing more recruits for the insurgents. The adoption by the government of collective punishment measures only further increased the resentment.

The government also created Civil Defence Aid Committees throughout Rhodesia, and offered instructions and help in the protection of farms by wire and guard dogs. In respect of the African population the division within government of opinion between those who believed massive force and firepower would keep the African population subdued and others who believed in reform measures including a measure of African advancement precluded any successful policy of rallying support such as that evolved by the British in Kenya in the 1950s.

The insurgents too had internal divisions due to poor leadership and supply difficulties arising from lengthening lines of communication. In addition to the ZANLA/ZIPRA split, an internal split within ZANLA developed, carefully fostered by Rhodesian intelligence who also supplied disinformation to the Zambian authorities hosting ZANLA camps. In the course of these machinations, Herbert Chitepo, the ZANU chairman in Lusaka, was killed by a bomb in March 1975, an event which led to intervention by the Zambian army, the closure of ZANLA's two camps in Zambia and the detention by the Zambian authorities of 1,300 or more insurgents, with a further 50 removed in internal ZANLA purges. This setback and the release from detention of Joshua Nkomo and Robert Mugabe by the Rhodesian government briefly created a more relaxed atmosphere for the rest of 1974. The Portuguese revolution led temporarily to a cessation of "hot pursuits" into Mozambique, but in Rhodesia a short-lived ceasefire brokered by Tanzania and Zambia collapsed following misunderstandings and shooting incidents. The main consequence was a tonic effect on the insurgents and a discouraging impact on the Rhodesian forces.

In 1975 ZANLA resumed incursions from Mozambique, and in reply Rhodesian forces returned to the pursuit of insurgents further and further into Mozambique. The war became increasingly dirty. The insurgents, avoiding the firepower of the security forces, concentrated on terror and the killing, maiming and torturing of men, women and children as a complement to politicization. Within the security forces excesses occurred in prisons and camps leading to torture and deaths. The security forces' "dirty tricks" included attempts to assassinate Nkomo, the fomenting of divisions between ZIPRA and ZANLA, between ZANLA and FRELIMO and within FRELIMO itself, and the provision by a devious route of poisoned uniforms to the insurgents, several hundred dying in great pain on their way to training camps. The counter-gang operations, too, deteriorated in standards, the gangs being taken over by the Army as the Selous Scouts and gaining an evil reputation for both braggadocio and brutality. Of greater significance for the future was the recruitment by the Rhodesian intelligence service of Mozambicans opposed for one reason or another to FRELIMO. These were used for intelligence gathering and other special operations and were to form the nucleus of a formidable guerrilla movement in Mozambique from the late 1970s onwards.

The mounting insurgent challenge brought increasingly severe pressures on Rhodesia's economy and society – as it was meant to do. In 1972 national service was lengthened from nine months to a year, and extended to include coloureds and Asians. The protected villages scheme was developed, nearly a quarter of a million Africans being concentrated in them, often in disease-ridden conditions. These pressures on the Rhodesian government, in particular from South Africa and also Zambia which was facing economic ruin as a result of the war, led to talks in August 1975 between Smith and nationalist leaders. The talks failed but Rhodesia was soon to fall under new and significant diplomatic pressure from the United States, with major consequences in the following year following much shuttle diplomacy by the American Secretary of State.

In January 1976 a short-lived new force, the Zimbabwe Peoples' Army (ZIPA), took to the field. ZIPA represented the disillusion felt by activists in both movements over the internecine feuding. Elements of ZIPA launched a new offensive in northeast Rhodesia in January 1976. Although 90 strong it achieved little; one member captured by the Rhodesians revealed plans for two further ZIPA strikes further south and with the advance warning these attacks were contained. ZIPA, however, was not trusted by FRELIMO, who detained several of its leaders, the remainder returning to ZANLA or ZIPRA.

ZIPRA had launched several penetration raids in April into northwestern Rhodesia from Zambia and Botswana, endangering the Bulawayo–Capetown railway line. To meet these new challenges the Rhodesians set up three new commands, *Thrasher* at Umtali, *Repulse* at Fort Victoria and *Tangent* in the northwest, and continued hot pursuit raids into both Mozambique and Zambia. The attacks, all poorly co-ordinated, led to heavy insurgent casualties. In January 1977 Moyo, a ZAPU militant, was killed in Lusaka in unexplained circumstances but leaving ZIPRA increasingly to fight its own war. In August an insurgent strike killed four Umtali White Territorial soldiers; in riposte a massive Rhodesian attack by personnel in FRELIMO uniforms and including Selous Scouts and former Portuguese *Flechas* destroyed a camp at Nyadzonia in Mozambique that included not only insurgents but also refugees, women and children. Some 1,200 people were killed.

This massacre had an unexpected effect, that of so severely alarming the South African government that it withdrew its remaining military personnel and imposed delays on fuel supplies reaching Rhodesia, thus effectively halving Rhodesia's ability to fight. Further, ZAPU and ZANU, while maintaining political independence, agreed to form a Patriotic Front (PF) for co-ordination in political negotiations. Leadership within the PF went to Mugabe, a ZANU leader fully trusted by FRELIMO. The Rhodesian government, now under crippling pressures, conceded the principle of a majority rule settlement and the British government convened a conference at Geneva in October. To mark the opening, and to pre-empt ZANLA from so doing, Rhodesian forces struck heavy blows at camps in Mozambique, capturing or destroying quantities of ZANLA equipment, including anti-aircraft and anti-tank guns, mortars and machine-guns.

Despite this spectacular success Rhodesia was to enter the third phase of the war in 1977 in a position increasingly desperate. In the event the Geneva conference failed to reach any agreed solution. More and more Soviet support was reaching ZIPRA via Zambia, more and more Chinese support reaching ZANLA via Mozambique. Capital and white settlers were leaving Rhodesia and the impact of sanctions was now being felt, though South Africa relaxed her pressures to ensure Rhodesian forces would not collapse.

A summary of the main events can only suggest their ferocity. The active insurgent challenge in April 1977 was estimated by the Rhodesians at 2,350; the total was to increase dramatically in the following 18 months. The year 1977 saw railway sabotage and a bomb explosion in the capital, Salisbury. In response a major raid into Mozambique to destroy a camp at Mapai followed in May. An even larger-scale Operation *Diago* was mounted against ZANLA headquarters base camps and refugee centres in Mozambique at Chimoio and at Tembue, the former 96 km, the latter 220 km across the border. Chimoio covered some 13 square km and was protected by anti-aircraft guns, earthworks and a FRELIMO unit of Soviet T-54 tanks. The preparations involved assembly areas in Mozambique and the complexity of the actual operations showed the growing sophistication of the campaign. A single decoy aircraft was sent over Chimoio to raise an alarm, after which the garrison's defenders, there being apparently no follow-up, returned to the centre. Three Canberras then bombed the camp, followed by 14 rocket-firing Hunter and Vampire aircraft. Three sides of the camp were then fenced in by parachute Rhodesian SAS and RLI troops, others followed by helicopter and the fourth side of the perimeter was sealed off by Alouette helicopter gunships carrying 20 mm cannon. The camp was obliterated, over 2,000 insurgents being killed for the loss of two Rhodesians; much the same tactics produced the same result at Tembue.

The dead, including a number of women and children, fuelled ZANLA hatred of the Rhodesian establishment. By 1978 ZANLA's attacking units were 100 or more strong, with a greater measure of determination and cruelty – extending to white women and children and geographically into Salisbury itself. In desperation Rhodesian security forces asked themselves fewer and fewer questions before opening fire; in one night attack on a village 74 people were killed, only one was an insurgent. In equal desperation Smith sought a deal with ZIPRA, but negotiations broke down and ZIPRA, using a Russian

SAM-7 missile, shot down an Air Rhodesia airliner, killing all survivors from the crash. The Rhodesian response was a four-day series of air/land strikes against ZANLA bases in Mozambique with, to follow, a three-day assault against ZIPRA bases in Zambia, Rhodesian aircraft even flying from air strips across the border. Once again the victims were largely refugees. The strikes failed to deter, and in November 1978 ZANLA forces destroyed a vast oil storage depot in Salisbury. Gwelo also saw gun battles and the railway between Salisbury and Bulawayo was sabotaged.

The last year of the war, 1979, opened with ZIPRA shooting down another airliner with heavy loss of life. In retaliation in February four Canberra bombers of the Rhodesian air force launched a raid into Angola, circumventing both the British-maintained Zambian air defence and the Soviet radar tracking system. The raid killed 160 insurgents and wounded several hundred more. Further heavy air raids against railways, road bridges and other economic targets in Zambia and Mozambique followed, all in the hope of coercing Zambia to support a moderate settlement. The raids met greatly improved anti-aircraft defensive fire from ZSU-23 mm guns and SAM-7 missiles supplied to ZIPRA by East Germany, the Soviet Union and Cuba and to ZANLA by the Soviet Union. Two helicopters, one South African and one carrying troops, were shot down and an RLI attack on a new Chimoio ZANLA base was very fiercely resisted. A Rhodesian SAS attempt in April to destroy ZIPRA's Lusaka headquarters was only partially successful as Nkomo was elsewhere, but a similar attack on ZIPRA's less important headquarters in Botswana was more successful. Overall, the Rhodesian command's last effort for a "Total War" was handicapped as much by the absence of its leading figures who were in London for the conference as by shortages of equipment and men. In late 1979 Rhodesian intelligence estimated insurgent totals as over 4,000 ZIPRA and 10,000 ZANLA deployed within Rhodesia, with a further trained 16,000 ZIPRA and 3,500 ZANLA across the border and 2,900 ZIPRA and 14,000 ZANLA training externally. ZIPRA had the equipment including tanks, bridging equipment, artillery and armoured personnel carriers, but used them only to defend base camps in Zambia and Angola and to bombard Kariba and Chirundu with mortars and field guns. To these totals must be added the many thousands of "passive wing" supporters, mainly ZANLA, known in Zimbabwe as *mujiba*, who supplied intelligence and sometimes shelter for the insurgents and laid mines; young boys would drive cattle in front of security force patrols to facilitate the escape of insurgents.

The Rhodesian organizational military response included the opening of new commands, *Grapple* in the centre, *Salops* in the Salisbury peri-urban area and *Splinter* around Kariba; a combined operation centre headed by General Peter Walls was set up to control all security operations.

In the field the Rhodesians turned increasingly to the laying of South African-made mines on insurgent approach routes across the Mozambique border; some of these were equipped with anti-lift devices and were sensitive to human sweat. Reconnaissance and transport vehicles were developed or adapted to withstand insurgent mines, these too now including photocell detonators, with varying degrees of success. South Africa supplied further numbers of Alouette III helicopters, which continued to operate unchecked by the Mozambique or Zambian air forces or defences. In Rhodesia itself the helicopters were used when an insurgent group was located in a "Fire Force" concept – a combination of a ground troops cordon, four or more helicopter gunships and perhaps a platoon parachute drop. Although Rhodesia deviously acquired some Soviet T-55 tanks, they were not used on operations. To meet the manpower needs Africans were conscripted into the army, though from 1978 many went to the auxiliaries being raised by the internal settlement political figures. Others boycotted the draft. Taxes rose, including a heavy defence levy in 1978. Large areas of the country were put under curfew and martial law and offences leading to the death penalty were extended, with courts martial empowered to impose the sentence.

The army had expanded to a total of 20,000, 14,000 of whom were white conscripts, the draft for whites extending to men up to the age of 60. The RLI recruited soldiers of fortune from several countries to maintain its strength. In addition to the Selous Scouts, two other new units appeared, one of horsed infantry and one of armoured cars which used Eland vehicles, a South African version of the Panhard AML-90, to good effect, on one occasion against Mozambique T-34 tanks. The reserve Rhodesia Regiment to which white conscripts were posted was also greatly expanded. The original one African battalion was increased to four of declining efficiency. Also of very dubious efficiency was the guard force for the protected villages. Evidence of the strain appeared in several other forms. One was the number of bitter quarrels between senior Rhodesian commanders. Emigration also increased, and war-weariness became ever more evident. Some irreplaceable pieces of equipment, too, were wearing out, in particular in the air force with its ageing late 1950s machines and in the older British Ferret armoured cars.

For Rhodesia itself the domestic consequences of the war were becoming catastrophic. In African areas authorities collapsed; looting was widespread, schools and clinics had to be closed, and the populace refused to pay taxes. Over half a million people were in protected villages. Conscription for whites and coloureds was having a disastrous effect on the country's economy in loss of job skills for those who chose to stay rather than leave. Smith's new answer was to be an "internal settlement", in which after negotiations in March 1978 certain leading non-revolutionary African leaders, notably Bishop Muzorewa and the former ZANU leader the Revd Sithole, were inspanned into a new

Executive Council supposedly concerned with the war but in practice virtually powerless against the white "establishment". Both Sithole and Muzorewa proceeded to raise small auxiliary private armies, which attempted to politicize their causes and leaders. The Patriotic Front rejected the "internal solution". The Rhodesian commanders were, however, able to draw some comfort from the fact that Nkomo's ZAPU appeared to be deliberately pulling its punches, only some 25 per cent of its 20,000 insurgents being deployed in the field in contrast to the 15,000 in the field of ZANLA, and even forbidding a projected Cuban invasion from Angola. ZAPU has since claimed that ZIPRA was being prepared for a final *Vernichtungschlacht* in late 1979 or 1980.

By the end of 1976 the auxiliaries of Sithole's ZANU and Muzorewa's United African National Congress (UANC) were fighting each other, the combined totals of the two auxiliary forces reaching 20,000 in the following year. Pre-emptive raids upon ZANLA-held areas in central Rhodesia and a massive deployment of troops and police enabled the elections, agreed as part of the internal settlement, to take place without any effective insurgent interference. The winner was Muzorewa's UANC, but the bishop proved an ineffective prime minister, unable to direct operations and in any case fatally undermined by the British government's refusal to accept the internal settlement and his administration. His "campaign for peace" amnesty offer backed by leaflets and skyshouts from aircraft over insurgent-held locations lost any credibility when it was accompanied by a violent repression of Sithole's auxiliaries, many trained in Uganda by the RLI. A strike at a ZIPRA base in Zambia and a daring raid by helicopter-lifted troops on ZAPU's intelligence headquarters in a suburb of Lusaka, both authorized by Muzorewa, were insufficient to reassert control fast slipping away from Salisbury.

At the August 1979 Lusaka Commonwealth Conference it was agreed, to the fury of Muzorewa and the Rhodesia white hardliners, to hold a conference of all concerned in London in the following month. In preparation for this the Rhodesian forces and insurgents both sought a military success. The Rhodesians sought to damage the transport infrastructures of Zambia and Mozambique so that they could no longer assist the insurgents in order that in despair they would moderate the PF at the conference. ZANLA was, however, now able to "borrow" heavier Soviet equipment from FRELIMO (who had themselves received it from Ethiopia) and began to shoot down Rhodesia's troop-carrying helicopters and aircraft. The most spectacular battle took place following a massive RLI and Selous Scouts incursion into Mozambique in September. In the course of this a large ZANLA base was destroyed after a three-day battle, but Rhodesians present commented that the fighting – conventional land warfare in all but name – was now on a scale in which, with their numerical inferiority and the insurgents, apparently endless supply of new recruits and more advanced equipment, they could not hope to win. Further, by the time the conference was sitting ZANLA had secured "liberated zones" with as much as a quarter of the population in Rhodesia itself, and increasingly viewed ZIPRA with suspicion of holding back its strength for assertion after the war ended.

After hard negotiating, the conference reached agreement providing for an interim return to British sovereignty and free elections in which the PF groups could participate. A ceasefire for 28 December was ordered. The total casualties of the long war will never be known, the official government estimate of 30,000 being unlikely to include all those killed in the bush or across borders. Of the commanders, Josiah Tongogara, who had succeeded Chitepo, proved an exceptionally able commander of ZANLA forces, well supported by his second-in-command, Rex Nhongo. Of the ZIPRA leaders, pre-eminent were the Soviet-trained Lookout Mafela Masuku and his intelligence chief Dumiso Dabengwa. General Walls commanded the Rhodesian Army, and later all Rhodesian security forces, with considerable skill despite his own reservations on the prospects of total military success and the political constraints imposed upon him. Despite virtually total tactical success throughout the campaign the Rhodesian security forces were strategically on the brink of defeat at the hands of the insurgents by late 1979. While the new weaponry and numerical superiority of the insurgents was a main cause, almost equally important was the blinkered approach of the Rhodesian political direction with its refusal to see the nationalist insurgent as anything other than an agent of Moscow or Beijing, and political concessions, when offered, were too little and too late.

Western Sahara 1973–6

Africa's smallest campaign to free a territory from European sovereignty exercised in a European capital took place in the Spanish Sahara; the issue at stake was in many ways more one of whom the successor should be. The campaign itself was very limited at this stage and sporadic, but as an overture to events that followed it was significant.[5]

After Morocco's independence in 1956 the Moroccan king, in need of an issue to rally national unity, immediately claimed the territory on historical grounds. At the same time he also claimed both Mauritania, which was still a French colony, and the small Spanish enclaves on the Mediterranean north Africa shore, all as part of a "Greater Morocco" project. The Spanish Sahara claim was backed up by a raid into the south of the territory by a group named

L'Armée de Libération du Grand Sahara, almost certainly Morocco-backed, which led to protective intervention by both Spanish and French troops. At her independence in 1960 Mauritania also made a claim for the territory, and a partition with Morocco was discussed.

Negotiations over the future of the territory dragged on until June 1970 when the Spaniards in Laayouny, the capital, were attacked, a number being killed. Sporadic violence continued, Spain declaring a state of emergency in 1972. In 1973 an insurgency movement, the Polisario (Popular Front for the Liberation of Saguia el Hamra and Rio de Oro), was founded with as its aim the ending of Spanish rule and the creation of an independent state by revolutionary violence. Small groups of Polisario insurgents began attacking small outlying Spanish garrison posts.

The period 1972 to 1974 saw intense Moroccan propaganda in support of her claim to the territory. Algeria, concerned at the growth in power of Morocco and hoping for an outlet to the Atlantic, objected and began to arm and train the Polisario. Libya also provided assistance.

Following further argument, in October 1975 the International Court of Justice ruled that no previous historical ties between the territory, Morocco and Mauritania precluded the people of the territory from determining their own future. Under intense domestic opposition pressure the King of Morocco, almost immediately in November 1975, despatched the "Green March" of 350,000 Moroccans escorted by some 20,000 soldiers into the territory to stake out his claim; this was met by 30,000 Spanish troops and hastily prepared minefields. The marchers were not able to enter the territory in any great depth, though in the north a clash occurred between Moroccan troops and the Polisario, each side losing a number killed.

Spain, which had been under United Nations pressure to decolonize for a number of years, then finally gave up any idea of advancing the territory to independence and agreed to set up a joint transition administration in partnership with Morocco and Mauritania. At the time the Spanish head of state, General Franco, was terminally ill, and the Spanish government had been alarmed by the growing strength of the Polisario. Under Spanish pressure the local legislature voted in favour of a partition and Spain withdrew on 28 February 1976.

The immediate declaration of independence for a Saharan Arab Democratic Republic, in defiance of Morocco and Mauritania, by the Polisario Secretary-General was the signal for the start of a bitter ongoing conflict, to be considered in a later chapter.

Chapter Four

Wars of integration and disintegration I: 1960 to 1980

The close of the Zimbabwe campaign marked the end of conflicts against regimes where ultimate sovereignty over a territory lay in a European capital city, Paris, Lisbon or London. There were of course countries, notably Ethiopia, whose capital claimed sovereignty over wide areas in which minority peoples lived under discrimination and who were in revolt against this status. But these conflicts were essentially the same as other post-independence conflicts in Africa, conflicts between indigenous African peoples, mostly black but some non-black. These conflicts initially concerned integrity or internal integration within the frame of the post-colonial state, but at the same time, and increasingly as time passed, the conflicts changed to local *lebensraum* struggles, often crude ethnic warfare designed simply to secure control of regional or local economic assets. Some conflicts reverted to nineteenth-century genocidal brutality. In both varieties war aims might be presented in ideological terms, but often, particularly in the latter variety of warfare, war aims represented nothing more than the personal fiefdom ambitions of a man or a clique not always even representative of the area concerned.

The first two decades of African independence, the 1960s and 1970s, saw large-scale civil conflict and strife in these forms in the Congo, Rwanda and Burundi, Sudan, Ethiopia, Nigeria, Chad and Lesotho, together with two inter-nation wars, those between Tanzania and Uganda and between Ethiopia and Somalia. Friction and some fighting in North Africa were caused by domestic problems and by the policies of Algeria and Libya. There was also smaller-scale warfare in a number of other countries. The 1970s saw ongoing conflict in Angola and Mozambique; these conflicts were increasingly a by-product of the South African political situation, and as such are considered in later Southern African chapters.

The Congo, Rwanda and Burundi 1960–78

Early examples of these new directions appeared as the Belgian Congo colony moved towards and then in July 1960 achieved independence.[1] The previous 80 years of European rule in the Congo had been at the outset disastrous and later unfortunate. The years of the personal rule of King Leopold of the Belgians were ones of ruthless economic exploitation enforced by cruelty and torture. The core period of Belgian official colonial rule beginning in 1908 had been one of a stifling overall paternalism, but with at local level toleration, and at times encouragement, of ethnicity-based self-help associations. The final three years had seen accelerating Belgian plans for a flag independence but with totally inadequate political, economic or administrative preparation of their Congolese successors. Smouldering memories of the Leopold era and Belgian heavy-handedness were to erupt into violence, beginning with serious rioting of the urban unemployed in Leopoldville in December 1958, 49 people being killed. The inspiration behind these riots was the largely Bakongo ethnic group's Abako movement, and its leader, Kasa-Vubu, who hoped for a restoration of the ancient pre-colonial Bakongo kingdom and was referred to informally as "King of the Bakongo".

The political history of the Congo in the tumultuous years 1959 to 1965 is intricate and complex, with changing patterns of alliances between parties, factions and ethnicities; the concerns of this work are the military operations that developed from these conflicts of interest.[2] Even before independence the tensions had led to inter-ethnic fighting, beginning in the Kasai province in mid-1959. The province was traditionally the home of the Lulua, a people resistant to change. Under Belgian rule considerable numbers of the more entrepreneurial Luba from the west of the neighbouring Katanga province had entered Kasai. Lulua ethnic leaders feared a Luba domination after the departure of the Belgians, and using spears, arrows and matchets, Luluas began to drive the Luba from the province's capital, Luluabourg. At the same time, Albert Kalonji, the Luba leader in the diamond-producing district of the Kasai province, and in the copper-producing Katanga province the leader of the majority Lunda people, Moise Tshombe, were both planning autonomy or secessionist movements in favour of their own ethnicity.

Within a few days of independence, attacks – often designed to humiliate rather than kill – opened on the Belgians, much larger-scale violence beginning with the mutinies of the former *Force Publique*, now the *Armeé Nationale Congolaise* (ANC), on 8 and 9 July. Belgium had failed to train a single Congolese officer, and the mutiny was scarcely surprising. Soldiers with weapons seized from armouries embarked on mob violence against the Belgians, numbers being injured, raped or, in some 20 cases, killed. Rumour later added to the numbers and the panic. The hoped for Belgian–Congolese partnership was irretrievably broken, internal security collapsed, and the fragile coalition government headed by Joseph Kasa-Vubu as president whose power-base was the Leopoldville area, and with the radical Patrice Lumumba whose power derived from his following in Stanleyville, Orientale province, as prime minister, fell apart. In Katanga Tshombe proclaimed independence. To save the lives of their own terrified and fleeing nationals Belgian troops were parachuted onto Leopoldville's airport, and they and others from Kamina were dispersed around the major centres of population. In Katanga Belgian troops, after a brief battle, disarmed the ANC troops in Kolwezi who were loyal to Leopoldville and began to assist with the raising and training of a Katanga defence unit for which mercenaries, Belgian, French or former French Foreign Legion, Rhodesians and South Africans, all too often with undesirable backgrounds, were recruited. In turn the arrival of the Belgian troops produced a hysterical over-reaction from Lumumba who formally requested a United Nations force.

This force, the United Nations Force in the Congo (*Opérations des Nations Unies au Congo* – ONUC), was authorized on 14 July as a stop-gap until the Congo had its own reliable forces. The Belgians were called upon to leave, which slowly and reluctantly they did from all areas except Katanga. Units from a wide variety of contributing countries, and of varying degrees of professional efficiency, arrived progressively over the second half of July and the early part of August. Kano was used as a staging post. The countries contributing infantry units were Ghana and Nigeria (whose units still included some British officers on loan), Tunisia, Ethiopia, Mali, Indonesia, Sweden, Malaya, Ireland, India, Guinea, Egypt, Morocco and Sudan, with Indian and Italian aircraft and a Canadian Signals unit. At its peak strength ONUC totalled 20,000 men. The Guinean unit had more political staff than effective officers, and the Ghanaian, Guinean and Egyptian units were prone to work more to their own government's agendas than those of the UN Force Commander. ONUC was initially and temporarily commanded by a British general, Henry Alexander, serving on loan with the Ghanaian army; he was succeeded by a Swedish general, Carl von Horn who fell ill after five months in command. Thereafter ONUC had no central commander, operations being commanded locally under civilian political direction.

The better units were despatched to the Kasai and other areas of disorder or inter-ethnic fighting; the less impressive were posted to guard government offices, airports and other key installations. In restoring order and quelling inter-ethnic fighting ONUC was generally successful, saving hundreds of lives. However, sometimes the methods used by units could be less than gentle, and on several occasions ONUC succeeded only in imposing a freeze on local conflicts which were resumed as soon as the UN unit had left the area. The force faced very great difficulties, being drawn from countries whose armies had no experience of working in an international force and, in most cases, little experience of peacekeeping or enforcement. The personnel came from 29 different nations and had, inevitably, problems of language, different concepts of staff procedures and no intelligence-gathering organization. The size of the territory presented great signals difficulties. Transport was in short supply, and spare parts even more so. The force's logistical difficulties were compounded by the ignorance of military needs and problems of the UN civilian directorate. Dr Bunche, the UN representative, for example, overruled the strong advice of von Horn and authorized the return of weapons taken from rampaging Congolese soldiers, thereby ensuring further rampaging.

The force was originally tasked to replace the Belgian troops, restore order and save life in all areas of the Congo except Katanga, a directive reflecting international disputes and Cold War attitudes. Following much pressure from Lumumba, the Communist world and some Asian and African countries, and to the fury of the Belgians, units were permitted on 15 August to enter Katanga. Threats from Katanga of opposing the UN units with force were quietly withdrawn when it was made clear that the UN forces were not empowered to replace the authority of Tshombe's breakaway regime and its right to maintain its own forces. Tshombe also insisted that units from Guinea and Ghana, whose governments had stated they would place their units under Congo government control to recover Katanga, were not to be permitted to enter the province. The units selected for the operation were Swedish, Moroccan, Irish, Ethiopian and Mali, all entering simultaneously from different directions. The political limitation inevitably enraged Lumumba, and members of the Canadian detachment serving with the UN force in Leopoldville were beaten up.

The second attempt at a provincial breakaway led to massacre. In August Kalonji moved on formally to proclaim an independent "Diamond State" in the Luba area of Kasai, with Bakwanga as its capital. Lumumba managed to assemble sufficient soldiers from the ANC which, together with some Soviet supplied lorries and transport aircraft and in alliance with levies of the Lulua-controlled Kasai provincial administration, succeeded in putting Kalonji and his "government" to flight. They occupied Bakwanga on 26 August and hoped to move on into Katanga. The Kasai Luba were not supported by the Katanga Luba, preoccupied as they were in defending themselves from attacks upon them by the Lunda-dominated Katanga government. The Luba paid heavily for being the minority in both provinces, some 3,000 being killed, the large majority in the Kasai, an action considered by the UN Secretary-General Dag Hammarskjold as verging on genocide. Massacres were particularly severe in the Bakwanga area, one reason being the total absence of logistic support for the ANC forces who, unable to move on into Katanga, turned on the local populace for food. UN units only arrived afterwards in September, and were permitted only to disarm ANC troops when these were caught acting illegally rather than undertake any general disarmament. The UN did, however, take two steps, both to arouse bitter political controversy but effective in defusing incipient civil war. At the request of President Kasa-Vubu ONUC forces took over the Lumumba-controlled radio station in Leopoldville and assumed control of all the airfields in the Congo, closing them to all traffic except that of the UN. These measures prevented further external assistance to Lumumba, and any attempt by him to wrest control of the capital from Kasa-Vubu. Conflict was thereby limited to rhetoric and the political and international stages, Kasa-Vubu and Lumumba both dismissing each other, and the ANC Chief-of-Staff Colonel Joseph Mobutu proclaiming himself head of a government of commissioners, so leaving the country with rival governments. The airfields were reopened for peaceful purposes under ONUC surveillance.

With the existence of rival governments, however, the country began to slide towards civil war. Western diplomacy, after violent controversy, secured recognition of Kasa-Vubu; Lumumba, as a consequence fearing for his safety, left the house protection of the ONUC in an attempt to flee to his power-base, Stanleyville, but was arrested on the way. One of his supporters, Gizenga, proclaimed a new Congo government of Lumumba's followers in Stanleyville, and ANC units, such as they were, divided between the two rivals. By the end of December Lumumbist forces took Bukavu in Kivu province, and in January they were able to repel a counter-attack from a force of Mobutu. Catching the local ONUC unit, a Nigerian battalion, off its guard, some 500 Lumumbist soldiers, mostly Katanga Luba and described as ill-disciplined and disorderly, then entered the north of Katanga, and an ANC unit at Thysville supposedly loyal to Leopoldville mutinied in favour of Lumumba. A small group of troops, almost certainly supported by Mobutu and possibly also by Belgians, attempted to mount a recapture of Bukavu from Rwanda, but this failed. Belgians in Kivu province began to suffer the same physical harassment as had occurred earlier in Leopoldville. The reaction of Kasa-Vubu and Mobutu to these events, a reaction facilitated by the United States Central Intelligence Agency, was to arrange for Lumumba to be flown to Katanga where a little later he was murdered, as was no doubt intended. The UN sought the recall and replacement of Belgian officers with the Katanga gendarmerie. As a riposte on 30 March the Katanga gendarmerie attacked and took Manono, but were repulsed by an ONUC Ethiopian unit when attempting to take Kabolo.

Bitter international controversy followed Lumumba's murder. Eventually a UN resolution was passed empowering the ONUC to take action against impending civil war or clashes with, as a last resort, the use of force. Hammarskjold interpreted this as authorization for the ONUC to occupy key points and disarm ANC personnel when necessary, an interpretation resented by Kasa-Vubu who declared total opposition to it. Attacks on UN civilian and military personnel in the Kasa-Vubu controlled Bakongo area opened in March. Military assaults were launched against ONUC detachments at Banana and Kitona, and against the port of Matadi through which supplies for the UN force were handled. An ANC force superior in numbers forced the ONUC Sudanese battalion to withdraw. The UN, deciding against a military reoccupation, was only permitted to re-enter the port – the territory's only port – following the constitutional settlement of August 1961 which with some American financial encouragement reconciled Stanleyville and Leopoldville.

Katanga remained, all the while strengthening its gendarmerie with re-cruits, more mercenaries and a handful of light aircraft. In August 1961 the UN sought to remove all the remaining non-Congolese personnel (the Belgians had earlier been withdrawn) from the Katanga gendarmerie, now over 20,000 strong against only 1,000 ONUC troops in the province. The military operation, Operation *Rumpunch*, began successfully, but was halted by the local UN representative following local and international rep-resentation, so enabling the large majority of mercenaries to rejoin after a brief period of concealment. A month later, in September 1961, after fruitless discussion, ONUC forces made a second attempt, Operation *Morthor*. The Katangese gendarmerie, now well-prepared, fought back, inflicting casualties on the ill co-ordinated advances of Swedish and Indian troops and launching counter-attacks in two areas, supported by bombs from a light aircraft. An Irish company was surrounded at Jadotville, and some of its members were taken as hostages. The ONUC failed to capture Tshombe, and his supporters in the Western world brokered a ceasefire, in practice returning Katanga to its status quo. Mobutu's ANC then attempted a two-pronged entry into Katanga. In October units advancing from Kasai were attacked by Katangese aircraft and in panic turned on the Belgian population of Luluabourg. Another force advancing into north Katanga from Stanleyville in November achieved nothing, turning instead to senseless violence and killing 11 Italian ONUC airmen.

A series of provocations by the over-confident Katanga gendarmerie and clashes with ONUC units led to a further UN attempt to end the Katanga secessions. The UN force had by now been increased to more than 12,000 troops, supported by Swedish jet fighters and Indian Canberra bombers. ONUC units were first, on 5 December, ordered to dismantle road blocks guarding Elisabethville. This provoked Katangese attacks, including mortar firing and sniping (on occasions from hospitals) onto the ONUC units.

ONUC air-to-ground strikes destroyed some of the Katangese aircraft and Katanga's small armoured force was prevented from approaching the capital. By 16 December the ONUC force, fully reinforced, was in total control of the perimeter around Elisabethville, the investing units being Swedish, Irish and Ethiopian. Tshombe was reluctantly forced into negotiations.

Most of 1962 was spent in protracted and fruitless talks and meetings between Tshombe and the central government, Tshombe having little real interest in an agreement. UN efforts to identify and order the expulsion of the mercenaries was frustrated by their being concealed on days of inspection. Incidents and clashes occurred at intervals with casualties among ONUC and the Katangese. In August the ANC, which had at last achieved a superficial reunification, launched an attack on the Katangese garrison in north Katanga and slowly gained an ascendancy, generally by the use of brutality.

Towards the end of the year a further series of events moved to crisis point. A further round of Katangese provocations and clashes coincided with the Indian government's urgent need for the return of its troops in the face of the Chinese threat to India's northern border. Mortar, machine-gun and rifle battles broke out around the largest Elisabethville mining company compound and a UN helicopter was shot down. In the last days of December and the first days of January the ONUC mounted Operation *Grandslam*. Swedish SAAB jets attacked Katangese aircraft on the ground, and ONUC forces entered Jadotville and Kolwezi and strengthened their hold on the Elisabethville suburban towns. The operations and the entry into Jadotville were justified on the grounds of securing freedom of movement, and the clashes with the Katangese as overcoming opposition to that securing. Katangese secession was ended, Tshombe formally capitulating on 21 January 1963.

Desultory fighting in several areas continued for a few months, but the draw-down of the ONUC could begin. In its four years of life 93,000 men from 35 countries had participated and 235 had been killed. The direction of forces by a small staff in New York responding to UN politics did not always accord with realities on the ground. The performance of units varied and many, particularly Africans, behaved badly; the Irish were poorly led into impossible situations and even the Swedish performance attracted criticism. But albeit over four years, the unity of the Congo was restored, paradoxically the slow process being useful in providing reassurance that the local economy would still prosper.

Warfare in the Congo, however, was to reopen in 1964. Early in the year a revolt broke out in Kwilu province, formerly Lumumbist. Despite Belgian and American assistance the ANC proved unable to cope, and only the intervention of a CIA-funded air force of mercenary Cuban exile pilots flying Harvard T-6 aircraft secured the province. More serious was the rising beginning in the eastern province as a revolt against ANC brutality, a rising later known as the Simba rising. It was labelled Communist by the Western world since it received weaponry and advice from the USSR, China, Egypt and Algeria. It was in fact an ethnic uprising, largely of Maniema, led by the self-styled General Olenga and inspired by drugs and potions administered by sorcerers and women fetishists who promised invulnerability. They wore a strange mixture of uniform and civilian clothes. At the outset they had few rifles, using instead clubs and matchets. They soon acquired rifles from the ANC and the Communist world. The Simba methods were as cruel as those of the ANC; after the capture of one town over 200 of its inhabitants were massacred. Many of the most cruel were young children. The Simba first took Kindu and, brushing aside the ineffective ANC despite its vastly superior numbers and equipment, entered Stanleyville after only a few small arms firefights. The Congo government, in desperation, had in July turned to its one effective political figure, Tshombe, who returned to the strategy he had employed in Katanga, the engagement of mercenaries. These at first were also ineffective and the Simba managed to take over a very large area of country. With the exception of an effective defence of Bukavu where, assisted by a former Katanga gendarmerie unit hurriedly flown in and some air support from CIA North American T-28 and Douglas B-26 Invader aircraft, the ANC killed over 300 rebels, the disintegration of the ANC continued. A revolutionary government established in Stanleyville openly treated the 1,200 Europeans and Americans it held as hostages and began the killing of well over 1,000 of the city's elite, by throwing them to the crocodiles in many cases. The Americans were under particular threat as a consequence of the effect of the CIA aircraft strafing of the Simba soldiery.

Faced with this situation and after much international debate a force of 600 Belgian parachute troops was flown to Stanleyville in United States C-130 aircraft, staging on the British-owned Ascension Island and at Kamina. The operation to rescue the hostages was difficult and daring.[3] Three hundred Belgians dropped on the Stanleyville airfield, seized the ground and cleared obstacles from the field. A further 220 men were then flown in who in armoured jeeps or motorized tricycles rushed into the city where executions of the hostages were taking place. The hostages, many injured, were taken hurriedly to the airport and flown out. The airport came under Simba attack and the CIA's T-28s and B-26s gave the Belgian troops close support in reply. Later in the day a mixed unit of Belgians, mercenaries, Cuban exiles and over 1,000 Katangese, together with a few British Ferret armoured-cars, arrived in the city in the name of the central government, having previously taken Kindu and surviving Simba ambushes in their approach march.

The assault, Operation *Dragon Rouge*, and a later similar but smaller-scale drop on the town of Paulia rescued 1,600 hostages though 61 were killed before the troops arrived. The mixed unit remained after the Belgian para-troops flew away from Stanleyville, but the number of Simba fighters and supporters massacred by the unit will never be known.

The day before the landing, Tshombe was replaced as prime minister and his successor was in turn ousted by Colonel Mobutu in a coup. Mobutu first used the expanded, if still undisciplined and badly trained, ANC together with the mercenaries to dispose of the Simba. These insurgents had in effect been fatally wounded by the Stanleyville operation and their movement was collapsing. The general pattern of operations appears to have been one in which if there were any serious fighting it was undertaken by the mercenaries with their CIA air support, while the ANC terrorized the civil population and killed any prisoners that the mercenaries, each now earning £200 per month or more, had left alive or untortured. By November the Simba uprising had been finally suppressed.

There then remained the question of the mercenaries, the last round in the Congo's first seven years of warfare. The mercenaries were serving in three groups, Five Commando, an armoured car and jeep mobile unit of South Africans and Rhodesians, Six Commando which was largely French, and Ten Commando under Belgian command. They met with a serious reverse at the hands of the Congo army at Kamanyola. Five Commando disbanded itself. Six Commando mutinied in June 1967 and a mixed body some 150 strong of some Five stay-ons, Six and Ten personnel together with 800 Katangese former gendarmes and levies all withdrew from Stanleyville. Fighting off both the ANC and the CIA's air-to-ground strikes, they pushed through to Bukavu where they proclaimed a "provisional government", evidently think-ing in terms of a mercenary state. No help for them came from the West or from South Africa. In desperation they continued to fight off the ANC for three months until they ran out of ammunition when they marched across into Rwanda, to the terror of the Rwanda government. From there the Europeans were finally flown home to Europe. The Katangese were repatri-ated, the fate of the majority remaining unknown.

Some, however, were to reappear in the next rounds of fighting in 1977 and 1978, by which time Katanga had been renamed Shaba and the Congo renamed Zaire. A 2,000-strong force, its motives being certainly to secure control of Shaba and possibly also to overthrow President Mobutu, moved into the province from Angola in March 1977. The force, styling itself *Front National de Libération du Congo* (FNLC) and led by Nathaniel Mbumba, was largely Lunda, and among its numbers were former Katangese gendarmes. Their advance was checked some 100 kilometres from the town of Kolwezi by the Zairean army, necessarily stiffened by 1,500 Moroccan troops hurriedly flown in by French military transports. The Moroccans then very quickly disposed of the insurgents.

A second, Cuban-supported, FNLC attack again led by Mbumba in May 1978 was very much more serious. A several thousand strong force of FNLC "tigers" armed with rifles, machine-guns, light mortars and rocket launchers invested Kolwezi. Some evidence suggests that small groups of insurgents with weapons concealed had arrived secretly in the city previously. Zairean army parachute troops recaptured and stoutly defended the town's airstrip but were not strong enough to overwhelm the insurgents. Mobutu appealed to France for help. Paris ordered the Foreign Legion 2nd Parachute Regiment (2 REP) to move to Zaire. The issue became urgent following the interception of FNLC signals directing the killing of as many of the 2,500 Europeans in the town as possible and the destruction of mining installations. American as well as French transport aircraft were used to fly the regiment, initially to Kinshasa, the former Leopoldville. Belgium also agreed to provide troops but did not sanction their use in the first attack.

The assault by 2 REP in the afternoon of 19 May will long remain a classic, if small-scale, example of professional competence and the worth of parachute troops. Despite a variety of difficulties – the long outward flight with fatigue and climate change for the soldiers, the absence of any light or flare guidance towards the dropping zone which had to be as near the European area of the town as possible to preserve the Europeans from massacre, the need to change parachute harness as the harness supplied by the Zairean army for the jump was American and different from that normally used by the French, over-crowding of the troops in the limited number of French and Zairean transport aircraft available, a 6 metre per second strong wind and the drop to take place from the low altitude of 200 metres – the drop of the Regiment's first wave of 200 men was accomplished successfully, despite FLNC fire. The whole unit was ready to advance into the town within 15 minutes, to find the reeking streets littered with over 300 corpses, black and white, and premises looted. The FNLC were taken by surprise and except for one brisk firefight near the police station, fled out of town in looted cars. By evening several dozen hostages had been freed, the European community secured and the Regiment's 250-strong second wave, including vehicles, had arrived. As the FNLC insurgents were distributed in small groups all over the area rather than concentrated in one location, the commander of 2 REP decided to wait until the next morning before further action. By the next day the Belgian unit had landed to strengthen the Zairean army's garrison at the airfield and evacuate the European civilians. The 2 REP then began a series of sweeps, first to clear the FNLC "tigers" out of the mining quarter of the town and next the other smaller neighbouring townships. On occasions they met with FNLC mortar, rocket-launcher and machine-gun fire from well-prepared positions. The FNLC insurgents often wore working men's clothes and were therefore not immediately recognisable; other hazards included elephants and cobras.

Nevertheless the legionaries inflicted some 250 casualties on the insurgents for the loss of only five killed, though a further 40 white hostages were found dead and mutilated. The soldiers carrying out these sweeps were by now fighting after five nights without sleep, a tribute to their thorough training. After a respite, the sweeps continued, repatriating dozens more panic-stricken Europeans until 7 June when the bulk of the regiment returned to France.

Zairean army units were briefly engaged in small-scale operations against an underground insurgency movement in the country's eastern provinces in 1979.

Linked to the Congo both by ethnicities and Belgian rule were the two small and poor interlacustrine states of Rwanda and Burundi. In each of these, two ethnicities formed the populations, the Paranilotic Tutsi and the Bantu Hutu. The agriculturalist Hutu first occupied the terrain; the pastoralist Tutsi arrived later. After friction and violence the two ethnicities settled into a social relationship part antagonistic and part symbiotic, with a common language and some intermarriage. In both, the Tutsi formed some 14 per cent of the population, the Hutu 84 per cent. In both, the Tutsi held a hegemony with a Tutsi monarch; authority was centralized in Rwanda, but more decentralized in a loose grouping of feudal Tutsi princes in Burundi. The colonial powers, the Germans to 1918 and thereafter the Belgians, based their rule on and strengthened the Tutsi ascendancy; this combined with population increase had created a political stage with winners and losers by the late 1950s. In both territories the new ethnic friction was to turn to ethnic warfare, over the years increasingly genocidal.[4]

The first outbreak was on 1 November 1959 in Rwanda following belated and clumsy Belgian attempts at democratization, with Hutu attacks on Tutsis and Tutsi reprisals. The violence continued for two weeks, some 300 being killed. Sporadic hunting down and killing of Tutsi in ethnic warfare of spears, clubs, matchets and house-burning continued. The Belgian authorities persisted with their perception of democratization, in practice the installation of a Hutu tyranny, throughout 1960 and 1961, hundreds of Tutsi being killed and thousands driven into exile or living in protected camps. In riposte small terrorist groups of Tutsi called *inyenzi* (cockroaches) by the Hutu launched largely ineffective attacks on the Hutu from across the border. Vicious Hutu reprisals followed. In July 1962 Rwanda became independent as a republic, the Belgians having abolished the monarchy in 1961 after exiling the last king. *Inyenzi* violence continued intermittently, but the different groups were sharply divided among themselves. In Uganda they were gradually brought under tighter control and those in the Congo, who had allied themselves with the Lumumbists, were disposed of when Mobutu's ANC reasserted control of Kivu province. A final desperate *inyenzi* attack was mounted from Burundi in December 1963, but it was repulsed and followed by the massacre of some 20,000 Tutsi. Thereafter tensions remained but ethnic warfare ceased in 1982.

In Burundi the monarch attempted to create some balance between the ethnicities in the government, but a crisis developed in 1965 following the assassination of a Hutu prime minister and a little later a massive Hutu victory in elections. The monarch refused to appoint a Hutu prime minister. Hutu in the gendarmerie attempted a coup, but its failure led to a purge of Hutu in the government. A Tutsi colonel, Michel Micombero, took power in 1966 and progressively strengthened Tutsi power. As a result a Hutu uprising followed in 1972 in which some 1,000 Tutsi were killed. In reprisal Micombero launched the largely Tutsi Burundi army with its firearms against the Hutu, in particular the educated. Tanzania and Zaire provided military help until they appreciated the nature of the massacres. Some 200,000 men, women and children were killed or died as a result of the operation, and a further 100,000 fled into exile in Tanzania. As in Rwanda, although violence then ceased, tensions remained.

Sudan 1963–76

The vast territory of Sudan became involved in the first of its civil wars seven years after formal independence in 1956. The underlying cause of this and succeeding conflicts in Sudan remains the disastrous linkage of the northern Moslems, who saw themselves as Arabs and formed two-thirds of the population, with the various southern Christian or non-Muslim African peoples together in one polity. This artifice of unification was the result of Britain's wish not to undermine their strategically important position in Egypt, whose monarchs claimed the whole area. The northerners had despised the southerners in the pre-colonial past, frequently enslaving them. In the formal colonial period, technically a condominium with Egypt but in practice a British administration, the internal administration of the south was until 1946 largely separated from that of the north for what had appeared at the time to be sound reasons.

Signs of trouble to come had already shown themselves with a pre-independence mutiny of southern soldiers, and in the years 1956 to 1963 lawlessness and banditry with occasional sniping at administration offices in the three southern provinces, mainly Equatoria. The military government of General Ibrahim Abboud, which had seized power in a coup in 1958, embarked on policies of spreading Islam and the Arab language together with the appointment of northerners to official posts and severe repression of lawlessness, all policies that heightened southern resentment to explosion point. A southern political movement aiming at secession was formed, but its leaders from a number of very different ethnic groups forced into exile quarrelled among themselves. Abboud's military officers too were involved in a succession of internal disputes and vendettas. To many southerners rebellion seemed therefore both opportune and necessary.

Real insurgency opened in 1963 following a meeting in September of the leaders of various outlaw bands which by then included some 500 from the original 1955 mutineers and a further 800 of the mutineers released from prison in 1961.[5] It was agreed that the various groups should merge into an insurgency movement which was at the outset called, interestingly, the Land Freedom Army, a title later changed to Anya-Nya, a term meaning viper's poison in several local vernaculars. The leading figures were soldiers and junior NCOs from the former British-trained Sudan Defence Force. The Anya-Nya tried to organize itself on British lines and training camps were opened in remote areas, but the movement always lacked good officers. At the outset the Anya-Nya possessed only some 200 firearms, many insurgents simply using spears and bows and arrows. At no time did it have signals communications and its only vehicles were those seized temporarily. It recruited mostly from the Dinka people and the Khartoum government tried initially to arm the other major southern people, the Nuer, against them.

A few small attacks were mounted from September 1963 onwards. The Anya-Nya's first major attack in January 1964 was, however, a costly failure. This attack, of 120 insurgents, was mounted against a Sudanese army barracks at Wau. A premature bugle call alerted the defenders, with the result that the attack was beaten off, 60 of the insurgents being captured, including the insurgents' leader who was later hanged. Alarmed by the size of the assault, the Khartoum government also moved four brigades, over 8,000 troops, into the two southern provinces. Later, units of the Sudanese army crossed the border into the Congo to attack a camp from which it claimed the attack on Wau had been mounted.

For the next nine months the Anya-Nya field commanders limited themselves to small-scale raids and attacks despite the hopes of a few of the southern political leaders that an attack of sufficient size to internationalize the conflict could be mounted. Still divided, only in September 1964 did a majority of the southern politicians move to full support of the insurgents. Anya-Nya was able to recruit notably from southern police and other government departments in which southerners knew that their days would be numbered. Overall, however, Anya-Nya at this stage did not represent a mass movement, and several southern chieftains were still opposed to violence. Weaponry, too, remained in short supply. The Khartoum government of General Abboud pursued severe reprisals following Anya-Nya raids and refugees in thousands fled to Ethiopia and Uganda.

Following two weeks of popular unrest in Khartoum the Abboud government fell in November 1964 and was replaced by a civilian government headed by Khatim al Khalifa who with the aid of a southern civil servant, Clement Mboro, sought a reconciliation. A brief ceasefire was agreed, though in practice often ignored. Further, a rumour that Mboro had been murdered led to rioting by southern labourers in Khartoum and the divided southern political leaders mostly rejected ideas of reconciliation, demanding instead full independence. A round-table conference achieved no result. At the same time the Anya-Nya, now some 5,000 strong, was able to recruit, sometimes by coercion, and to buy, steal or otherwise acquire weaponry from the defeated Congolese Simba taking refuge in Sudan.

In June 1965 the Khalifa government resigned and was followed by a government headed by Mohammed Mahgoub, which took immediate steps to ensure that Sudanese refugees in Ethiopia should not use the country as a military or political base. Mahgoub tried to continue the reconciliation policy but Anya-Nya shooting affrays and severe government reprisals at Juba and Wau ensured failure. From July 1965 the Sudanese army, with now over 12,000 men deployed, embarked on ferocious repression, including aircraft bombings targeting in particular medical centres and burning down villages. A major consequence was the spread of disease which in turn aroused more southern resentment and support for the Anya-Nya cause. The Anya-Nya insurgents' reply was still limited mostly to occasional attacks on police posts. The Anya-Nya were also faced with a short-lived rival insurgent organization, the Azania Liberation Front (ALF), the still divided political leadership and the preference of individual Anya-Nya field commanders to pursue their own plans rather than work to a common overall strategy devised by the nominal commander of the Anya-Nya National Armed Forces (ANAF), General Emilio Tafeng. Weapons remained scarce with only one-fifth of the 10,000 insurgents possessing a firearm, discipline was weak with recruits choosing their units rather than going where they were told, and there was recurrent banditry and settling of vendettas.

Mahgoub resigned in July 1966; his successor as prime minister, Sadik al Mahdi, defined his policy as "pacification with persuasion". The scale of operations increased slightly with the Sudan army mounting sweeps. Both the army and the Anya-Nya sustained a small number of casualties in local clashes but generally the Anya-Nya took to the safety of the forests on being warned by the local populace of an impending sweep. In May 1967 after further political turmoil in Khartoum and an inconclusive election in the south, Mahgoub returned to head a government which remained in power for the next two years.

The strains, political and ethnic, within the southern political and military leadership led to further divisions, Tafeng leaving the Anya-Nya to head his own Anyidi Revolutionary movement while yet another, the Suer Revolutionary Government, proclaimed its rule over the Congo border areas. In Khartoum politico-religious rivalries had reduced the government to virtual impotence with the consequence of a military coup in May 1969 led by Gaffar al Nimeiry.

General Nimeiry's most urgent task was that of establishing his own authority, first against rival left-wing officer plots and then in March 1970 against the powerful Ansar community, the followers of the nineteenth-century Mahdi. In the suppression of the Ansar, Nimeiry was forced into street fighting in Omdurman and the use of over 4,000 troops, armour and Soviet air-to-ground strike aircraft piloted by Egyptians to storm Aba island, the Ansars' redoubt. Challenges to his authority continued, however, and in July 1971 he was briefly overthrown by a group of left-wing officers. Soldiers loyal to him secured his release and return to power three days later.

Although after the events of July 1971 Nimeiry was to turn against the Soviet Union and the political left, both he and, earlier, Mahgoub had embarked on extensive purchases of Soviet weaponry, including T-34 and T-54 tanks, armoured personnel carriers, field and light anti-aircraft artillery, MiG-17 and -21 aircraft and Mi-8 helicopters. Soviet instructors arrived in considerable numbers. As the quality of instruction was poor and there were frequent purges of cadres, the end result, the professional standards of the army, remained indifferent.

A distinctive feature of warfare in south Sudan was, and was to remain, the difficulty of obtaining reliable reports. The remoteness and inhospitable nature of the terrain precluded television and almost all on-the-spot journalism; in this period both sides used the remoteness to advantage, the insurgents to exaggerate, the government to conceal. With his developing military and air force capabilities Nimeiry increased the pressure on Anya-Nya; Anya-Nya in return alleged bomb or machine-gun massacres of whole communities. Certainly air attacks in which substantial numbers of people were killed were mounted against insurgent settlements in 1970 and 1971; equally certainly Anya-Nya groups attacked convoys, bridges and government stations killing northern soldiers. A week-long battle took place at Morta, in Equatoria province, in September 1970. Some 3,000 troops, some flown in by helicopter, attacked Morta, their attack supported by artillery and air-to-ground rocket fire. The Anya-Nya defended the area with vigour, bringing down a MiG-17 and two helicopters, the pilot of one being a Russian. Eventually after suffering losses themselves, the Anya-Nya faded away into the forest. A very successful insurgent attack certainly took place in December 1970 when an Anya-Nya group of 118 surprised a government post at Pachola held by 450 soldiers and police. Opening the attack with a light mortar strike, the Anya-Nya claimed to have killed 157 soldiers and seized a rich haul of weapons and ammunition. Some reports suggest Israeli help, particularly in minelaying, was given to Anya-Nya.

The year 1971 saw dramatic change. Most notable was that, for the first time, south Sudan produced a leader who could command general allegiance, Joseph Lagu, a southern Christian who had been commissioned into the Sudan army and deserted to join Anya-Nya, becoming a successful insurgent leader in Equatoria province. He persuaded both Tafeng and his declining Anyidi group and another small splinter faction, the "Nile Provisional government", to serve under an Anya-Nya Armed Forces (ANAF) High Command. After promoting himself to major-general, he next expanded his following into a Southern Sudan Liberation Movement (SSLM), and from a base in the Immatong mountains began to organize a system of administration in areas the ANAF controlled.

The fighting entered a final and particularly violent phase with Nimeiry's MiGs and helicopters machine-gunning and firing rockets into villages and troops setting about killing ordinary people after first kidnapping them so blame could be attached to "bandits". Egyptians and a few Russians were again reported to be serving in air and ground units, now totalling over 16,000. The Anya-Nya, however, had also greatly increased its strength to about 10,000. Its capabilities now included mines, mortars, grenades and a few Warsaw Pact automatic weapons as well as old British rifles. Its forces were divided into three brigades, one for each of the three southern Sudan provinces, Equatoria, Upper Nile and Bahr el Ghazal.

It would seem from covert diplomatic feelers that early on in his rule Nimeiry realized negotiations with the insurgents were inescapable, but like de Gaulle in Algeria he thought a sharp prior military reverse for them would improve his negotiating stance. In December 1971 a Sudanese army three-brigade offensive was mounted to contain the spread of Anya-Nya activity in Bahr el Ghazal province. For the most part the Anya-Nya slipped away; some crossed the frontier into Uganda and there were several clashes on both sides of the border.

At the same time, however, and in the early months of 1972 contacts and secret negotiations initiated by the World Council of Churches and followed up by others were taking place, the southern negotiators including representatives from the SSLM and the Anya-Nya. These meetings resulted in ceasefire declarations by both sides in early March, conceded reluctantly by some Anya-Nya as full independence was not attained. Nimeiry proclaimed autonomy for the south, dismissed some hardline ministers, granted an amnesty and promised to absorb Anya-Nya personnel in the Sudan army or police. A conservative estimate of the dead in the years from 1955 to 1972 is 500,000, the majority from disease or malnutrition. Some 1,190,000 refugees were enabled to return from Ethiopia, Uganda and the Congo, or to emerge from hiding in forests. Despite Moslem unrest involving bloodshed in Khartoum Nimeiry appointed Lagu as Sudanese army commander in the south. In the heady atmosphere of reconciliation it seemed that North and South had learnt to live with each other.

Nimeiry had to face two further revolts in the 1970s, both by the Mahdist faction supported by Libya. The first in 1975 was quickly put down. The second revolt, involving large convoys of lorry-borne insurgents entering the country from Libya, led to street fighting in Khartoum. This fighting lasted two days, several hundred people were killed and Nimeiry had to call upon Egyptian air and military help.

Ethiopia 1965–80

The Ethiopia of Emperor Haile Selassie was a ramshackle polity including provinces acquired in the nineteenth century together with the former Italian colony of Eritrea acquired after the end of the Second World War. The Empire was dominated by the Christian Amharic Shoa of the central Addis Ababa area. Eritrea was seen as particularly important as it provided Ethiopia with its only port, Massawa, but the Ethiopian regime, in particular its military, was, however, oppressive, brutal and corrupt. Revolts were to break out in three areas, Eritrea, Tigré and Oromo.[6]

Under the United Nations sponsored arrangements, Eritrea in 1956 was federated with Ethiopia and given local autonomy. In the late 1950s, Haile Selassie's government, seeking full control, began preparations to end the federal status. Initial resistance appeared in the form of the Eritrean Liberation Movement (ELM), formed in 1958, which hoped that a province-wide civil disobedience campaign would create opportunities for a coup. Initially Moslem, ELM gained followers from Christian areas. Its strategy, however, achieved no result and in 1960 a Moslem Eritrean Liberation Front (ELF) was formed in Egypt. In 1962 Haile Selassie abolished Eritrea's autonomy and the ELF decided to open a full insurgency campaign. It first turned on the ELM, which had actually moved to mount one attack on a police post, but had lost support and many of its adherents after a student strike that had led to mass arrests.

A number of ELM then moved on to join the ELF, broadening its base from its southwest Eritrea origins, from where it had been able to recruit personnel trained by the British in the 1940s. Other ELF insurgents were trained in Syria and China. But the ELF remained Moslem-dominated, supported by Arab countries and discriminating against Christians. Its internal structure, too, of four, later five, zones reflecting local ethnicities, lacked any effective horizontal co-ordinating linkages, with the results of patronage and warlordism. In total the ELF at this time had over two thousand insurgents in the field and was launching attacks on bridges, government offices, army camps and police stations with the aid of weaponry supplied by Libya. Most attacks represented small insurgent successes; one at Keren in 1968 was, however, a bloody failure. In addition insurgent cells carried out selected assassinations in cities. The Ethiopian government's response, the formation of a 1,000-strong elite counter-insurgency force, Commandos 101, Israeli-trained, was able to attract numbers of Christian recruits. ELF actions were met by increasingly heavy repression, including killings, shelling and aircraft bombing, and the establishment of free-fire zones on the Sudan border and Red Sea coast. This repression in turn led to large-scale ELF surrenders and desertions. In 1969–70 splits within the movement led to internal fighting and many deaths, continuing until 1972.

The most effective of the splinter groups, the two People's Liberation Front (PLF) groups, in September 1973 formed a new movement, the Eritrean People's Liberation Front (EPLF), but it too initially faced internal strife, finding it necessary to execute members of extreme left and local parochial factions.

Civil war between the two movements prevented the Eritrean insurgency from fully profiting from Ethiopia's "creeping revolution" which opened in 1973–4 and for which the imperial government's failure to suppress insurgency in Eritrea, together with mutiny in the Eritrean-based units, had been important causes. From May to July 1974, though, a series of insurgent ambushes and assassinations took place and were met by brutal repression and the massacre of civilians. One of Ethiopia's new military leaders and titular head of state, General Aman Andom, himself an Eritrean, then visited Eritrea offering an amnesty and a programme of reform. As part of the liberalization Andom permitted freedom of movement in an attempt to bring mass popular pressure to bear on the two insurgency movements to end the fighting; he also tried to use the EPLF against the ELF. This strategy enjoyed only a brief success as Andom remained insistent on retaining Eritrea within Ethiopia. In consequence and despite ongoing clashes (in one in October over 600 insurgents were killed) the two movements managed to co-ordinate their activities to mount a threat to Eritrea's capital, Asmara. Andom, discredited, was murdered in November and military leadership was increasingly taken by the Marxist-Leninist Colonel Mengistu Hailemariam. In December the combined insurgent movements struck at Asmara, hundreds of guerrillas engaging in street fighting. In response in January 1975 Mengistu launched a ferocious military offensive against the two insurgency movements.

Mengistu's punitive offensive in particular targeted Eritrean youth with, predictably, a result the reverse of that sought, large numbers, including

Eritrean policemen and sailors, joining the insurgent movements. These concluded a formal military co-operation agreement. In February 1975, however, an attempt to take Asmara failed after a bloody three-week battle, and a primarily ELF force suffered a mauling at the hands of Mengistu's army. In the event the EPLF proved much better organized to withstand Mengistu, establishing local administrations in the western areas that it controlled. By late 1975 the EPLF was fielding some 11,000 insurgents in an effective armed force which compared favourably against the more numerous 20,000-strong ELF. Mengistu's army had been forced to withdraw from a number of smaller stations, garrisons of at least a battalion-size being necessary for survival. In addition the EPLF was further helped by small numbers of Afar and Tigré insurgents.

The government's response was to organize a mass mobilization. Some 35,000 peasants were given a very basic military training, any weapon that was available and a briefing for a "Peasants March" to defend the Faith against an Islamic jihad. The EPLF and ELF attacked their camps on the way, killing hundreds. Further insurgent successes followed; in July 1977 both movements had liberated large areas, and after a pitched battle in which the Ethiopians lost over 2,000 killed and a further 2,000 taken prisoner, the EPLF took Keren. Fortune then swayed as the Somali invasion preoccupied Ethiopia's forces. (This invasion is considered later in the chapter on pp. 102–104.) The two movements still working together, albeit uneasily, occupied further large areas of Eritrea in late 1977, placing Asmara under siege and threatening Massawa and Assab. After the dramatic Soviet-backed Ethiopian military recovery, the Ethiopian–Cuban army counter-attacked with a force of over 100,000 men with warship bombardments in the Massawa area, forcing the two movements to withdraw again to remote country and mountain safe areas. The withdrawals led to recriminations, and these in turn led to a return to civil war. The EPLF drove the ELF out of the northeastern Sahel province into exile in Sudan and thereby into further splits and terminal decline, leaving the EPLF free to carry on the struggle in the next decade.

The province of Tigré had a tradition of revolt against the Shoan hegemony of Haile Selassie's government; this tradition had included a major revolt in 1943. The province remained quiet for the remainder of Haile Selassie's rule, but in the turmoil of the Ethiopian revolution a new movement, the Tigré People's Liberation Front (TPLF) emerged. Supported by the Eritrean EPLF, the TPLF embarked on insurgency and established control over the rural areas of the province and one town. But like the EPLF and ELF it suffered from the restored power of the Ethiopian army after the end of the Somali war. It was, nevertheless, able to withstand an advance of some 10,000 Ethiopian troops supported by Soviet armour and aircraft, and by 1979 the movement had regained some of its former initiative. It occupied substantial areas of the province, attacking and killing large numbers of government troops, and appeared well placed to continue the fight in the 1980s.

The southern province of Ethiopia, Bale, saw two Oromo revolts, the first being a slow spreading insurgency beginning in Wabe in April 1964. Over the next months insurgent control extended over central Bale and spread into neighbouring areas. The insurgents, as elsewhere, targeted police and military outposts for their attacks. The leader of the revolt Wako Gutu, tried to enlist Somali support, with some success. The Oromo ceased fighting in 1970, but Somali guerrilla activity continued, and led to a brief reappearance of Oromo insurgency under an Oromo National Liberation Front (ONLF – later shortened to Oromo Liberation Front (OLF)). With the collapse of the Somali invasion, the fighting, which had been dependent on Somali support, again ceased.

Nigeria 1967–70

Britain in East Africa and France in West Africa demarcated and structured coastal colonies and inland colonies. In West Africa, however, the British elected to link an inland region with several coastal ones to form the colony of Nigeria. The inland region happened to be the one inland region in West Africa supporting a large population. In the colonial era that inland region's pattern of trade was changed from one of leather, ivory and slaves traditionally trans-Saharan, to one of groundnuts and cotton dependent on access to the sea. Therein lay the resolve of the post-independence federal government of Nigeria to preserve the British-created linkage, and, essentially, the prime cause of the most dreadful and devastating of the wars to affect a post-independence African state in this period.[7]

There were of course middle-distance contributory causes: the vast size of Nigeria and the difficulties of ruling the many different ethnicities in its 55 million population, the constitutional arrangements left by the British favouring the largely Moslem Hausa-Fulani North; the North's subsequent political distortion of, and the overall corruption within, those arrangements; the exploitation of oil in the southeast, in Nigeria termed the East, which combined with the inability of the East's economy to absorb its entrepreneurial school leavers and graduates, led to local secessionism; and finally a measure of encouragement for the secessionists from the de Gaulle government in Paris, aspiring to replace British oil interests in the region by those of France.

In addition there were foreground catalysts that led the Eastern Region of Nigeria with its 12 million population, mostly but not all Ibo, to break away under the name of Biafra. Foremost among these were the pogroms and killings of Ibo labourers in the North as part of the North's reaction to the killing of its political and religious leader, the Sardauna of Sokoto, by an Ibo army officer in the January 1966 military coup; the personal ambitions of the Ibo soldier, Colonel Ojukwu, serving as the post-coup military administrator of the East; the breakdown of all national and international conciliation efforts; and finally the plans of the post-coup federal military government headed by General Yakubu Gowon to recast Nigeria into a federation of 12 states, so breaking the Ibo cohesion.

The Nigerian army in 1966 was relatively small – 9,000 men in only five or six battalions together with a few other major French Panhard armoured car and artillery units. Several of its better trained officers were killed at the time of the January coup which had resulted in the assumption of power by General John Aguiyi-Ironsi, or at the time of the second coup in July 1966 from which after a brief period of turbulence Colonel, later General, Gowon had emerged as the nation's head of government. In composition, the soldiers in combat arms had been mainly from the North or the middle of the country known as the Middle Belt, while support and logistic service personnel were generally southerners – a division reflecting Nigeria's education imbalance. After the July, August and September 1966 pogroms in the North, Ibo officers and soldiers withdrew or defected, fleeing back to Iboland in the Eastern Region with their weapons. Other weapons were supplied to them by France's two most subservient African client states, the Ivory Coast and Gabon. When, therefore, on 30 May 1967 Colonel Odemegwu Ojukwu proclaimed the independence of Biafra both sides had some nucleus of an army. The federal army had begun a rapid expansion bringing it to between 35 and 40,000; Biafra had approximately 2,000 former Nigerian army personnel reinforced with some 20,000 new recruits. It also had the equipment of a battalion that had been stationed at Enugu, together with a few Saracen armoured-cars and 105 mm howitzers.

The federal military made the mistake of underestimating its opponent and believing the secession could be ended with a short, sharp "police action". This action actually involved six battalions of the hurriedly expanded and hurriedly trained Federal Army 1 Area Command advancing after preliminary artillery barrages into Biafra from the north on 6 July 1967. Their attack was two-pronged: one involving some of the best federal troops, mostly northern Hausa, was directed against Nsukka, the second further east against Ogoja. Nsukka was quickly taken, with Ogoja also by mid-July. Thereafter the federal Nigerian advance was stalled by logistic difficulties.

It was now in any case clear that a full-scale civil war had opened, and both sides developed a war strategy. The federal strategy was to prove decisive in the long run. Using the federal naval forces, which they possessed, the

Nigerian navy mounted an assault on and captured the oil terminal port of Bonny. In this operation they were aided by British oil company pilot vessels. In addition to its economic significance, the seizure of Bonny, which stood between the Atlantic and Port Harcourt, denied the use of Port Harcourt to the Biafrans for the import of food and purchased weaponry, a crucial blow.

Biafra's strategy for August 1967 was to prove a sad disappointment. The Biafran commander, General Philip Effiong, launched a three-battalion attack designed to bypass the westward flank of the federal forces at Nsukka, cross the Niger at Onitsha and strike westward into the Mid-West region and on to Lagos. The Biafrans believed the population of the Mid-West region, which included a number of Ibo and Yoruba, would support them; to facilitate this a Yoruba brigadier, Victor Banjo, was given command of the assault. At first all went well. The units in requisitioned lorries dashed into the Mid-West region taking Benin, crossed the western border, and after a brisk battle took a small town, Ore. The way to the capital Lagos, only 100 miles away, was then held by only one federal battalion of recruits. But the Biafran strategy was wrecked by the personal ambitions of Banjo who saw himself as head of state of a greater Southern Nigeria after assassinating Ojukwu. In early October Banjo turned his columns back and the opportunity was lost. Banjo was arrested and executed. All that Biafra gained was loot, in particular some £2 million taken from banks in Benin.

Caught off balance by the Mid-West invasion, the federal army then effected a reorganization: 1 Area Command in the north became 1 Division; 2 Division under Colonel (later General) Murtala Mohammed was formed for the Mid-West retaking Benin City on 24 September; and 3 Division, later 3 Marine Commando Division, was created in the south under Colonel Benjamin Adekunle.

The federal army's 1 Division then, on 4 October, began an offensive aimed at capturing the Biafran capital, Enugu. The offensive opened with a heavy artillery barrage, and within a week Enugu had been occupied with the Biafrans withdrawing to their new capital Umuahia. Federal pressure also forced the Biafrans to withdraw across the Niger bridge at Onitsha, which city they could only hold with difficulty and under periodic federal artillery bombardment. In the east there was another withdrawal to a line on the Cross river following a federal advance on Calabar supported by an assault from the sea.

The Federal pressure then temporarily eased while their army was refitted and expanded; the difficulties it faced of distance, climate and terrain were formidable. The reorganization produced some 70,000 men for the three Divisions, together with British rifles and ammunition, and Saracen armoured personnel carriers and Saladin armoured-cars. Spain provided bombs for the federal air force, initially dropped from Dakota transports but later from Soviet-supplied Ilyushin-28 bombers, adapted MiG-17 fighters and Czech L-29 Delphins. The delay also gave the Biafrans respite to prepare airstrips and import weaponry, but they possessed no effective anti-aircraft capability, either in the form of interception aircraft or artillery other than Bofors guns, a weakness to cost them severe casualties as the Ilyushins flew above 10,000 feet. At the outset Biafra had one old American Second World War bomber and a few helicopters. The bomber quickly became unserviceable, an airliner adapted for bombing blew up and hand-grenades dropped from the helicopters made little impact on battles.

Re-equipped, Murtala Mohammed's 2 Division commenced operations aimed to take Onitsha. The first assaults, in December 1967, were attempts to cross the Niger; these met heavy machine-gun fire from the Biafran defence, costing the federals hundreds of casualties. Murtala then changed to an attack along the Enugu–Onitsha road, this after very heavy fighting proved successful. Once in Onitsha, however, fresh difficulties arose for Murtala as his depleted division could not maintain control of the Enugu road, and supply across the Niger was hazardous, particularly after the Biafrans under their ablest general, Achuzie, recrossed the river further south and were able to harass supply columns. Only the use of armoured vehicles and the Biafran lack of artillery enabled the Division to hold the city and in June 1968 Murtala, who openly blamed federal headquarters for his difficulties, was replaced by Colonel Haruna. The Division never really recovered from its maulings.

Adekunle's 3 Division, an ethnic mix in which perhaps Western Yoruba dominated, put its new strength to better effect in the southeast. After diversionary attacks, some incurring heavy casualties but compelling the Biafrans to distribute their troops along the western creeks, Adekunle, a commander of fiery temperament, mounted a massive river crossing from Calabar to the western bank of the Cross river to threaten Port Harcourt. The offensive to take the city began at the end of April; the city was first bombarded by the Division's artillery. One of its escape roads, that to Aba, was cut; the other to Owerri became crowded with fleeing refugees – although not in Iboland, Port Harcourt was a largely Ibo city – so preventing Biafran reinforcements, with the result that the city fell in May.

May, June and July 1968 saw intense fighting in the delta swamps as Adekunle advanced northeastwards from Port Harcourt, taking Aba in August and Owerri in September. In the northeast, Mohammed Shuwa's 1 Division, a division of Northern and Middle Belt soldiers, in a cautious advance took Abakaliki and Afikpo. It seemed the Biafran cause was lost. But towards the end of the year, to the discomfiture of the federal forces, they made a recovery, tenaciously holding the Uli airstrip, surrounding the federal forces in Owerri and advancing towards Aba. The recovery was facilitated by the arrival of French weaponry via Gabon and the Ivory Coast.

This recovery brought about a stalemate for several months in which operations by both sides were limited to small-scale raids and some limited gains by Shuwa in the north. The federal government was content to let the stranglehold of its economic blockade take an increasing toll on Biafran morale. In April Shuwa's 1 Division opened a large-scale offensive aimed at taking the Biafran capital Umuahia which fell to them in May. The federal success was, however, offset by the Biafran recapture of Owerri and the unexpected arrival on the scene of a new Biafran air asset, a small force of MF1–9B Minicon light aircraft directed by a Swedish supporter of Biafra, Count Carl von Rosen. The Minicon arrived via Gabon and were able to launch exceedingly effective air-to-ground rocket attacks on Nigerian aircraft on the ground, oil installations and ordnance parks. Federal aircraft flown by a variety of pilots from Egypt, East Germany and the USSR concentrated on trying to destroy the vital Biafran Uli airstrip.

Following the loss of Owerri, Adekunle was replaced by General Olusegun Obasanjo, to prove the ablest of the federal commanders. Adekunle had earned an evil reputation for the excesses committed by his troops and the opportunity to remove him was a political advantage for the federal cause.

The end of 1969 saw the beginning of the collapse of Biafra which until then had fought with great determination. In January 1970 Obasanjo's troops broke through the Biafran positions east of Owerri and, using their armoured vehicles with considerable skill, raided and created havoc in Biafra's rear areas. Owerri fell on 9 January, followed shortly by the federal capture of Uli. The Biafran position was now hopeless. Ojukwu fled to the Ivory Coast leaving his army commander Effiong to surrender. So ended Black Africa's first major war fought with modern weapons in which all the generals were Africans who had to command, sustain and supply large forces.

The federal cause was victorious for several reasons. First and foremost was the federal army's superiority in numbers – over 120,000 by the end of 1968 – and its ability to equip those numbers with the basic weaponry needed for the war, most importantly rifles and ammunition, and Saladin armoured-cars and Saracen armoured personnel carriers, used principally and successfully to hold ground acquired rather than in the attack. For this supply the federal government had been able to rely on Britain. Prime Minister Wilson assured Parliament that only weapons traditionally supplied to Nigeria were being made available to the federals; he did not, however, expand on the quantities. The infantry weapons and their ammunition, far more than the showy Soviet aircraft, armour and artillery, were the battle-winners. The federal blockade, cutting Biafra off from the sea, from the Norwegian stock fish after the capture of Port Harcourt and from the Middle Belt meat needed to balance the East's traditionally heavy carbohydrate diet, was as important as the interdiction of weapons supply to the Biafrans. The will to fight on was destroyed by hunger and death from kwashiorkor and other protein deficiency diseases.

Both the Federal and the Biafran armies were on paper organized on the British pattern, with distinctions between arms and services, and in formation and unit order of battle – though in many cases divisions, brigades, battalions and other units were well below British strengths in terms of men. The British pattern, however, appeared often in fairground mirror-image chaotic distortions. Personnel of both sides engaged in corrupt practices, particularly as the war progressed and opportunists saw chances of sales and profits from military equipment, many joining both armies simply to enrich themselves. Pay was claimed for non-existent or dead soldiers. Both armies looted areas they occupied.

On the federal side the general headquarters was not always in close touch with events on the ground. The three divisional commanders were, in effect, uncontrolled feudal warlords; they requisitioned recruits, stores, vehicles and buildings as they pleased, sending accounts to GHQ which rarely settled them. Each division kept a logistics staff at major ports, the winner being the first staff to rush up the gangway of a ship bringing equipment; divisions also had their own overseas purchasing teams. One observer described the federal army on the march as the "best defoliation agent ever known", soldiers were often inebriated or high on marijuana. Women accompanied the columns in various, mostly dubious, capacities. Attacks opened with an artillery bombardment, almost a code signal for opponents to withdraw; there followed a noisy assault wasting quantities of ammunition on quite often a deserted position, and a tactical victory would then be proclaimed. Vehicles carried fetishes of bones and feathers. In the Biafran army juju soothsayers promised immunity from federal bullets. Some were taken on to formation establishments, even being commissioned as chaplains receiving pay, accommodation and vehicles. But the sum total of their influence was an increase in Biafra's own casualty rate.

The Biafran army was generally rather better officered than the federals where such odd practices as battalion commanders ordering all the men of their own ethnicity to the rear prior to an attack, or simply taking good care to ensure they themselves were absent, were frequent. The October 1967 fall of Enugu, however, may have been caused, at least in part, by a deliberate Biafran shelling of their own capital to create panic. In both armies, the appurtenances and privileges of rank often counted more than the duties and responsibilities.

Despite the federal army's shortcomings and chaotic command, the federal military machine managed somehow to work. The command structure was generally, if not always, maintained; the soldiers usually, if not always, received food and ammunition. Aircraft sometimes found their target, even if they did not hit it; sometimes they lost their way. Signals networks generally worked, as did signals interception by both sides for intelligence gathering. Engineers repaired or improvised bridges, and lower formation and unit commanders were capable of imaginative tactical thinking and planning, including diversions and feints.

The federal head of state, General Gowon, a strict Christian, issued orders forbidding any form of genocide in reprisals. The orders were more often disobeyed than obeyed, in particular by Adekunle. There were also Biafran excesses. The economic blockade of Biafra, which Gowon attempted to alleviate in respect of civilians, is estimated to have killed at least 500,000, while propagandists for Biafra of varying repute have claimed far larger totals. The military casualties of both sides in total have been estimated as between 90,000 and 120,000.

Immediately the war was over Gowon directed that there should be no triumphalism and no medals, that oil profits should be channelled into the reconstruction of Iboland, that Ibos should be reabsorbed into the army and public service, and that Biafran currency be in part exchangeable for that of Nigeria.

In historical terms it was a bizarre war, its ferocity as extraordinary as the magnanimity of its victor.

Chad 1968–79

Another vast African country, much of Chad is semi-desert with mountains in the north but with areas of good vegetation in the south and southwest. In contrast to the Sudan, these southern areas populated by negro peoples, many Christian, represent the wealth, such as it is, of Chad. The peoples of the arid north, Moslem and mostly nomad, feel kinship with North Africa.

The French left Chad in 1960 with an independence government southern dominated and headed by President François Tombalbaye. In the first years of independence this regime proved unable to cope administratively, especially after several years of drought, and there were a number of plots and local rebellions aiming to overthrow Tombalbaye. In 1968 an insurgent movement, styled Freedom and Liberation for Chad (FROLINAT) that had been formed two years earlier, began a rebellion in the northern Tibesti, Borkou and Ennedi areas. Tombalbaye appealed to Paris for help.

Chad had been the first French colony to opt for de Gaulle in 1940 so the appeal was not one de Gaulle could ignore. In April 1969 the French despatched 3,000 Foreign Legion troops and, later, *Troupes de Marine*. Zaire sent a small military unit, Israel a training team and the United States provided logistic equipment. The conflict, however, worsened with increasing military support for FROLINAT from Algeria and Libya, including tanks and anti-aircraft missiles. FROLINAT groups captured important northern towns, including Bardai and Faya-Largeau. By 1972 some 50 French and 500 Chad soldiers had been killed in the fighting. For her own reasons – not to forfeit all hope of a share in Libya's oil – France scaled down her military effort in 1971 and 1972, and in 1975 Tombalbaye was overthrown and killed in a coup, his successor being General Felix Malloum. France was, however, still present, and to be further embarrassed when the wife of a French develop-ment official was abducted by FROLINAT, forcing the French authorities to deal directly with them, to the fury of Malloum who briefly closed down the French bases. French effort now took the more discreet form of several hundred "advisers" and French personnel in Chad uniform, both serving to buttress Malloum against conspirators to overthrow him. The "advisers" were not supposed to become involved in the ongoing fighting. They nevertheless were so involved on several occasions, notably in delaying the fall of a Borkou town, Ounianga Kebir, in 1977 and generally securing the southern half of the country.

From the mid-1970s the pattern, hitherto the relatively simple one of the south and France versus the north and Libya, became more complex. Libyan regular forces entered and proclaimed the annexation of the Aozou strip in the extreme northwest of Chad, believed to be uranium-bearing. A powerful FROLINAT force, styling itself the Second Army, advanced southwards with Libyan units in discreet support. In February 1976 FROLINAT forces again occupied Faya-Largeau, the most important town in the north, inflicting a heavy defeat on the Chad army. But Libya's clear self-interest led to splits within FROLINAT and in March the Libyan head of state, Gadaffi, agreed to a ceasefire in return for undertakings to effect political reform by the govern-ment of Chad. The ceasefire was not acceptable to some FROLINAT groups who began a move on the capital, N'Djamena. Libyan equipment supplied to them included AK-47 rifles, 81 and 120 mm mortars, grenade rocket-launchers and cannons.

The French reacted sharply, despatching 2,500 soldiers – mostly *Troupes de Marine* infantry and artillery with Foreign Legion and *Marine* armoured-car detachments, ten Jaguar air-to-ground strike aircraft and gunship and trans-port helicopters – in March 1978. These together with Chad's own units repulsed the northerners in a series of sharp clashes. In one, near Ati, Chad troops surrounded a 1,000-strong FROLINAT group which were then bombed and machine-gunned by French aircraft. Criticism in France of the scale of the operations and casualties incurred, however, led to a further

French effort to mediate in August 1978. These efforts eventually resulted in a Chad administration dyarchy headed by Malloum as president but with a Toubou leader of a FROLINAT faction, Hissene Habré, as prime minister, with the Chad army expanded to include the Northern Armed Forces (FAN) and the followers of Habré. A continuing French military presence mounted fast-moving long-distance patrols supported by helicopters in a strategy called *nomadization*.

This French presence remained unacceptable to several of the FROLINAT factions, notably the largest led by Goukouni Oueddai, also a Toubou but of a different clan to Habré, and with resumed Libyan support for FROLINAT fighting continued. The French hoped their presence could be limited simply to holding the south with its, in their eyes, lawful government. For this some 2,000 French soldiers, Jaguar air-to-ground strike aircraft and an electronic surveillance system were all deployed. Whatever chance of success these arrangements might have had was negated by a rift in the Malloum–Habré dyarchy, Malloum falling increasingly under the influence of a southern colonel, Wadal Kamougué, bitterly opposed to Habré. Habré, however, had used the dyarchy period to provide his FAN followers with French weaponry delivered as aid, and after some bloody engagements in which he defeated the formal Chad army and with some support from Oueddai, Habré entered N'Djamena in February 1979. The French forces present, who were prepared to fight Oueddai, were not deployed to contain Habré – or stop the local bloodshed which soon extended into Negro versus Moslem mutual massacres in several areas; the French estimated that deaths totalled 10,000. Chad was now effectively divided into three, a north under FROLINAT once again divided into factions, the centre under Habré and the south under Malloum and Kamougué. Intense Sahel and Nigerian diplomatic activity and pressures led, after much wrangling, especially within FROLINAT, to the formation in March 1979 of a Government of National Unity (GUNT). The GUNT head of state, Lol Shawa, was a leader of one of the ten factions that had broken away from FROLINAT, the Chad Liberation Movement (MPLT); Habré and Oueddai were both ministers. The French agreed to withdraw in favour of an all-African force, but before they could do so the GUNT came under attack from Malloum and Kamougué in the south, which had been excluded from it, and more importantly a massive assault involving 2,500 Libyan regulars together with FROLINAT groups opposed to the GUNT. The two challenges were contained by the temporary alliance of Habré, Oueddai and the French, and a further reconstruction of the Chad government followed, this time Oueddai becoming president with Kamougué as vice-president and Habré a minister. It seemed at last a government representing all regions of the country had been formed. Oueddai, too, was prepared to accept the Libyan annexation of the Aozou strip, thereby satisfying Gaddafi's interests in the affairs of Chad. In the hope that accordingly the French would no longer see any need to continue supporting Habré he somewhat precipitately dismissed him. Oueddai thereby set the stage for further rounds of civil war and violence within his country in the next decades.

Lesotho 1970–4

The small land-locked and mountainous kingdom of Lesotho experienced brief civil strife and a period of unrest from 1970 to 1974. Violence erupted after an election held in January 1970. From independence in 1966 to the election Lesotho had been ruled by Chief Leabua Jonathan and his Basutoland National Party (BNP). The regime claimed that Lesotho's geographical situation, entirely surrounded by the Republic of South Africa, necessitated accommodation with Pretoria, and South Africa had responded with help in several fields.

In the election, the BNP was narrowly defeated by the Basutoland Congress Party (BCP), a result unacceptable to Jonathan who declared an emergency, suspended the constitution and the courts, and had the BCP leader Ntsu Mokhehle arrested. A little later the king of Lesotho, Moshoeshoe II, was placed under house arrest and subsequently exiled. Jonathan mobilized his 500-strong police mobile force which included many British officers, and was further provided with police reinforcements, helicopters and light aircraft by South Africa.

In February an opposition force, initially of some 1,000 men, opened a rebellion in the hills, their leader Clement Leeper being a former senior police officer. Fighting in February was sporadic, but in March Jonathan's police mobile force mounted a major sweep against the insurgents, their headquarters and their bases in caves near Maseru. The government forces used helicopters and aircraft, killing a large number, at least 150, of the insurgents. The remainder retreated further into the hills from which they launched occasional strikes at government posts and police stations. These attacks met with decreasing success and increasing casualties. The police mobile force's repressive measures were severe, including killings, the beating up of villagers and the burning of villages, particularly in the eastern mountains. By the end of April the insurgency movement had been suppressed.

There was a brief recurrence of anti-government insurrection by followers of Mokhehle in 1974; the police mobile force harried and hunted the insurgents in the hills on the Lesotho/Orange Free State border. Mokhehle and some of his followers escaped to South Africa, while others were killed in the operations and a number arrested. Lesotho then remained calm until 1979 when the country became involved in the southern African turbulence and violence created by South Africa's apartheid policies.

Ethiopia and Somalia 1977–8

The internal security difficulties faced by Ethiopia have been set out earlier in this chapter; this section examines Ethiopia's involvement in full war with a neighbouring country, Somalia. Following Somalia's check at the hands of the Kenyans, the attention of the country's military rulers turned towards the Somali-populated Ogaden area of Ethiopia, the most sensitive of Somalia's long-standing irredentist claims. At this time, to the mid-1970s, it suited Soviet Union foreign policy to build up the military strength of Somalia. The Army in 1977 was estimated to total 30,000 with seven tank battalions, 22 mechanized or motorized infantry battalions, two special force units and supporting artillery. Equipment included 200 old Soviet T-34 tanks, 100 of the newer T-54/55 tanks, 350 armoured personnel carriers, 180 field guns or howitzers, anti-tank and anti-aircraft artillery and a few surface-to-air missiles. The air force was reputed to possess 55 combat aircraft, the most important of which were Ilyushin-28s and MiG-15s, -17s and -21s. Some 4,000 Soviet personnel were at work training the Somalis in 1976.

Incidents on the border, notably in 1964 with a series of clashes, occurred all through the 1960s and again in 1973.[8] A little later, sponsored by the Somali government, a Western Somali Liberation Front (WSLF) appeared. Its members received Somali government arms and training, as did Ethiopian Oromo dissidents in the Ogaden and Eritrean and Afar dissidents in northeastern Ethiopia. All three groups were increasingly active as Ethiopia's "creeping revolution" weakened the authority of Addis Ababa. By the end of 1976 the WSLF, about half of whose members were volunteers from the Somali army, had gained control over much of the Ogaden. Events came to a head early in 1977 when Mengistu Hailemariam expelled all American military advisers. Faced with Eritrean insurgency poised to take Massawa and cut him off from the sea, Mengistu was unable to reassert authority in the Ogaden where by June the WSLF had forced the Ethiopian army back into the mountain strongholds of Diredawa, Harar and Jijiga. General Siad Barré, the military ruler of Somalia, believed he could now secure a complete victory, and committed Somali regular army T-34 and T-54 tanks and mobile infantry with some use of Somali air power, to raids on two Ogaden towns. The Somali air effort was, however, limited by an acute shortage of spare parts and the Ethiopians claimed to have shot down over 20 MiGs. The WSLF, under Hassan Mahmoud, took Jijiga in September and began to threaten the important city of Harar, having taken the Kara Marda pass. Somali-backed guerrillas penetrated even further into Ethiopia, in one battle only 240 km from Addis Ababa, killing a large number of Ethiopian soldiers. The Ethiopian 3rd Division mutinied; both it and the 4th Division were reduced to remnants, much Ethiopian equipment was lost, and shortage of spares rendered other assets unusable. The Somali advance was, however, finally checked by the Ethiopian heavy artillery and constant air strikes, and a successful counter-attack in November provided a respite for Harar, though the city was once again threatened by a final but unsuccessful Somali attack in January 1978.

Mengistu had now to reverse his military priorities to avoid an irretrievable loss of the Ogaden. He was enabled to do this successfully by a breathtaking 180 degree turn in Soviet policy. Moscow's long-term strategic aims had included an effective presence on or near the western Indian Ocean to threaten Western oil supplies. To 1977 Somalia appeared to offer the best prospects, but the larger size of Ethiopia and the Marxist-Leninism of Mengistu led to a policy reappraisal, brought to a head when Barré rashly expelled all his 6,000 Soviet advisers in November 1977, a move which ended any hope of the Soviet Union acting as an arbitrator.

The speed and efficiency of the Soviet military response under General Vasili Petrov was remarkable.[9] Weapon deliveries begun earlier in mid-1977 were accelerated, equipment arriving in a 60-aircraft airlift or via South Yemen (formerly Aden) and Assab. To man the T-55 and T-62 tanks, ASU-57 airborne assault guns, BMP and BMD armoured personnel carriers and the artillery units, Cuban troops were flown in and given hurried updating training; Soviet pilots flew in over eighty MiG-21s and MiG-23s together with some 30 helicopters. The Cuban troop total eventually reached 11,000 by March 1978; they were commanded by Major-General Arnaldo Ochoa Sanchez. At the start of the counter-offensive Ochoa was able to field a parachute battalion, one mechanized and two other infantry regiments, a tank regiment and several 122 mm and 152 mm field gun artillery units, the Soviets adding one of BM-21 multi-barrelled rocket launchers. Ethiopia provided three divisions of hastily recruited and virtually untrained illiterate troops, with some rather better artillery batteries and a parachute battalion.

General Petrov was greatly assisted in his command and control by his intelligence assets – former Soviet advisers to the Somalis, unimpeded air reconnaissance, signals intercepts and a satellite beamed to his headquarters. He and Ochoa were therefore well equipped for their aim – the total ejection of the Somalis from Ethiopian territory. The operation was to proceed smoothly and provide an almost unique example of a sophisticated conventional European battle fought on the African continent. Petrov's first move, at the end of January 1978, was the use of Ethiopia's American F-5 and Soviet MiG-21 strike aircraft to disrupt essential supplies for Somalia's armoured units by the bombing of ordnance field parks and the Hargeisa–Jijiga road. The land offensive involving over 55,000 men opened some ten days later. A flanking force composed of the Cuban parachute unit, artillery and the Ethiopian 10th Infantry Division struck eastwards to secure the flank and block the Djibuti–Diredawa railway line. The main force assaulted the by now well-prepared WSLF positions, held by 8,000 men with T-55 tanks and 122 mm guns in the mountains around Harar. Close air support and the use of ground saturation BM-21 multiple rocket launcher artillery produced initial success but the Ethiopian attack was checked by the WSLF before Jijiga, where the decisive battle of the campaign was to be fought.

Petrov decided to fight this as an air–land battle, three airborne assaults being mounted. The first led off with a parachute unit drop on a village north of Jijiga, but bad weather prevented the landing of follow-up helicopter troops. The unit was withdrawn and redeployed to assist clearing the railway line. A second, this time effective, combined parachute and helicopter assault followed on 2 March, the railway line was cleared and the way opened for the 10th Ethiopian Division to move around the rear of the WSLF's Jijiga defences. The third assault landing was to provide the vanguard for the attack on the WSLF's rear, 100 helicopter sorties delivering 70 ASU-57 guns with infantry in BMD airborne armoured personnel carriers. The WSLF were then attacked in front and in the rear, and were quickly overwhelmed, suffering heavy casualties. With this defeat the WSLF campaign came to an end, its surviving followers fleeing back into Somalia and Barré formally announcing the withdrawal of his regulars.

Both sides suffered many thousands of dead and injured. The war forced some 700,000 refugees to flee into Somalia and more followed the Ethiopian reoccupation of the Ogaden. The WSLF continued guerrilla warfare in the rural areas of the Ogaden, with the Ethiopian and Cubans holding the towns and continuing the bombing of small Somali settlements on both sides of the border throughout 1978 and 1979.

Tanzania and Uganda 1978–9

The brief war between Tanzania and Uganda in 1978–9 was not comparable to that between Ethiopia and Somalia in sophistication of operational art. Although both sides' armies were equipped with reasonably up-to-date conventional warfare weaponry, neither army, in particular that of Uganda, was able to use the equipment to full advantage.[10]

The war was caused by the demands of the increasingly unbalanced military dictator of Uganda, General Idi Amin. Amin had seized power in a coup in

February 1971. He was a northwest Ugandan Muslim of massive physical size and strength but of very limited formal education; he had been commissioned from the ranks and had reached the rank of colonel at the time of his coup. One of his first actions was to order the massacre of hundreds of Acholi and Lango soldiers whose loyalty he distrusted; sometimes the killings were preceded by clashes within barracks. Immediately after the coup Amin also began to lay claim to land on his country's borders in Rwanda, Kenya and Tanzania. With clearly aggressive designs the Ugandan dictator also embarked on a massive expansion of the Ugandan army. By 1978 the Ugandan army had reached a paper strength of 20,000 (from a population of 12 million). It was organized into two brigades, each of four battalions with one additional mechanized battalion, one commando unit and an artillery regiment. The equipment included 10 T-34 and 15 T-54 tanks, some older M-4 American tanks, Soviet reconnaissance vehicles, modern Czech OT-64 armoured personnel carriers together with some elderly Soviet BTR-40 and BTR-152 armoured personnel carriers, a small number of Soviet BRDM light armoured personnel carriers, a few worn British Saladin and Ferret armoured cars, an artillery unit of Soviet and Chinese 122 and 75 mm guns and an engineer unit.[11] A small number of Soviet MiG-21 aircraft and light helicopters were the nucleus of Uganda's air force, together with a few transport machines. Much of all this equipment had very quickly become unserviceable as the Ugandan army had been expanded rapidly, and almost all of its pre-coup best officers killed or in exile for daring to oppose, or even criticize, the blood-thirsty nature of Amin's rule. Battalions (often only 200 men) were commanded by men who had been junior NCOs prior to the coup. The aircraft were flown by Libyans or Palestinians, but a few Ugandan soldiers had been sent to Brno to learn how to handle the OT-64s.

Amin's first target was Tanzania, whose Peoples Defence Force (TPDF) was also expanding to a ground force total of 17,000, organized into one tank, two artillery, one engineer and ten infantry battalions. The equipment included Chinese T-59 medium and T-62 light tanks, some Chinese K-63 and Soviet BTR-152 and BTR-40 armoured personnel carriers, Soviet and Chinese 76 mm field guns and 122 mm howitzers and other miscellaneous mortars and light anti-aircraft guns. The TPDF's air assets were similar to those of Uganda – a small number of MiG-21 and MiG-17 aircraft together with transport machines and a few helicopters. Tanzania's equipment was generally better maintained, though there remained an acute shortage of personnel adequately trained to use it.

Full-scale war did not break out until 1978, but there had been a succession of border clashes from 1971 onwards. In September 1971 Amin alleged that guerrilla supporters of the former civilian government of Uganda were crossing the border from Tanzania and killing Ugandans. Using this allegation as justification Amin ordered a Ugandan military raid into Tanzania, on the way briefly occupying the border town of Mutukula and looting and killing civilians in the town and surrounding area.

In September of the following year a large body of Ugandan insurgents including former soldiers and policemen again crossed from Tanzania, but they were heavily defeated by the Ugandan army. In retaliation for the incursion Ugandan aircraft bombed Bukoba and Mwanza before a ceasefire was arranged. Over the next five years Amin's megalomania and thirst for blood increased. Many hundreds of Ugandans were killed – including many more Langi and Acholi soldiers regarded as suspect by Amin. Uganda's Asians were expelled and increasingly bombastic territorial claims made. Events came to a head in October 1978 with a failed coup attempt and unrest in Uganda's greatly expanded army, in particular unrest and mutinies in the army's elite units, the Simba (Lion) mechanized battalion at Mbarara and the "Suicide" battalion at Masaka.

Amin immediately alleged a Tanzanian invasion and launched a probing reconnaissance raid across the border with air attacks on Bukoba and settlements along the Kagera river. On 30 October the Ugandan army invaded Tanzania in force, using tanks and artillery. Catching the Tanzanians by surprise they advanced as far as the Kagera river, meeting only weak Tanzanian opposition. The attackers looted and killed, the Tanzanians later alleging some 10,000 dead. Amin then laid claim to the Kagera salient area, some 1,820 square km, that his army had occupied, but in the face of a counter-attack by Tanzanian artillery bombardment and under intense international pressure he withdrew. The Tanzanians were ordered to halt at the frontier.

Amin's troops again attacked in December, and this time the Tanzanians were permitted a "hot pursuit" across the border. In early January the Ugandans made a further attack, also repulsed, but it determined the Tanzanian government to act firmly. As a first move, and in the hope of OAU help, it was decided to push the Ugandans back to the garrison towns of Mbarara and Masaka, but to go no further. They also hoped there would be further attempts within Uganda to remove Amin, and they needed time to make military preparations, including the recall of reservists and the crash training of volunteers and militiamen. Amin also completed his preparations. His last-minute reinforcements included some 2,000 Libyan military reservists, many past their first youth.

Accordingly the Tanzanian entry into Uganda later in January was very slow and cautious, but they evidently realized that an advance limited to the two garrison towns would not destroy Amin, and the advance gathered more momentum. The vanguard of the invading force, for political reasons and to avoid Tanzanian casualties, was a unit of some 1,000 Uganda National

Liberation Army (UNLA) armed exiles under Major-General Tito Okello and Lieutenant-Colonel David Oyite-Ojok. Under the Tanzanian field commander Major-General David Musuguri were five infantry brigades, 201, 205, 206 (Drywood), 207 (Black Mamba) and 208 (Slippery Fish), each probably some 1,000–1,500 men, more the equivalent of a Warsaw Pact motor-rifle regiment than a British brigade. Attached to the force was a Mozambique field artillery unit. Their advance, preceded by a heavy artillery bombardment, remained slow, based on foot-soldier speed rather than the armoured vehicles which they possessed; the slow speed, based on experience in Mozambique, certainly kept casualties low.

The original plan had provided for a two-pronged assault, one force to advance along the coast towards Entebbe and Kampala via Masaka, the other to advance inland towards Mbarara. The plan was then extended to include a swing by the inland force northwest to Fort Portal and finally a return east towards Kampala. This strategy proved very successful. The Ugandan army, unpaid in many units, demoralized and lacking ammunition, generally offered weak resistance, an additional difficulty for them being sabotage behind their own lines. Being either untrained or poorly trained, the Ugandans opted to fight around or from within their wheeled armoured personnel carriers, so making themselves targets for encirclement and Tanzanian anti-tank weaponry.

Only in three of the opening engagements, at Mutukula and Lubaya, did the Ugandans show any resolution. At Mbarara Major-General Mayunga's 206 Brigade had a stiff fight before it destroyed Amin's elite Simba battalion. Masaka fell on 24 February, Mbarara a day later. The most competent professionally of the engagements were the Tanzanian 208 brigade's assault on Entebbe airport on 7 April, led by Major-General Mwita Mara, and the subsequent investment of Kampala, taken with UNLA units in the lead following an artillery bombardment of Amin's defences and troops, mainly Libyan, the repulse of a Ugandan counter-attack and the successful ambush of a Libyan column. By mid-April Kampala's suburbs were finally cleared and the remnants of Amin's forces were in flight northwards through Jinja. Libyan reinforcements, estimated at between 1,000 and 3,000 men, and a 1,000-strong unit of Moroccans were unable to reverse the course of the war. Ugandan army units either mutinied or fled, some 8,000 arriving in Zaire and Sudan.

Both countries' air forces were committed to small-scale operations. Two Libyan Tupolev Blinder bombers bombed Mwanza, achieving virtually nothing. The Tanzanians' 30 mm anti-aircraft guns shot down a number of Ugandan aircraft and destroyed a Libyan transport full of troops as it attempted to land at Entebbe. The pilot had not realized the airport was in Tanzanian hands.

Casualty figures are far from clear. The Tanzanians admitted to the loss of 435 men; the Libyan contingent probably suffered a rather higher number. Ugandan casualties were very much higher but are unlikely ever to be known. Overall, the result was a complete victory for the Tanzanians and UNLA. Amin fled into exile and Tanzania, exerting influence through a large garrison not withdrawn until 1981, was able briefly to ensure a new government in Kampala in accord with its own interest. Further events are set out in a later chapter.

North Africa

Events in North Africa in the period 1956–80 were initially concerned with internal domestic issues; they then became increasingly responses to the claims of Algeria and the actions of the Libyan leader, Colonel Gadaffi.[12]

Morocco faced an insurrection in the Rif mountains in the years 1958 and 1959, and over 20,000 troops were needed for the suppression. In 1962 Moroccan troops entered the Colomb-Béchar area of Algeria, and over the next year Moroccan forces occupied a substantial area of Algerian territory. Some sharp fighting with Algerian troops supported by Cuban units, in which the Moroccans generally proved the better, led to negotiations and the subsequent demilitarization of the area. In the 1970s two military coup attempts against the monarchy, one in 1971 and one in 1972, occurred, both resulting in bloodshed. These were followed by the insurrection of a small group of Libyan-backed insurgents in the Atlas mountains, also suppressed by the military. There then followed the events in the Western Sahara already noted.

Tunisia saw unrest in the form of a general strike followed by severe rioting in January 1978. Troops had to be deployed in the streets and over 100 people were killed. In January 1980 a group of 60 armed insurgents entered Tunisia from Algeria, and military operations for their death or capture lasted several weeks.

The most vigorous military operation in North Africa in this period was, however, the large-scale punitive operation mounted by Egypt against Libya in July 1977. The Egyptian government had become exasperated with Libyan troop concentrations and border incidents. The operation involved the penetration of Libyan border territory by Egyptian armour, an airborne troop occupation of the Giarabub oasis deep inland, and aircraft strikes against Libyan air bases and radar posts. The Libyans, apparently taken by surprise, lost a number of men, tanks and aircraft, while the Egyptians suffered only a few casualties.

Small-scale operations

A number of other newly independent countries found themselves faced, at or shortly after independence, with destabilization. In some cases this arose from the unsound political or constitutional legacy of the departed colonial power, in others from groups of religious fundamentalists, mutinous soldiers or industrial labour protesters that challenged law and order. Those that led to a military involvement are outlined here; they will confirm the Clausewitz doctrine that war is a continuation of politics by other means.

At independence the three East African territories that had been under British rule, Tanganyika, Uganda and Kenya, all possessed small armies modelled on the British pattern and with a number of British officers on loan, including all the army commanders. Zanzibar had no army and only a small barrack police force, again British officered.

The Zanzibar revolution, which broke out on the night of 11 January 1964, was one of the African population, largely indigenous but also including a significant percentage of mainlanders at work in the island, rebelling against the Arab political hegemony. This hegemony was reflected in the constitution drawn up by the outgoing British colonial regime; an election under the constitution failed adequately to represent the African majority. The revolutionaries, with the aid of some mainlander ex-policemen that the Zanzibar government had dismissed, seized the police armouries and very quickly overcame the weak resistance offered by the government's police mobile force. With the insurgents armed with rifles and Bren guns, the revolution soon became largely a one-sided ethnic conflict, Arabs being attacked, detained, forced to flee in dhows or be killed, with only a few able to defend themselves with sporting weapons. The total number of Arabs killed will never be known, but it would certainly amount to several thousand.

The turbulence in Zanzibar, some rash internal political incitement from Kambona, the Tanganyikan Minister for Defence, a demand for increased pay and the continuing presence of British officers were the main causes of a mutiny in the Tanganyikan army that broke out on 20 January 1964, beginning with a battalion in Dar es Salaam and spreading to the army's second battalion at Tabora. British personnel were arrested and in some cases roughly handled before being flown off to Nairobi. The mutinies sparked off a breakdown of order along the Tanganyikan coast, with Asian and Arab traders being attacked. The Tanganyikan government requested British help in the restoration of order; a Royal Marines commando of 600 men together with a squadron of light armoured cars were already on their way from Aden in a Royal Navy aircraft carrier. The mutineers were surrounded by a detachment of the Marines flown in by helicopter; when the mutineers refused to surrender the Marines, using rifles and anti-tank rocket launchers, stormed the barracks. The remainder of the force then landed, rounded up remaining mutineers and restored order. The British force was then withdrawn and replaced temporarily by a Nigerian battalion.

The Tanganyikan mutiny was followed almost immediately by mutinies in Uganda and Kenya, both of whose governments requested help from the British units still in Kenya. A British battalion was flown to Entebbe where on landing the troops deployed for an assault on the airport, to the great surprise of an official Ugandan government reception party. The unit was then moved to Jinja, where they seized the guardroom and surrounded the two mutinous Ugandan battalions who surrendered and gave up their weapons without a fight. In Kenya a Kenya Rifles battalion mutinied at Lanet and seized some weapons from the armoury. A detachment of 75 men was sent from a British artillery regiment at Gilgil, some 30 km away. They recaptured the guardroom and armoury after a brief exchange of fire in which one mutineer was killed. The Kenyan officers then attempted to persuade the mutineers to surrender, without success. To avoid casualties to soldiers and their families the British gave the mutineers a night for reflection; the next morning the majority agreed to hand in their weapons to the Kenyan officers. A minority, however, refused and temporarily reoccupied the armoury, necessitating its recapture by the British gunners supported by Royal Engineers scout cars.

Common to each suppression was the fact that the British knew well both the barrack layouts and the structures of the mutineers' units, and were readily available with few logistic problems.

In the first three years of independence the Kenyan army had a small-scale but difficult campaign to fight. Somalis laid claim to a large area of northeast Kenya, a claim rejected by the Kenyan government. In 1963 the Somalis then embarked on the "Shifta War". Bands of a dozen to 100 Somalis, in which several, but not all, were armed with old rifles, roamed, ambushed and raided in the areas claimed by Somalia. The difficulties of high scrub terrain impeding vision, and the ability of the lightly armed Somalis to move very quickly, up to 80 km per day, made pursuit very difficult. A number of the Somalis had served in British colonial units, their ambushes could be very effective and the Shifta were often able to draw on local compatriot support for food and shelter. Some Shifta moved by camel. The Shifta attacks were never co-ordinated in any overall plan although some 1,000 Shifta were involved at the campaign's peak in 1964. To contain them the colonial government, and after 12 December 1963 the independent government of Kenya deployed some five infantry companies – 700 men – comprising soldiers, police patrols, the police general service unit and the police air wing. Patrols were sent out, but most success resulted from the response to ambushes where the Somali inferiority in fire power was quickly evident. Occasionally on large operations the Kenyan troops — still with a number of British officers — would mortar an area in which it was believed Shifta were hiding. Logistic support for the five companies was always a difficulty, particularly after the Shifta acquired a small number of mines. At the outset supply was by horsed transport but, after several ambushes, by 60-vehicle convoys escorted by a 100-strong infantry company. The Shifta injected a dimension of psychological warfare by the emasculation of any soldiers they captured. Counter-measures included stock confiscation, which proved counter-productive, and eventually the enforced concentration of the Somali population in three large controlled zones.

The operations continued until 1967 when agreement to end the Shifta raiding was reached. The Kenyan government's casualty figures for the four years claimed 1,650 Shifta killed at a cost of 69 Kenyan troops and police and 500 civilians.

A small 1960–61 military commitment, involving a British army presence of one battalion, was that of peacekeeping in the Southern Cameroons while a plebiscite was held to decide whether the area should remain part of Nigeria or, as the majority came to decide, rejoin the Cameroun Republic. Unrest and violence had broken out, the activists being members of the ALNK (*Armée de Libération Nationale Kamerunaise*), a descendant of the former UPC. The ALNK, some of whose members had trained in China and North Africa, sought to end all ties with both Britain and France. British military intelligence was efficient and led to the discovery of the base camp of an ALNK unit described as the 1st Mobile Battalion.

In the last months of Northern Rhodesia's existence as a British territory a fundamentalist Christian breakaway group created so serious a local threat that the military had to be called in. The group called itself the Lumpas and was led by one Alice Lenshina (Lenshina derived from "regina" or queen). Lenshina forbade her followers from membership of political parties, a ban that brought her into direct conflict with Prime Minister Kaunda and his ruling political party. Clashes leading to deaths broke out between Lumpa followers armed with axes, spears and old guns (in some cases muzzle-loaded) and the police in the second half of 1963. The Lumpa then withdrew to stockaded villages to fight back against police and troops stormed Lenshina's own stronghold; after one further battle near Lundazi and a few other local clashes Lenshina gave herself up. The fighting then ended, with the official total of deaths at 491. A second, less significant, insurgency movement led by Adamson Mushala, aimed at the overthrow of President Kaunda, broke out in the late 1970s. Troops as well as police were needed for its suppression.

Uganda experienced two cases of ethnic warfare resulting from the meltdown of "colonial glue". The British had enlarged the kingdom of Toro in the early years of the century; two ethnicities, the Amba and the Konjo, were included in this enlargement. Protest in the 1950s turned to violence in 1964 when hundreds of Toro spearmen from all over the kingdom turned on the Konjo, killing a large number, almost certainly several hundred men, women and children. Ugandan police and military arrived too late to prevent the slaughter. In 1966, when, following constitutional changes effectively ending its autonomy, the kingdom of Buganda declared its secession from Uganda, President Obote, who had declared himself president in place of the kabaka, or king, of Buganda, ordered the Ugandan army under Colonel Amin to occupy the kabaka's palace. Fighting ensued but the kabaka's followers, most of whom had only sporting weapons, were overcome and the kabaka fled to Britain.[13]

In Swaziland, at the time still a British protectorate, the destabilizing force was an industrial labour group presenting demands on a mix of political and employment conditions. On 10 June 1963 some 3,000 men clashed with the police in Mbabane. A battalion of Scottish infantry was ordered to fly to Mbabane from Nairobi. It arrived on the 13th, restored order in Mbabane and then immediately moved on to the asbestos mining centre of Havelock, some 16 km away. The troops mounted an early morning cordon enabling the police to make searches and arrests, a tactic then repeated on a sugar plantation. Goodwill was restored by the unit's bagpipes and drums.

French troops had been used to end small-scale unrest in Gabon and Congo-Brazzaville in 1960 and, as already noted in Cameroun, both before and after independence, French units were committed to end inter-ethnic conflict in Mauritania in 1961, to restore order in Gabon in 1962 and in Chad in 1962–3 and to repress a military revolt in Niger in 1963. More serious destabilization took the form of an attempted military coup in Gabon in 1964. The President of Gabon, Leon M'Ba, had called an election for February of that year but just before the election date Major M'bane at the head of the local military, seized power and invited Aubame, the leader of the opposition to M'ba, to form a government. French *Troupes de Marine* parachute troops were at once flown in from Senegal, on a justification of a bilateral defence agreement to restore M'Ba. This was achieved with only limited fighting, two French and 19 Gabonese soldiers being killed.

Another former French colony, Benin, was the scene of bizarre fighting in 1977. The events have never been satisfactorily explained and included an attack on the palace of President Kerekou by soldiers described as airborne and with light skins. The attack was a failure. Moroccan involvement, with perhaps support from elsewhere, seems the most likely explanation, as Benin had been championing the Polisario cause.

The year 1979 saw mounting domestic protest against the excesses of the self-styled and self-crowned "Emperor" Bokassa in the "Central African Empire". Students and others demonstrated in the streets. Bokassa sought support from Zaire which sent a military unit to restore order, a large number of people being killed in the process. Further intolerable abuse of power, including the beating to death of over a hundred teenagers, followed. France decided unilaterally to act, despatching a 1,000-strong regiment and restoring a republican government.

Chapter Five

Southern Africa to 1983

The dominant theme in the affairs of southern Africa from the late 1960s to the early 1990s was the apartheid policy of the government of South Africa and the implications and consequences of that policy for states adjoining South Africa. It is appropriate, therefore, to treat the various 1970s and 1980s conflicts in the region together, as all were either wholly or in large part reactions to Pretoria's policies. Apartheid, especially in the vertical apartheid form creating demarcated "independent homelands" of Prime Ministers Hendrik Verwoerd (1958–66), and John Vorster (1968–78), was in many respects a white version of traditional African warfare: areas were to be delineated by pressure or by force within which the white population with all its mineral and agricultural wealth was to be secured by a white or white-controlled military, as frontiersmen. Non-whites were essentially to figure only as labour and be reduced in number as far as possible in these areas.

The policy increasingly aroused African opposition within and outside South Africa to an extent that by 1977 South African leaders were talking, in terms reminiscent of the French military of the 1950s, of a "Total National Strategy" to combat the "total onslaught in South Africa", all in the name of *Suiwer Afrikaner Kalvinistiese Christilike Nationalise Geloof*, a pure Afrikaaner Calvinist Nationalist Christian faith. One general commented: "We already exist in political, economic and ideological circumstances usually associated with a state of war." This state of war was fought with semi-religious fervour, strengthened by an apparently unshakeable belief in the racial superiority of the white man, in internal military and police repression, and in intelligence and "dirty tricks" special operations which included, among others, sabotage, telephone tapping, blackmailing, abduction and forgery in South Africa and neighbouring states. It was also fought by supporting client factions or open civil warfare in neighbouring states, so attempting to keep the external threats

115

either of exiled ANC supporters or of critical regimes out of South Africa itself. As will be seen, these different theatres of conflict all impacted upon each other.

In fighting its wars, the South African government possessed the major asset of an industrial base that could be turned to arms manufacture, increasingly necessary as, after the December 1963 UN Security Council ban, other nations refused or became unwilling to supply Pretoria with weaponry. The country's industrial capability extended to the manufacture of first-rate artillery, armoured fighting vehicles and early jet fighters, but could not extend to later more sophisticated aircraft. South Africa also had the wealth and developed technical education systems to enable her to afford, man and maintain some of the sophisticated electronic equipment, aircraft and armoured fighting vehicles necessary for the external wars. The country's weakness was the shortage of, and risks to, white manpower, a highly charged political issue.

1960–74

The internal conflict moved from protest and civil disobedience to overt violence in March 1960 when South Africa's police, faced with an angry demonstration at the township of Sharpeville, lost their nerve and opened fire on the crowd, 67 people being killed. The two African nationalist political parties, the African National Congress (ANC) and the Pan-African Congress (PAC), were then both banned. Each formed an underground military wing. That of the ANC was called *Umkhonto wa Sizwe* (Spear of the Nation); it became closely linked with members of the banned South African Communist Party. The PAC's rival underground movement was called *Poqo*. Members of both movements went abroad for insurgency training, but neither made much initial impact. Conditions in many of the foreign training camps were brutal, women combat trainees suffering particularly severely.

The South African government was able, therefore, to continue its unde-clared but very real internal frontiers war. Between 1960 and 1970 over 1.5 million people regarded by the government as "surplus Bantu" were forcibly resettled. The government strengthened its security machine by increasing the numbers in the police force, extending its powers and, in 1968, centralizing all the security services under a Bureau of State Security (BOSS). Nelson Mandela of the ANC was placed on trial in 1964 and sentenced to life imprisonment.

The next phase of African reaction took two forms. One was the formation of the Black People's Convention by Steve Biko; the other, in 1973, a wave of strikes. The strikes proved very successful in economic terms with increases in wages and the recognition of African trade unions, both enhancing African assertion.

South Africa's earliest activities and policies during the liberation campaigns in Angola, Mozambique and Zimbabwe have already been noted. Forewarnings of her future military commitment in South West Africa – Namibia – had also begun to appear even before the collapse of Portuguese colonial rule. The South African government held, despite all international pressures, that the territory should continue to be ruled under the terms of the original League of Nations mandate, integrated with South Africa. Local protest against South African rule turned to violence in 1959, when the Ovambo Peoples Organization (OPO), resisted a government-formed population removal from a suburb of Windhoek. During a campaign of civil disobedience, police opened fire on marchers in a demonstration, killing 11 and wounding over 50, mainly Ovambo.

The Ovambo organization evolved in 1960 into the wider SWAPO (South West Africa People's Organization) which in 1962 launched a military wing, the People's Liberation Army of Namibia (PLAN), sending young men to Tanzania, China, Algeria, North Korea, Egypt and Ghana for insurgency training. PLAN to the end in 1989 remained largely Ovambo; another organization, the Caprivian African National Union (CANU), set up another very small insurgency group based across the border in Zambia. Early insurgent incursions were feeble, achieving nothing. The first effective assault was in 1966 when a white farm was attacked, but the assault met an effective riposte when helicopter-borne police destroyed the only operational base, complete with underground shelters, that PLAN was ever to establish, at Ongulumbashe. The police killed and captured a small number of insurgents. From then to 1968 PLAN's threat was limited to periodic small group attacks along the northern rim of the territory, mainly targeting traditional leaders and headmen. South African policing remained effective and in May 1967 PLAN's commander-in-chief, Tobias Hainyeko, was killed. In 1968 two rather larger group assaults were mounted but with still only limited success and at the cost of 178 PLAN insurgents killed or captured.

The next decade ushered in a new and more deadly dimension with the use by PLAN of Soviet-made mines. Five policemen were killed and 35 others injured in 1971–2, with more to follow until the police mastered precautionary procedures. A fighting unit of black police was created in 1972 for the Caprivi strip, areas of which soon became a free-fire zone. Also in 1972 PLAN staged a propaganda coup, taking photographers to the site of a Portuguese village massacre in Angola and laying the blame on South Africa, and in both 1972 and 1973 PLAN mounted a series of small-scale ambushes and attacks on police patrols and camps. By the end of 1973 despite logistic and helicopter gunship support from the South African Air Force, the situation in the territory had deteriorated to such an extent that in April 1974 operations were transferred from the police to the military, the South African Defence Force (SADF). The transfer was effected discreetly, as the League of Nations mandate forbade any militarization of the territory. Small-scale clashes continued, usually caused by PLAN attempting to move groups northwards to safety in Angola where they were linked with the UNITA faction.

1974–83

The events in Lisbon in April 1974 saw a dramatic and fundamental change in, South Africa's military position with the collapse of the Portuguese counter-insurgency operations in Angola and Mozambique. Immediately vast new frontier problems opened for the South African forces. Externally these problems became acute, leading South Africa to intervene in force. Internally a major repercussion was the need to control manifestations of the new African assertion in the most violent riots in South Africa's history to the time, the Soweto riots of 1976.

South Africa possessed a direct common frontier with Mozambique, and a South West African frontier and considerable economic interests in Angola, particularly investment in the Cunene dam hydroelectric project at Ruacana Falls on the border in the south. The Portuguese revolution was followed by instability in both territories.[1]

In Mozambique, Mozambicans who prior to the revolution had been recruited by Rhodesian intelligence to operate against FRELIMO turned initially into intelligence gatherers for Rhodesia. They then expanded, the expansion including some former FRELIMO personnel, into a guerrilla organization, openly hostile to the FRELIMO government, RENAMO (*Resistència National Mocambicana* – the movement also appears as MNR, or *Movimento Nacional da Resistència de Mocambique*). In Angola, as already noted, attempts to coerce the three rival insurgent movements, the MPLA, FNLA and UNITA, into a coalition had all failed with each later proclaiming its own government.[2] After independence the left-wing Portuguese government briefly supported the MPLA, as with weapon deliveries did Cuba, while the USA provided money and military equipment to the FNLA via Zaire. South Africa began to support UNITA which, although mostly pushed out of the southwest of Angola by the MPLA, opened attacks upon the FNLA, driving them out of Huambo in December.

The chaos caused by thousands of refugees arriving in Namibia and the identification of Cuban weapons had already led South Africa to more direct intervention. In August 1975 a unit of the SADF crossed the Cunene, brushing aside UNITA opposition and occupying the whole Ruacana Falls with its nearby Calueque power station areas. UNITA and the SADF then found common cause, the SADF training a UNITA group in conditions of the greatest secrecy. In early October a mixed SADF and UNITA force mounted a larger incursion into southern Angola, moving into the area between Lobito and Nova Lisboa.

The MPLA counter-attacked with three small columns but the SADF force was reinforced by the formidable Eland armoured cars hurriedly flown in, whose 90 mm guns provided a capability of tank-killing as well as reconnaisance, and the MPLA were repulsed. The SADF then decided to develop its operations, though the aims remained confused, some staff wishing to limit the aim to that of containing SWAPO, others seeking to weaken the MPLA. There were also arguments arising from political fears over possible casualty lists and American criticism. Two further columns were improvised, of mixed SADF, FNLA Chipenda faction and Caprivi Bushmen transported in vegetable lorries. These occupied Mocamedes, Benguela and Lobito after a series of small-scale battles. The SADF used 81 mm mortars, and 106 mm recoilless guns to reinforce small arms; a little later a few 25 pounder field guns were provided. But the SADF stopped at the Queve river in the face of strong MPLA and Cuban defence positions and their own supply difficulties.

The Soviet Union – among whose motives were air base facilities over the southern Atlantic – reacted swiftly to support the Marxist MPLA government in Luanda. Soviet immediate support included aircraft and ship loads of military supplies, including T–34 and T–54 tanks, PT–76 amphibious light tanks, MiG–21 interceptor fighters, BM–21 multiple-barrelled rocket launchers, Soviet and East German technical staff and an initial 1,000 Cuban soldiers. By the end of the year the total of Cubans was over 12,000, with the MPLA force of 20,000 additionally strengthened by some 6,000 of the former Katangese gendarmes.

Their first success was in November when Roberto rashly launched an ill-assorted and ill-equipped force of his own FNLA followers, some Portuguese and Zaire Bakongo, from the north in an attempt to take Luanda by independence day, 11 November. The force, which unwisely followed the line of a road, was met by BM–21 ground saturation fire, creating panic. Despite SADF air support from three Canberra bombers and the loan of some artillery, Roberto's assault faltered and turned to rout, the SADF's own artillerymen being evacuated by sea.

This operation, effectively finishing the FNLA, freed the MPLA from fighting a two-front war. It turned its attention to UNITA and ejected UNITA forces from all the towns they had controlled; at the same time SWAPO's PLAN broke with UNITA to link with the MPLA. The end of any prospect of a non-MPLA government also determined the SADF, plagued by manpower shortages and logistic difficulties, to withdraw from Angola. There was also again concern over casualties – these had to be notified – but only on 1 December did Pretoria admit that its troops had been operating deep into Angola. The process of withdrawal included a severe mauling of a Cuban–MPLA force, several hundred being killed by SADF artillery and Eland armoured cars at a bridge over the Nhia river, and several other lesser clashes in which superior SADF training and Eland armoured car firepower inflicted casualties on Cubans or MPLA. The withdrawal, skilfully conducted by General André van Deventer, was completed in February 1976. The revised South African strategy was to be one of controlling the border to which the MPLA had quickly advanced, and supporting UNITA in the bush; for this period conscription of white males was extended and reservists recalled, but training levels remained low for some time.

The year 1976 saw intensification of both the internal and external wars. From March 1976 co-ordinated if still low-level PLAN insurgency was launched into South West Africa from Angola and Zambia. In addition to Angola Zambia provided PLAN with food and supplies. The Zambian government also took a firm line with dissidents within SWAPO, first imprisoning Andreas Shipanga, a senior but dissident SWAPO leader, and his followers and then some 1,800 further dissidents. PLAN was, however, a little handicapped by its opposition to UNITA and the MPLA's requests for help in disposing of it.

For the border war the South Africans manned battalion bases, patrolled in convoys and existed with supplies and unit rotations (the latter carefully noted by PLAN). The police moved in the top-heavy but effective Hippo lorries which were protected by sandbags. Local black and bushman manpower was used as trackers and to detect mines, sometimes with specially trained sniffer dogs. Mounted infantry were used in pursuit, as on occasions were parachute troops or helicopter-lifted detachments. PLAN operated in groups of 40–60, subdivided into teams. PLAN's tactics were summarized by the SADF as "shoot and scoot" rocket and mortar bombardments, cross-border fire, ambushes, attacks on loyal headmen and the use of mines. Twenty-one SADF soldiers were killed during the year. PLAN casualties were considerably higher. Skirmishes and local clashes occurred regularly: in one case the SADF attacked a SWAPO camp in Zambia which attracted international protest. Towards the end of the year the SADF cleared a 1 km-wide free-fire zone, fenced off with wire, on 420 km of the Angolan border.

A much more deadly challenge to the South African government was the internal unrest of June 1976, generally known as the Soweto uprising. This began in Soweto on 16 June, and was followed by three weeks of battle between rioters and police. These battles then spread from the suburbs of Johannesburg to Pretoria and other cities in the Cape and Natal, continuing sporadically until the end of the year. Official figures gave a total of 360 killed by the police or other security forces, with large numbers, mostly under 18, arrested and convicted. Unofficial figures assert a greater number killed. The uprising served notice that South Africa had now moved to a state of undeclared civil war, with large numbers of young Africans disappearing to reappear abroad, mostly in ANC but some also in PAC training camps.

The repression, presented to the South African peoples and the world at large as necessary responses to Communism, continued into the next year, 1977, and culminated in the suppression of 18 "Black Consciousness" organizations. Over 40 of their leaders were arrested. Biko himself had earlier died from torture and injuries at the hands of local police in Pretoria and Port Elizabeth; other deaths followed. The deaths were not authorized by the South African government but ministers remained indifferent to the events, thereby arousing local and world criticism and revulsion. The most serious consequence for South Africa was the reaction of the French government. To this time France had opposed the international arms boycott. Paris now announced it would join the boycott, so denying South Africa further deliveries of modern interceptor fighter aircraft. The South African air force's ageing early Mirage aircraft were soon to prove inferior to the modern Angolan/Cuban MiGs supplied by the Soviet Union, and when the Mirages were shot down they could not be replaced. The loss of air superiority was eventually to prove a very serious blow.

On the northwestern border small-scale clashes occurred throughout 1977. PLAN groups based in Angola laid ambushes and mines and mounted occasional small arms or mortar attacks on SADF border posts, which reacted in kind. The SADF also continued to use San (bushmen) trackers to great effect. PLAN was receiving supplies of weapons and equipment from Cuba, but its standard of training remained poor with consequent loss of life, and its groups found food supply difficult to maintain. PLAN concentrated on heavy politicization of ordinary people. Operations in the Caprivi strip were less significant, but in both areas both sides sustained casualties, those of PLAN being much the greater. Generally PLAN sought to avoid pitched battles but one three-day clash in October was notable for its size. Over 80 insurgents, crossing into Ovamboland, encountered a small SADF patrol which called up helicopter and armoured-car support. The fight moved over 20 km into Angola ending with the SADF destroying two PLAN bases and killing 61 insurgents for the loss of six SADF men. SADF estimates held that by the end of the year there were between 250 and 300 insurgents operating in South West Africa with over 2,000 more in camps in Angola and 800 in camps in Zambia.

The South African overt strategy, that of the very able General Jannie Geldenhuys, was based on trying to retain local acceptability, the creation of a local South West Africa Territorial Force (SWATF) with African military units under white officers, and the destruction of PLAN's logistic and supply lines in Angola. For this latter work a special unit, 32 Battalion, was created that in deep penetration tasks would operate in PLAN uniform for attacks or the guiding in of South African air strikes.

Developing also was the covert strategy of South African aid for UNITA's recovery in Angola and for RENAMO in Mozambique. UNITA's groups were transformed from bush guerrillas into a full insurgent army, with uniformed regular infantry units and specialist sub-units, supported by semi-regular locally recruited groups and a highly efficient intelligence-gathering system. A training camp for UNITA personnel was opened at Grootfontein in Namibia and other South African help was provided for the movement in different ways. UNITA began to harass and then effectively to close down the Benguela railway and mount a new wave of attacks on PLAN groups and bases, declaring itself at war with SWAPO as well as the MPLA. The MPLA government in Luanda expanded its army to over 45,000 and drew increasingly on the support of the Cubans, now totalling 18,000 men. With this force it was able to contain the incursions in the north by the FNLA which were dwindling in number and effectiveness, and also reassert authority in the Cabinda enclave where the FLEC were in any case weakened by leadership vendettas.

RENAMO was developing into a very different movement from UNITA. Its Rhodesian origins have already been noted but it soon gained a considerable following in Mozambique as it presented opposition to FRELIMO's utopian policies of commune villages, control of all trading and marketing, and nuclear families, enforced on an unwilling peasant populace with the deliberate humiliation of traditional authorities. Other supporters of RENAMO included urban entrepreneurs, some Portuguese and losers in internal FRELIMO faction vendettas. RENAMO encouraged people to move away from the villages into areas they themselves controlled. Initially RENAMO operated in small groups with little or no central co-ordination. Its weaponry was at the outset captured FRELIMO small arms but more often spears and matchets with wood silhouettes of AK-47s, later developed into a home-made gun called a *pataka* which could fire captured ammunition down a metal tube mounted on a wooden stock, the cartridge set off by a metal and elastic striker. More effective weaponry from Rhodesia began to reach

RENAMO in 1976 and 1977. By 1978 RENAMO had, with its Rhodesian support, bases inside Mozambique from which attacks against FRELIMO and ZANLA camps and infiltration trails were launched. An ambitious plan was devised of cutting Mozambique into three. Events in the following year, however, were to thwart this strategy.

The suppression of the unrest of 1976–7 left the internal domestic conflict in South Africa in stalemate for seven years. Vorster and his successor as prime minister, Pieter Botha, both slightly eased a few of the harshest features of apartheid while continuing to press forward with the policy as a whole. They were successful to the extent that, until 1983, the war remained one fought outside South Africa, on its glacis. In South Africa itself the only major ANC achievement was a car bombing outside the South African Air Force head-quarters in May 1983, killing 11 officers.

International pressure in the form of UN-sponsored negotiations seeking to compel South Africa to withdraw from South West Africa dragged on, while the years 1978 to 1983 saw increasingly hostile international criticism. The year 1978 opened with an intensified number of border incidents – patrol clashes, casualties from mines, assassinations of anti-SWAPO personalities and the first appearance of an RPG-7 in PLAN hands. May and August, however, were to see two considerable battles. In May the SADF launched a parachute attack of 250 men on a major PLAN base at Cassinga, 250 km inside Angola, with simultaneous attacks by two small mechanized battle groups on PLAN bases in and around Chetequera, some 25 km inside Angola. The battle groups were composed in the form to be standard for several years, a mix of Eland armoured cars and Ratel armoured personnel carriers that also carried a 20 mm cannon. All three of the target areas were protected by Russian-style trench and bunker systems. Some 1,200 PLAN members, insurgents and trainees, along with some wives and children, were in the Cassinga base, along with a total of some 900 insurgents in the two other target areas. As a consequence of the international arms embargos the SADF had lift capacity – aircraft for the drop and helicopters for recovery – of only 250 men for Cassinga.

Cassinga was first attacked from the air. The parachute troops despite stiff resistance then stormed the base killing numbers of insurgents and others, and wounding many more. The helicopter evacuation was more difficult. A mixed Angola-Cuban force comprising a few old T-34 tanks and BTR-152 armoured personnel carriers had to be beaten off with the help of South African Impala, Mirage and Buccaneer aircraft. The two other attacks achieved the same results. SWAPO alleged that Cassinga was only a refugee camp and publicized the women and children among the dead but there is no doubt that the insurgent casualties – numbering over 1,000 – were a very heavy blow upon PLAN.

The second considerable local success for the SADF took place after a PLAN Zambia-based 120 mm and 82 mm mortar bombardment of Katima Mulilo in Caprivi in August. Two SADF mobile columns with Eland armoured cars riposted, one aiming for a PLAN base 30 km inside Zambia, the second harassing the retreating insurgents. The columns were supplemented by drops of a small number of parachute troops and others lifted in Alouette helicopters, together with support from light artillery and Canberra and Buccaneer bombers. The result, some 16 insurgents killed, reduced the scale of PLAN operations in Caprivi for some time and opened a quarrel between PLAN and CANU. Confident in its success the South African government held elections in South West Africa: boycotted by SWAPO, these were won by moderates acceptable to Pretoria, though not to the international community. Nevertheless, talks with UN diplomats over the territory's future were resumed, the two military issues being those of a demilitarized zone and the withdrawal of the SADF.

Military operations in 1979 were on a reduced scale. PLAN mounted a 250-man attack on the SADF base at Nkongo in February, while in March two small SADF columns struck at PLAN bases, one column in Angola and one in Zambia. Neither of these operations proved very effective for either side. For the remainder of the year there were intermittent clashes, with PLAN continuing the mining and sabotaging of telephone, water and power systems. PLAN's heavy casualties at the hands of the SADF, 915 killed in the year (against 50 South African dead), together with UNITA attacks on SWAPO lowered insurgent morale and led to desertions. But evidence of the spill-over of South Africa's apartheid policies was also to be seen in bomb incidents in Lesotho, in the ongoing civil war in Angola and, with the approaching end of the independence campaign in Zimbabwe, in the transfer in Mozambique of a large number of RENAMO personnel to direct South African control. This transfer was opportune for RENAMO which had been under severe pressure from the FRELIMO army, losing Manica and northern Sofala, and being cleared effectively from everywhere north of the Beira–Zimbabwe railway. In these operations RENAMO's charismatic young commander André Matsangaissa was killed, and the movement's bases in the Gorongoza mountains lost to them. Matsangaissa, who used the services of a spirit medium, was believed to be invincible to bullets. His death had to be explained as the consequence of a rocket attack. A leadership struggle followed which was only finally settled in a shoot-out in Zimbabwe in June 1980 when Matsangaissa's deputy, Afonso Dhlakama, killed his rival Lucas M'Langa and assumed command of RENAMO, at that time reduced to fewer than 500. Under South African control numbers quickly recovered, especially when the South Africans provided a training camp in the Transvaal and helped create a new RENAMO firm base in Gaza province to which units were airlifted after training.

The next year, 1980, saw continuing and now more regular rather than intermittent border clashes, with a few deeper PLAN penetrations into South West Africa. In May the SADF under the command of General Charles Lloyd launched a major attack on SWAPO command and PLAN bases spread in and around Chifufua, over 100 km inside Angola. Three battle groups including light artillery, one supported by a parachute company and supplied by helicopters, were deployed. The operation lasted a month and led to sharp infantry fighting; on their withdrawal one group was attacked by an Angolan army column. This operation was followed by several more smaller raids, some helicopter-lifted into Angola and attacking SWAPO and MPLA posts, these now often being held jointly. SADF figures claimed that the year cost the insurgents 1,447 men against their own loss of 100; these figures do not include the smaller but steadily increasing casualties inflicted by UNITA groups, some of which included South African special forces personnel. UNITA groups had been badly mauled by Angola-Cuban forces in April but by August had recovered sufficiently to inflict severe sabotage damage on oil installations at Lobito, and were reasserting control in both the southeast and centre of Angola.

The next three years saw intensification of the conflict, with discreet United States support for the SADF and UNITA in turn leading to powerful direct Soviet military support for the Angolan–Cuban forces, the campaign becoming an exposed hot facet of the Cold War. Until 1983 the advantage lay with South Africa. The developed SADF strategy of "Total Onslaught" aimed at forward defence by creating a *cordon sanitaire* in southern Angola by means of air and mechanized force attacks upon SWAPO lines of communication and headquarters deep in Angola. PLAN had to pull back, entrench and fortify its bases and, under its new commander and chief-of-staff, Dimo Hamaambo and David "Ho Chi Minh" Namholo, move to conventional war organizations and tactics. As PLAN's former forward bases were now untenable, insurgent groups had also to carry weapons, food and water for much longer distances before entering South West Africa, and later while withdrawing. In some areas the local populace, so terrified by the SADF and the specially created and ruthless local police formation, Koevoet, withdrew their support for PLAN. To add to SWAPO's problems the Caprivi insurgents, CANU, went over to the South African sponsored government.

In 1981 the pattern of frequent border patrol and ambush clashes continued with in August a massive South African offensive aimed at the destruction of Angolan–Cuban military bases, newly installed radar and anti-aircraft missile sites and command posts in the border area of Angola and further inland. Fighter bomber strikes were followed up by thrusts by two mechanized columns which broke up an Angolan artillery, tank and motorized infantry force. The Angolan force, unwisely, wasted its Soviet T-34 tanks in largely static roles as self-propelled guns. The SADF columns then temporarily occupied two large bases at Xangongo and Ondjiva capturing or destroying Soviet supplied armour, guns and ammunition, killing over 1,000 PLAN and Angolan personnel, and seizing much valuable intelligence material. A smaller-scale air and mechanized column offensive took place in November striking at PLAN bases at Bambi and Cheraguera, 120 km inside Angola, and the year ended with South African air attacks on targets in Moxico province. The SADF claimed to have killed over 2,500 insurgents in the year at a cost to themselves of only 56. South African help enabled UNITA to defeat a weak Angolan attack on Mavinga in March and to put to rout a much stronger two-regiment attack in May. In Mozambique RENAMO, with now a regained strength of some 5,000, became very much more active, attacking railway lines and roads and the Cabora Bassa power station, cutting power lines and establishing control in large areas of Manica and Sofala provinces. In November, however, Mozambique government forces overran the main RENAMO ban at Garagua. In January SADF special forces raided houses in a Maputo suburb where ANC members were believed to be living, and there were also several raids on houses used by ANC members in Lesotho. Most bizarre of all was tacit South African support of an attempt to topple the left-wing government of the Seychelles. The attempt was made by a 44-strong group of mercenaries all recruited in South Africa, the majority South African and including a South African intelligence officer. The Seychelles police and gendarmerie crushed the attempt without having to draw on the help of a Tanzanian garrison unit.

In 1982 operations in Namibia, so named now even in South African nomenclature, continued at the same level but with the SADF beginning to suffer heavier casualties both on the ground and also in the air as the Angola-Cubans were now deploying SAM-3 and SAM-6 anti-aircraft missile systems. The border clashes continued. In March a Puma and Alouette helicopter-borne force destroyed a new PLAN forward base, but in April PLAN gained some success and much propaganda value from an attempted nine-group incursion into Namibia. Six of the nine groups were either stopped or wiped out on their way in; the remaining three, however, slipped in and mounted ambushes, acts of sabotage and attacks on farms for two months before all were rounded up. At the same time the SADF and the special Koevoet police unit came under increasing criticism, domestic as well as international, for excesses and cruelty. July and August saw a series of raids by small teams of parachute troops and other special forces personnel on SWAPO command headquarters, one over 200 km inside Angola. The SADF claimed to have killed 1,286 insurgents for the loss of 77 of their own personnel in these operations during the year.

Other operations in South Africa's overall war in 1982 included a SADF special forces raid on houses in Maseru, Lesotho in December when 42 people including women and children were killed. It was again alleged ANC insurgents were living in the houses and planning attacks on "soft" targets such as supermarkets. There was also an opening of cross-border shooting on South Africa's border with Botswana. The SADF-supported UNITA resisted a seven-regiment Angola-Cuban attack in July, and in November UNITA launched its own offensive towards Lumbala and Cangombe while also harassing the Angola-Cubans in other areas. In Mozambique RENAMO's operations became even more effective in disrupting the economy of Mozambique and her inland neighbours with ongoing attacks on oil installations and railways, in particular the Beira corridor, and RENAMO's adaptation of a UNITA tactic – that of attacking, abducting and occasionally killing European expatriates. At the same time, however, the shallowness of RENAMO was beginning to become apparent. The movement had no meaningful ideology or political programme. A frequent target of RENAMO attacks were the government's social service, schools and health centres, as if to purge society of them, with terror as a substitute for ideology. Some RENAMO leaders drew on, or manipulated, traditional spirit superstitions. In the areas RENAMO occupied, the group leaders were usually from another area, using the local notables as interlocutors. People were moved forcibly from villages, and the old, infirm and recalcitrants quite ruthlessly killed, tortured or mutilated. Children of parents who refused to co-operate were boiled alive. The villages were burnt, food seized or levied as a "tax" and the young, aged 15 sometimes, forcibly drafted into military service by initiation rites, often involving a killing, and drugs. A 5,000-strong Mozambican army offensive, supported by Zimbabwe air-to-ground strikes and detachments from Zimbabwe's North Korean trained 5th Brigade, achieved little success. South Africa's ally was becoming a sociological and military monster.

The following year, 1983, was to be the last in which the SADF was able to do much as it pleased; the background was, however, one of mounting UN and international pressure and meetings seeking agreement for South African withdrawal and full independence for Namibia, together with ferociously hostile propaganda compounded by rumours and by accusations of atrocities by both sides. The worst excesses, of torture sometimes inspired by sexual perversions, were perpetrated by Koevoet against civilian supporters of SWAPO in Namibia itself. In a special forces raid in January the SADF breached a dam in Benguela province with serious consequential flooding and loss of electric power. PLAN mounted a major assault in February involving

1,700 men in 14 companies from its East German trained Volcano force. The assault took the form of a long and bloody rampage deep into Namibia, including white farming areas. SADF containment and pursuit lasted for two months, in which the Volcano force lost over 300 men, a mauling which brought operations other than minor border raids to a halt for several months. UNITA took the town of Cazomba on 17 August, thus finally severing the Benguela railway line. The capture was the result of an eight-day battle in which UNITA's three battalion-sized units, supported by captured pre-1939 Soviet 76 mm field guns, defeated the Angola–Cuban defenders despite their air support from MiG-21 air-to-ground strikes and Mi-8 helicopters used as gunships. UNITA, by the end of the year, was in control of some 20 per cent of Angola, including the Cazomba salient which shielded Kavango from PLAN attack, and had a firm base in the southeast. PLAN personnel had to be redeployed to defend other areas of Angola. The UNITA success, however, led to the arrival of a further 5,000 Cuban troops bringing the total to well over 20,000, and quantities of more modern Soviet equipment including T-62 tanks and missile launchers, and in September and October UNITA lost control of towns in central Angola. The Cubans were mostly employed on static defences, so making Angolan manpower available for front-line combat.

In October and November, SADF intelligence, in the form of signals intercepts, reconnaissance flights and small deep-penetration reconnaissance teams, began to pick up indications of a planned insurgent strike of over 900 men supported by Angolan troops. A pre-emptive attack was therefore launched in December involving four SADF 500-strong mechanized battle groups tasked for penetration, supported by smaller motorized infantry groups to sweep the areas close to the border. The attack included air strikes, upwards of 80 aircraft in the air at once on some occasions, upon command head-quarters bases and arms caches some 300 km inside Angola. One town bombed by South African Mirages was Lubango, one purpose being to create fear that the town, Hamaambo's PLAN command headquarters, might be a target for ground forces. An Angolan force ambushed a small South West African Territorial Force unit and other Angolan units were drawn in to rescue PLAN groups under SADF attack. The SADF successfully occupied Cassinga but the new dimensions of the fighting were, however, brought most firmly to the SADF's attention when it attacked a major PLAN base at Cuvelai. The town was protected by 16 minefields and artillery firing air-burst shells; weather conditions were rain and mud. While the SADF attack was in progress a relief force of an Angolan regiment and two Cuban battalions with T-54/55 tanks being used in a mobile role appeared. The SADF battle group only won the fight by superior tactics. It seems that the SADF considered remaining in southern Angola but intense UN pressure led to the adoption of contingency withdrawal plans. Withdrawal of the raiding groups involved mine-clearance and emergency bridge-building, but was completed by mid-January 1984. The SADF claimed to have destroyed 25 tanks and inflicted heavy casualties.

In Mozambique South African support for RENAMO developed further the crippling of the country's economy, with RENAMO insurgents active in all provinces except Cabo Delgado which had a Tanzanian garrison. Zimbabwe troops guarding the Beira railway line were less successful with acts of sabotage continuing. The SADF carried out two further special forces raids in Maputo, allegedly in search of ANC activists, evidence of the growing ascendancy in the South African government of its "dirty tricks" organizations, the SADF Directorate of Military Intelligence, the Directorate of Covert Collection and the Civil Co-operation Bureau.

FRELIMO operations against RENAMO were eventually mounted in Zambezia and Inhambane provinces, the latter with some small success, but generally Mozambique's war-weary and under-fed FRELIMO units lacked motivation. Neither side sought a pitched battle and encounters were often more occasions for skirmish and show rather than combat. The government used its MiG aircraft and helicopters to noisy but little real effect. RENAMO's internal anomie became more evident – many of its followers were simply fighting to exist and existing to fight in a society as destabilized as that in which the similar pre-colonial *ruga ruga* had rampaged a hundred years earlier. Neither its formal leader Dhlakama nor its South African backers had more than the loosest control over at least 50 per cent of the 7,000 or so RENAMO fighters. The ordinary populace took to the bush, leaving a little food for RENAMO raiders in villages – even constructing false villages for the purpose. In this way of life, known as *shoshorona*,[3] families hid under rocks or in caves, moving daily to avoid the RENAMO or the government forces which were equally cruel and rapacious in areas they reoccupied. The most fortunate were those who lived near a large government military base and could organize a village home guard. Paradoxically, RENAMO was gaining its early objectives, as FRELIMO was becoming more pragmatic and allowing people to leave villages to return to their home farming areas, but RENAMO's ferocity and inability to rule the areas it occupied were already costing the movement support.

Chapter Six

Southern Africa 1984 to 1997

It appeared at the end of 1983 that, although heavily committed, South Africa was still in overall control, with her wars either on or beyond her frontiers. The years 1984–8 were, however, to prove a watershed. The country had to face an internal implosion, the costs of the border fighting in lives, manpower and money began seriously to bite, and the correlation of forces tilted away from the SADF. The Force's technical professionalism became insufficient to control the larger numbers opposed to it, with their modern Soviet equipment that South Africa could not match on account of the UN arms bans. From 1985 on, South African policies and strategy appeared more and more defensive, by the end of the decade rearguard. In the border war field commanders became more cautious, taking a step-by-step approach to ensure that if there was some internationally negotiated ceasefire they would not be caught at a disadvantage.

Internally, in South Africa's heartland the magnitude and increasingly anomic nature of black unrest unmistakably signalled that South Africa's "Total National Strategy" had failed. As apartheid crumbled too, an entirely new ethnic warfare appeared: over who should be the negotiators with the government and perhaps the heirs to that government.

1984–90

In 1984 constitutional changes offering some concessions to Indians and coloureds but not to the black population led at the end of the year to rioting and strikes in the black townships throughout South Africa. Early in 1985 these were followed by rent strikes, boycotts of white owned businesses and student strikes, all part of the ANC's overall strategic aim – ungovernability.

131

The military wing of the ANC, *Umkhonto*, had its own direction headed by Chris Hani, which worked in close co-ordination with the National Executive Committee of the party. The ANC leadership, headed by Oliver Tambo, was based in Zambia.

After the ending of apartheid, the ANC was later to claim its strategy had never been that of targeting civilians and that killings – except of military personnel – were the work of maverick groups. This may have been the case but the number of deaths serves to illustrate the culture of violence that apartheid created. The violence intensified and on 21 March police opened fire on a demonstration at Uitenhage, killing 20. The tempo increased further during the year and in 1986 with attacks on local government offices, police personnel and bars frequented by military personnel. The larger black townships soon became ungovernable, with "necklacing" (tyres soaked in petrol placed around a victim's neck and then ignited) of men suspected of collaboration, attacks on whites and, in Natal, attacks on Indians. In the townships groups of young "comrades" enforced the boycotts and ordered the punishments following "trials" in "peoples' courts". These groups of "comrades" and their behaviour led to opposition groups of migrant workers and others who in return formed vigilantes, their own self-defence groups. These attacked comrades and burnt their homes, with tacit police approval. The comrades and vigilantes soon became labels for groupings in the Inkatha war, considered later in this chapter. In contrast to the 1976 exodus of young black men to join the 8–10,000 in insurgent groups training abroad, on this occasion the young remained within South Africa to further trouble – a paradoxical consequence of the Nkomati Accord. Massive general strikes took place in May and June 1986 and again in May and June 1987. The government claimed 230 terrorist attacks took place in 1986 with 235 in 1987. No accurate figures of people killed exist but an estimate of 2,000 by the end of 1987 can fairly be made. Approximately 24,000 people were arrested – and a considerable number tortured. Troops were moved in to support the police in many areas.

President Botha was obliged to accept a militarization of his government. The State Security Council had already virtually replaced the cabinet as the most important policy-making body; its executive arm, the National Security Management System of military, police and intelligence officers with at local levels 11 Joint Management Centres, came to have virtual free reign over operations.

The magnitude of the unrest and the near-panic it aroused corrupted still further the already badly corroded officers of the South African government at all levels. Chemical and biological warfare agents were developed and have been alleged to have been used on a small scale both in Angola and within South Africa itself. From later statements it appears that in 1988 President Botha himself had sanctioned a special force terrorist attack on the offices of the Council of Churches in Johannesburg, offices which harboured a number of anti-government organizations, and that the Cabinet had authorized the supply of booby-trapped explosives to anti-apartheid activists.[1] Other senior police officers had quietly arranged for the killing off of known government opponents. By 1997 235 former policemen had admitted responsibility for the deaths of more than 200 people, with others seeking amnesty for 30 bombings and 20 abductions. Several mass graves of ANC activists in total containing over 250 bodies were unearthed. Such was the "epidemic of the mind" that white police interrogators would say a prayer for success before commencing a torture session. The theory that there was a South African government "hidden agenda" to create trouble by provocation so that it could be turned to its own advantage is, however, unproven.

The scale of the violence was in fact making it clear that apartheid could not be saved by limited political reforms. International criticism and pressures further undermined the government. The cosmetic changes made by President Botha totally failed to recapture any black acquiescence. Relying on the support of the military to counter the still apartheid-minded administration, Botha's successor as president, De Klerk, made his historic announcement on 2 February 1990. The ban on the ANC and other proscribed organizations would be lifted, Mandela released from prison and talks with black leaders on a new constitution based on a universal franchise would be opened. This speech and new policy effectively marked the defeat of the South African whites' attempts forcibly to secure their position by demarcated apartheid frontiers; the repeal of specific apartheid legislation, in particular the Group Areas Act, and the "independence" of the "homelands" followed, as did an ANC renunciation of armed struggle.

Nevertheless, just as the domestic situation had called for the severest repression, the years of South Africa's retreat were to call for very vigorous military covering action, the SADF deploying over 9,000 men on the Namibia/Angola border.[2]

After protracted negotiations an agreement, brokered by the United States, was reached in Lusaka on 16 February 1984. The agreement provided for a zone in southern Angola to be demilitarized, with withdrawal by both the SADF and the Cubans and PLAN. The disengagement was to be monitored by joint Angolan and South African military monitoring teams. The strength of UNITA, however, was to be the agreement's undoing. The Angolan government's forces, even when strengthened by some 30,000 Cubans, were still dependent on SWAPO's PLAN followers. Neither UNITA nor PLAN had any intention of giving up the fight; in consequence the war continued albeit in a slightly lower key for a while, over 500 insurgents being killed in the year 1984. Joint monitoring teams attempted to implement the withdrawals, Angolan troops actually clashing with PLAN on one occasion. But motivation on the part of the Angolans soon dwindled, faced as they were with SWAPO political militancy which many, both military and civilians, still actively supported. The diplomatic rounds of negotiations failed to advance the peace process, the South Africans insisting on a Cuban withdrawal but at the same time maintaining covert support for UNITA for whom the year 1984 brought considerable successes. These included units striking to within 280 km of Luanda, cutting an oil pipeline in Cabinda, attacking a northern diamond industry town and appearing for varying lengths of time in large areas of the territory.

South Africa's policies in Mozambique appeared also to be successful. RENAMO fighting and destruction obliged Mozambique to come to the conference table in March to conclude a deal, known as the Nkomati Accord, by which Mozambique agreed no longer to support or harbour ANC political figures or insurgents, in return for which South Africa agreed to end support for RENAMO. The accord was generally respected by Mozambique and, despite political protestations of innocence and an official joint declaration in October, largely disregarded by South Africa. RENAMO activity paradoxically increased all over the country after the October Pretoria declaration, equipment, including long-range mortars delivered before the declaration being made available for use. The Mozambique government replied with a brisk military campaign in which it claimed to have killed 1,000 insurgents but this setback in no way limited RENAMO activities.

The Lusaka ceasefire agreement gave Angola a brief period of calm before its final collapse following PLAN–SADF border clashes that escalated from mid-March 1985; the monitoring teams were formally disbanded in May. SADF personnel were involved, and killed, in an abortive raid in May on an oil complex in Cabinda, the Angolans reported repeated South African violation of their air space, an SADF special force raided ANC premises in Gaberone, Botswana, and in June the SWATF launched a two-day foray into Angola, which it sought to justify on grounds of riposte for PLAN mortar attacks. A smaller raid into the Kavango area followed later. PLAN, in reply, but facing a worsening recruiting situation, converted one of its semi-regular units to small group bush insurgency and sabotage.

The heaviest fighting of the year, however, was that of the Angola-Cuban forces against UNITA which had established a firm base and headquarters at Jamba in the extreme southeast of Angola. While such a base and command centre gave UNITA a number of political and logistic advantages, Jamba inevitably became the prime Angola-Cuban military objective in the following months and years, obliging the SADF to underpin the defence of Jamba as otherwise PLAN would have been able to extend its zone of operations. UNITA opened 1985 with an over-ambitious attempt to envelop the capital, Luanda. Using pseudo-groups specially trained by the East Germans, the

Angolans first sought to infiltrate UNITA and then in July, aided by Soviets and Cubans, commenced a major offensive involving PLAN's semi-regulars and some ANC insurgents as well as Angola-Cuban armour, artillery infantry and air-to-ground strikes by MiG-21s, MiG-23s and helicopters. The offensive was two-pronged, against the Cazombo salient and against Mavinga as a stepping stone to Jamba in the southeast. Fighting was stiff, but the Angola-Cubans advanced steadily.

As a response to the PLAN insurgency and sabotage, in September the SADF had mounted a limited raid into southern Angola, a raid of fast-moving mobile patrols, trackers and air support. Although not specifically intended to reduce Angola-Cuban pressure on UNITA, it had that effect; the SADF raid enabled Savimbi, the UNITA commander, to concentrate his forces to save Mavinga with its strategically important airfield at the expense of withdrawing from Cazombo. The SADF assisted him with air strikes and an artillery unit as well as with much logistic support, with the result that the Angola-Cubans were stopped 32 km from Mavinga, and with the rains approaching, were obliged to withdraw. UNITA's fortunes revived, insurgent attacks on the Angolan government forces in Cazombo were resumed and American aid was promised to supplement that already received from France, Morocco and Zaire, as well as South Africa. At the end of the year, a small SADF column again raided the Angolan base at Cuvelai, 200 km inside Angola. Angolan losses during the year were estimated to be some 2,500 killed or wounded, eight fighters, six Mi-24 helicopter gunships, several smaller helicopters and transport aircraft, six tanks, 26 other armoured vehicles and at least 100 lorries. UNITA lost about 500 killed and 1,500 wounded.

In Mozambique, despite repeated South African denials of continuing support for RENAMO, the FRELIMO government remained very hard pressed, RENAMO groups controlling and continuing to recruit forcibly in many areas and in April destroying a railway bridge linking Mozambique with South Africa. The total of Zimbabwean troops assisting the Mozambique forces was raised to over 6,000; combined Zimbabwean and Mozambican forces scored one success with the capture of a RENAMO provincial headquarters in Sofala province, but overall RENAMO ended the year in a position of strength.

The first four months of 1986 saw the same scale of fighting in Southern Angola – border clashes, casualties on both sides but much more severe for PLAN, and two- or three-unit SADF hot pursuits into Angola backed by air-to-ground support. UNITA units lifted by SADF aircraft ranged far into the north of Angola engaging in daily clashes with the Angolans and effecting a spectacular and highly profitable capture of a major northern diamond town. In early June a daring South African fast patrol boat raid wreaked havoc in the port of Namibe, missiles destroying all installations and frogmen sinking Soviet freighters bringing in weapons.

Exasperated, the Soviets had already made their plans, with the Soviet general who had commanded in the Ogaden, Petrov, again in command. On 27 May another large-scale onslaught on UNITA was launched involving some 20,000 Angolans and Cubans, 7,000 PLAN and 900 ANC, all guided and directed by 2,000 East German specialists mainly in intelligence and signals, and 1,000 Soviets in a variety of command, staff and technical duties. Two powerful columns pushed into east-central Angola, a third, slightly smaller, struck southeast, including and supported by a full range of very modern Soviet equipment. Initially the assaults made considerable headway, but a combination of UNITA assaults on lines of communication for the flank, improved UNITA weaponry now including Stinger anti-aircraft and anti-tank missiles, light and heavy mortars and multi-barrelled rocket launchers together with logistic overstretch brought the assault to a stop. Despite Cuban air strikes, in August UNITA invested Cuito Cuanavale with the support of South African artillery, the special force 32 Battalion and air-to-ground strikes. The town was not occupied but the military base, its large ordnance park and its radar installations were destroyed, and its demoralized Angolan garrison subjected to propaganda broadcasts from helicopters.

South Africa's interventions in the affairs of her neighbours continued in early 1986. In Lesotho, Chief Jonathan had moved to anti-South African rhetoric and policies. His fate was sealed by a three-week blockade of the country in January co-ordinated by South Africa, leading to a military coup and a government more amenable. Later land and air attacks on buildings near Gaberone in Botswana were to follow. Most serious of all were air and land raids in Zambia and Zimbabwe aimed at collapsing the Eminent Persons Group's efforts at mediation in South Africa. In Mozambique RENAMO's destruction of the country's economic life, particularly the railways, continued remorselessly. RENAMO retook Casa Banana, which was only restored again to the government with the aid of Zimbabwean troops. Despite earlier covert Malawi help for RENAMO, a Malawi unit had to be brought in to assist protection of the Nacala rail link. In November RENAMO occupied five towns in northern Mozambique. Most serious of all, in circumstances never clarified but coinciding with a major RENAMO offensive, in October 1986 the president of Mozambique, Samora Machel, was killed in an air crash on a return journey from a meeting with the presidents of Zambia and Zimbabwe. Whether as a consequence of Machel's death or of the Nkomati agreement, it does appear that South African official help for RENAMO dwindled in late 1986, though unauthorized help from South African sympathizers continued. RENAMO's disengagement from South Africa had now begun and the movement's further activities are set out in the last section of this chapter.

The final two years of the South African involvement in Angola were to see the largest European warfare style tank and air battles on the African continent since 1943. Assessment of them is complex as the Angolan side, for propaganda reasons, exaggerated SADF strength, while South Africa, also for its own reasons, was generally reticent, particularly over two further special forces raids into Zambia and Botswana. Also, all the combatants – the SADF, the MPLA, the Cuban president (who was more ambitious than the Cuban military), the Soviets, SWAPO and UNITA – were all fighting with an eye to secure an advantage at the international negotiating tables. On the border itself the year 1987 opened with border clashes and several SADF and SWATF pre-emptive sweeps, while UNITA returned to harassment of north-central and northeast Angola, including again a diamond area. Strengthened by American equipment arriving by air at Kamina in Zaire, UNITA also trained several hundred FLEC insurgents, so reviving activity in Cabinda. It was claimed, probably correctly, that in exasperation the Angolans used chemical weaponry against UNITA. South African intelligence identified a Cuban colonel who was a specialist in chemical warfare, and also specialist Vietnamese military tunnel engineers. April and May saw intensification of the Soviet build-up, the big Antonov AN-12 transports firing off flares to confuse UNITA's American Stinger missiles before landing or dropping supplies. In July a bloody clash followed an ambush of an SADF column near the border.

In August the Soviet command let loose the most powerful Angola-Cuban offensive yet, involving 13 regiments – over 20,000 men – in an attempt to bring UNITA, with its American backing, to battle and destroy them in a Dien Bien Phu style *Vernichtungschlacht*.[3] One column, from Lucasse, of five regiments with close air support was tasked to strike towards Cangamba and Lumbala, a second of three regiments at Munhango was to hold central Angola while a third, of four regiments, was to link up with a fifth already deployed and with close support from the air move towards Tumpo (east of Cuito Cuanavale) and then on to Mavinga. The first column was stopped by UNITA harassment and attacks on its front and flanks. The third column took Tumpo and slowly, 4 km per day, began to move on towards Mavinga.

Direct South African intervention was again needed to secure these bases vital to UNITA. Initially limited to a battery each of multiple rocket launchers and 120 mm mortars together with two infantry companies, further SADF help was soon necessary. This help included a mechanized infantry/armoured car (Ratels, now with 90 mm guns) battalion group, a light artillery battery, a battery of G-5 radar-guided towed 155 mm guns, and further mortar and multiple rocket launcher batteries, along with UNITA infantry. Air support was provided by Mirage F-1 fighter bombers and Canberra bombers dropping "smart" bombs, developed in South Africa, on bridges and pilotless drone aircraft used for air photography. In September and early October these now powerful SADF forces cleared out a hitherto successful Angolan crossing of the Lomba river and in follow-up operations destroyed 47 tanks and most of one regiment, a turning point in the war for 1987.

The SADF commander, General "Kat" Liebenberg decided to follow up this success with a pre-emptive strike on a regrouped Angola-Cuban three-regiment force assembling for a second attempt to take Mavinga. For this, further reinforcements were committed, including a squadron of Olifant tanks, a South African version of the British Centurion battle tank, and a troop of G-6 155 mm wheeled self-propelled medium guns. This offensive opened on 9 October with air and artillery bombardment of Cuito Cuanavale, which was both the major Angola-Cuban air and land base, a key point to any advance on Savimbi's headquarters at Jamba, and a vital link in the developing Soviet radar early warning system. Cuba later claimed that several SADF attempts to take the town and proclaim it a UNITA capital had been repulsed, but it seems that the SADF's aim may simply have been to deny the use of the base and airfield, additionally forcing Angola-Cuban aircraft, heavy consumers of fuel, to fly further before striking at them. They also estimated that assaulting and occupying the town would cost unaccept-able casualties, that in the town they would present a target and any occupa-tion would goad the Cubans into fresh adventures. This operation was followed by stiff fighting early in November when a combined SADF and SWATF force mauled an Angola-Cuban regiment, killing over 500 and destroying 33 tanks. The South Africans then announced that they would withdraw, but the arrival of the ablest Cuban field commander, General Cintra Frias, together with units of the elite Cuban 50th Division and the first Soviet T-62 tanks in the area led to a decision to maintain artillery bombard-ment of Angola-Cuban lines of communication to Cuito Cuanavale, and provide support for renewed UNITA action in central Angola while conduct-ing a phased withdrawal elsewhere. In one engagement a 900-strong UNITA unit captured four T-55 tanks, shot down a Mi-24 helicopter gunship and recaptured Munhango.

The year 1988 opened with the virtual destruction in a night attack by the SADF of an Angola-Cuban regiment, but also with a significant Angolan success against a UNITA unit in the Tumpo area; at the same time the notably efficient SADF artillery continued their extreme range bombardments, at one point over 200 shells a day falling on Cuito Cuanavale. In February, in the second battle of Tumpo the SADF mauled one Angola-Cuban regiment and UNITA forced another to withdraw from its position to one less favourable. But in the face of fire from 58 artillery pieces, the SADF was unable to retake Tumpo. The whole Angola-Cuban offensive, however, remained stalled. It had cost, in six months, over 4,000 dead, 94 tanks, eight MiG-23s, three

138

SU-22s, four MiG-21s, several helicopters, rocket launchers and armoured personnel carriers and 400 logistic vehicles destroyed, with important SAM-8 and SAM-9 anti-aircraft missiles captured by the South Africans. Twelve regiments had to be committed, leaving UNITA free to retake the Cazombo area and to roam elsewhere in Angola. South African losses were 31 whites killed, and two Mirage aircraft, three Olifant tanks and four Ratel troop carriers destroyed. UNITA personnel casualties were undoubtedly very much higher.

March saw a further SADF check at the hands of Cintra Frias in the third battle of Tumpo, and an attempt to clear a particularly well defended sector failed with the loss of three more Olifant tanks in a minefield, and vigorous Angola-Cuban air-to-ground strikes and artillery fire.

Cuba proclaimed that its holding of Cuito Cuanavale and the successes at Tumpo were a great military victory; one reason for the propaganda, however, was the hope that a prestige success would edge the MPLA towards negotiations. The South African position was in any case now hazardous; it was estimated that Angola-Cuban infantry in southern Angola, many in units equipped with Soviet BTR-60 armoured personnel carriers, now totalled 11,000 with over a hundred tanks, T-55s, T-62s, some of the newer Soviet T-64s with greatly improved anti-armour gun power and for the first time Soviet divisional artillery FROG 7 missiles (Free Rocket Over Ground), with a range of over 70 km and a 450 kg high-explosive warhead. In addition there were three mixed PLAN–Cuban units near the border, and MiG-21 and -23 aircraft flying into Namibia at heights beyond the range of SADF anti-aircraft systems. By June the totals had risen to 17,000 Cubans and 5,000 Angolans. There seemed a real danger of an invasion of Namibia. The war was becoming unpopular in a South Africa increasingly preoccupied with internal unrest. Further recall of reservists and mobilization in the face of this danger led to the war being even more heavily criticized.

Criticism intensified after a ferocious Cuban–South African clash in late June in the Calueque area. A Cuban mechanized battalion column supported by T-55 tanks and SAM-6 track-mounted anti-aircraft missiles began a southward advance, and a South African mechanized battalion group with batteries of rocket launchers, 120 mm mortars and towed 155 mm artillery, Ratels fitted with 90 mm cannon, mortars and missiles and a squadron of Olifant tanks went out to meet the Cubans. The fight, the SADF's last major operation, opened with an exchange of artillery fire, followed by an armoured vehicle fight in which both sides lost vehicles but with the advantage to the South Africans, the Olifant proving superior to the T-55s, and the Cubans withdrawing. The picture then changed totally following a strike by four MiG-23 aircraft with parachute-retarded bombs, 12 South Africans being killed and the SADF column now obliged to withdraw. It was clear South African air superiority was finally lost, and that the country's only surface-to-air missile systems, the French-manufactured Cactus vehicle-mounted rockets, 20 mm guns and a few hand-operated missiles, were inadequate.

Negotiations at international levels continued: the Soviets were tiring of their costly support; the United States, while supporting UNITA, remained sharply critical of South Africa; in Cuba the number of young men killed for no clear purpose was being questioned. A provisional agreement providing for a ceasefire, a staged northward redeployment and then withdrawal of the Cubans and free elections in Namibia was reached in July. It was developed further in August when, by the Geneva Protocol, lines beyond which Cubans and PLAN would not remain were agreed with arrangements for a Joint Military Monitoring Commission (JMMC). The South Africans then began a withdrawal from Angola which was completed by the end of the month. Special force incursions into Botswana, Swaziland and Zimbabwe, which had been repeated in 1987 and 1988, were halted at the same time.

UNITA operations, however, continued, the USA asserting that it would continue to provide support while the Cubans remained in Angola. In July UNITA mounted a powerful and successful raid on the Benguela railway line near Huambo. In August–September UNITA initially defeated an eight-regiment Angola-Cuban attack on Munhango, but by mid-September they had been forced out of the town, and out of the Cangamba region as well, with heavy losses. The Cuban participation was in contravention of the Geneva Protocol. UNITA's remarkable power of recovery was, however, again evident with a resumption of attacks in October, with sharp fighting in several regions and the halting of a major Angola-Cuban offensive in December. UNITA's strength in 1989 was estimated at 40,000 trained men in combat units as small as 20 men, or as large as 100, with a further 30,000 semi-regulars and irregulars. UNITA dominated larger areas of the country than the government but held only a few small towns in the southeast. Its chief-of-staff, General Demosthenes Chilingutila, and his deputy, General Ben Ben Arlindo Pena, were notably able field commanders.

Violations of the ceasefire, predictably, occurred leading to small-scale border shoot-outs, SWAPO-PLAN intimidation and abductions, particularly of children, all together with the Cuban failure to withdraw troops behind the agreed line. After negotiations, sometimes bitter, in December formal agreements were concluded by which all Cubans were to be withdrawn 300 km north of the border and specified numbers returned home, South African aid to UNITA was ended, the SADF in Namibia was to withdraw to two specified bases and not exceed 1,500, the SWATF and the infamous Koevoet were to be disbanded, and Namibia was to have a free election. Later, to supervise the transition to independence, a UN military force was to take over security responsibility.

The agreement provisions were not put into effect without initial minor border incidents and misunderstandings. More serious were four-pronged incursions of over 900 PLAN insurgents into Ovamboland on 1 April, followed by a second large incursion a week later. Sharp fighting and the deployment of SADF Ratel 90s and helicopter gunships followed for some time, over 250 insurgents being killed. It would seem that SWAPO had wrongly believed the SADF for the most part had been withdrawn and the SWATF demobilized, and that therefore the way was open for them to invade, establish bases and perhaps move on further into the territory before the arrival of the UN supervisory force. Under intense international pressure SWAPO instructed its insurgents to report to the newly arriving UN military centres, but most insurgents did not, preferring to withdraw discreetly.

With the arrival of the UN force the South Africans proceeded with their withdrawal from Namibia, the SWATF was disbanded and the long border war was over. South African estimates of the total casualties were 11,291 Angola-Cuban and PLAN soldiers and 1,087 civilians for the loss of 715 SADF and SWATF personnel, totals that exclude the casualties in UNITA's operations.

In reviewing the war Angolan and Cuban propaganda endlessly reiterated that the battles around Cuito Cuavanale represented a historic defeat of the SADF, ending a myth of white supremacy. The Angola-Cuban failure to take Jamba despite their huge numerical and air superiority was conveniently overlooked. The rhetoric also greatly exaggerated SADF and SWATF strengths in Angola, alleging over 9,000 when in fact they never exceeded 3,000 actually across the border at any one time. The Cubans, more directly committed in the fighting in the last four years having wrested command and direction away from both the Soviets and Angolans, certainly needed such propaganda to cover the very poor performance of their forces up to 1988. Most of the Cuban soldiers were badly trained and led; in Angola they were often very badly fed. No statistics of the number of Cuban soldiers killed were published, but the total was high, possibly as many as 10,000.

Although the Cubans possessed almost all of the weaponry of Soviet motor-rifle divisions, their tactical handling of armoured fighting vehicles was until 1988 generally poor. They were often indiscreet in their signals which the SADF intercepted. Vehicles were badly maintained. The Cuban pilots of the MiG-23s and SU-22s remained tightly controlled from the ground, flying high with consequential limited target acquisition and accuracy. The success rate of the 111 anti-aircraft missiles fired was only 4.5 per cent. Cuba's President Castro blamed his expeditionary force commander, the victor in the Ogaden war, General Onchoa, for the lack of success. Criminal charges, almost certainly trumped up, were brought against him and he was executed.

Onchua's predecessor in Angola, General Rafael del Pino, who had lost a son in Angola, had defected to the United States a little earlier.

South Africans assessed the PLAN units as well skilled in fieldcraft, tracking and camouflage; individuals were physically tough and brave. Their military skills, however, reflected poor training while internal discipline was very harsh. In the last years of the campaign three joint Cuban–PLAN battalions were formed.

The SADF units included increasing numbers of coloureds, Indians and black soldiers, among them an entire Zulu battalion. Their patrolling – foot, horse, vehicle, riverine or helicopter-lifted – was of a very high standard. The SADF also quickly learnt the techniques of mine detection and protection of vehicles, the Buffel mine-protected armoured personnel carrier being a notable success. Two special forces merit mention, the 32 Battalion mixed-race deep-penetration unit including a number of Namibians and Angolans, and a specialized tracking unit, SWASPES. In the later stages of the campaign 32 Battalion was equipped with the formidably effective Valkyrie 127 mm multiple rocket launchers mounted on German light armoured UNIMOG vehicle chassis copied from a captured Soviet BM-21. Evidence points to the use of chemical warfare methods by the SADF in the form of poisoning of clothing or uniforms which were then allowed to fall into PLAN hands, or of water supplies. One of the most notable military achievements of the SADF in the campaign was the success, despite all the difficulties of distance and terrain, of its logistic support system. SADF intelligence gathering, human, signals and air, was also exceedingly efficient.

The SWATF eventually totalled some 30,000. It comprised a Reaction Force of a motorized brigade in which one of the three battalions was mixed race, six light infantry battalions, five recruited from Blacks and one from bushmen, an area force of part-time soldiers and logistic sub-units. Two of its all-volunteer units mutinied in 1987, the mutineers of one of the units being mostly Ovambo and in the second unit the closely related Okavongo. The mutineers alleged that they had been used in advances with white units following in order to reduce white casualties. Certainly in the later Cuito Cuanavale fighting there was increasing SADF use of non-white personnel, and the soaring costs both in money and casualties were major factors in pushing South Africa towards negotiations. These reflected the military situation, being on a "no losers" basis.

The Inkatha War 1986–90

While South Africa was fighting a sophisticated high technology war on and across her borders, within the Republic, first in Natal but later spreading to

Transvaal, a crude regional war of a very different nature was developing. Over the eight years of this war the total cost in lives was to prove only a little less than the 22 years of the border war.[4]

The war began as one between the supporters of the United Democratic Front (UDF) and its ally the Congress of South African Trade Unions (COSATU) with a membership of over 900,000, and the Inkatha Movement together with its ally, the United Workers Union of South Africa (UWUSA). The UDF–COSATU grouping generally represented a modernizing movement totally opposed to apartheid; as a front it comprised some 600 youth, welfare, civic, women's and recreational organizations. It claimed, not without justification, to represent the vast majority of black people, but its intolerance towards any rival led it to violence. It was still the victim of the South African government's repressive measures, Pretoria regarding it as the internal wing of the banned ANC.

Inkatha was a Zulu cultural and increasingly political movement, founded in 1975 by Chief Buthelezi. Its strength lay in KwaZulu, and in the Kwa Zulu Assembly all members were Inkatha, as was the case in many local government councils. Inkatha also received some covert white right-wing support.

The conflicting parties did not challenge the existence of a South African state itself; their war was an armed conflict for political control of particular territorial areas, these being seen both as essential leverage for power within the post-apartheid state, and as a day-to-day struggle to secure land or job opportunities necessary for survival in the socially fragmented conditions of South Africa. For these reasons, although in rhetoric opposed to apartheid, Inkatha was quite prepared to operate within the apartheid system as being more disposed to confirming their control in specific demarcated areas. Each side claimed that the war, and most of the battles and clashes during it, was caused by the other. The war should also be seen at least in part as a by-product of the violence and turbulence in South Africa over the previous 20 years.

The vocabulary of the war was singular. On the UDF side there were "activists" – leaders – and "comrades" or *amaqabane* – rank and file, some only 15 years old. Activist turnover was rapid, leaders being restricted or detained by the police or killed by Inkatha. The comrades came to be infiltrated by *comtotais*, thugs who committed crimes under a political label and proved impossible to control. Within Inkatha the armed members were known as *amabutho* or "vigilantes". They claimed to be responsible citizens ensuring law and order, but their behaviour was the reverse. The UDF renamed geographical areas to suit their cause with names such as Moscow, Cuba or Tanzania; by so doing they believed they were creating a new reality and expunging the old. Both sides hurled or chanted abuse, in word or song, against the other.

The UDF drew recruits widely, many from COSATU. Inkatha's recruits were provided by the Zulu social structure. Chiefs and headmen, salaried as such by the Pretoria government, had almost feudal powers in the dispensing of favours such as marriage or market licences, or, more basically, in providing money, food and drink. They became known as the "war lords" and some without doubt used coercive powers such as threats to burn down houses to enforce recruitment. In the nineteenth century Zulu territory had been deliberately fragmented to ensure white control; these fragmented pockets, the majority controlled by the KwaZulu warlords and linked to the Zulu monarchy, were Inkatha's formidable power base.

A third participant in the fighting was the South African Police who saw Inkatha as an ally against the UDF, while the latter came to see Inkatha, and not the apartheid regime, as the main enemy. Police partisanship appeared constantly: they would be slow, or fail altogether, to answer UDF appeals for help; they would tell people to leave areas sought by Inkatha, saying they could not be protected; they would escort vigilantes and look the other way at Inkatha meetings or assemblies of fighters that transgressed, or were about to transgress, the law; if Inkatha was in trouble they would arrest comrades while any Inkatha arrested would often be quickly released.

From 1987 the police were reinforced by *kitkonstabeli*, young men who received a short six-week training. Many were Inkatha members. At a national level the government, until the early 1990s, was largely indifferent to the death of blacks. The government dismissed the events as "tribal conflict" or "black on black", so concealing the real issues; the word "war" was too embarrassing.

The weaponry at the outset was rudimentary. The comrades used clubs with metal heads, sword-sticks and a few home-made guns. Inkatha was only little better equipped, with iron bars, canisters of stones, stabbing spears, matchets, petrol bombs, "kwasha" home-made guns and a number of shotguns. The comrades might on occasions wear yellow T-shirts with UDF or COSATU slogans; Inkatha would wear khaki shirts with UWUSA slogans or red headbands. In the wrong area, wearing such shirts could mean death. Inkatha also included an Inkatha Women's Brigade and a Youth Brigade.

The aims of the fighting were at first local. UDF activists in street committees would harass Inkatha members, forcing them to move, or would mount "gauntlet" attacks on Inkatha followers from settlements on either side of a road. Inkatha would invade territory not previously occupied by its own supporters, seeking to redraft the political geography and land resources of the area. The area would then be subjected to ethnic cleansing, Inkatha even extending killings to the parents and relatives of their opponents. The processes were simultaneous and two-sided – any person in an area whose controlling faction he refused to join was seen as a justifiable target. Neutrality became impossible. Refugees fled from scenes of fighting, over 60,000 being dispossessed by 1989. The basic nature of the fighting affected every aspect of life: schools, work, transport and recreation.

The fighting itself developed to low-intensity war, informal and irregular, endemic in the rural areas, more sporadic in built-up areas. Task forces, large or small, would be assembled for a particular purpose and disperse afterwards. Patterns of attack and retaliation developed. Casualties were generally the result of small bands seeking out particular targets such as individual families or a bus full of opponents. Later, when more guns were available, cars would speed through an opponent's area spraying the flimsy houses with bullets.

From small beginnings in 1980 with more serious clashes in Pietermaritzburg and Durban in 1985, conflict became serious in 1987 after a forcible Inkatha recruiting campaign. Inkatha task forces, 200–300 strong, invaded areas in the Natal midlands to secure control; people began to flee townships and villages; families who had lived amicably with their neighbours became inflamed with passion and joined in the fighting. In the rural areas, particularly on the Pietermaritzburg–Durban corridor, land was the target, while in the towns the targets were small but specific urban zones. Success was secured by patrols, and clashes most frequently occurred at the borders of areas or zones such as roads, ditches or yards. On the roads, cars and buses could be weapons or targets. To 1990 the fighting was limited to the greater Pietermaritzburg area, the Edendale Valley and the adjoining Vulindlela, and the Natal Midlands, the UDF attacking areas where for historical reasons Inkatha was weak.

The first Inkatha operations in 1987 failed to secure some of the rural areas they held and made no progress in the townships. In January 1988 with some police help, Inkatha reoccupied the Vulindlela rural areas they had lost and mounted a raid on the township of Ashdown, killing a number of people. The police banned the UDF. The war then entered a less mobile phase for 18 months, each side consolidating the land it held with smaller groups raiding across the informal borders – the average death rate was 50 or more per month. In late 1989 the fighting spread to the Durban area where the increase of population bore particularly heavily on scarce land, often in the hands of the urban counterpart of the "warlord", the 'shack-lord".

South Africa 1990–7

In 1990, following the release of Mandela and the unbanning of the ANC, conditions were to change sharply and the scale of this civil war spread. The price of success or failure appeared to the combatants to inflate, with the imminence of a black government. Fighting intensified, and an appeal for reconciliation by Mandela, who by now had been released, was ignored. Inkatha armies, several over 3,000 strong, now well armed with rifles and sub-machine guns and ferried by the KwaZulu police, rampaged through the hill areas around Pietermaritzburg in the "seven Day War" of March–April. The SADF deployed 2,000 troops (many brought straight back from Namibia) to try to enforce a peace.

Worse, however, was to follow as a consequence of ANC followers harassing Zulu urban labour and of a change in Inkatha strategy. Buthelezi and the movement came to believe that, to affirm the status that they sought of being the country's third largest political group, they must extend their activities. Accordingly, renamed as the Inkatha Freedom Party (IFP), the conflict was spread to the Transvaal Reef townships in the Vaal Triangle, East Rand, West Rand, Soweto and Johannesburg itself. The IFP became overtly ethnic, arguing the unbanned ANC, which had supplanted the UDF, was Xhosa-driven, set to dominate the Zulus. Reluc-tance to join the IFP among Zulus was met by coercive recruitment and the bussing of IFP vigilantes up from Natal. The fighting centred round 56 hostels housing some 175,000 single working men, mainly Zulu, a group with the least to lose. Some of the hostel complexes housed up to 20,000 men in squalid conditions. The hostels became ethnic fortresses, to be defended or used as sally ports for attacks on Xhosa squatter camps and other settlements. Trains and their passengers were another frequent target. The weaponry, too, became more deadly with the acquisition by both sides of AK-47 rifles, grenades and limpet mines. The death totals spiralled, 7,000 being killed in township violence between February 1990 and July 1992. In one case, at Boipatong, more than 40 people were killed in one massacre in June. The Reef fighting tended to fluctuate in scale, related to national political developments. The Natal fighting continued as sustained violence.

The government made some limited attempt in September 1990 to try to halt the violence with curfews and barbed wire, but overall the indifference and police partiality continued, this despite revelations that the government had been covertly funding Inkatha and training some of its "hit squads" in secret camps in Natal and Caprivi. Examples of police discharging tear gas on IFP opponents or failing to intervene to protect ANC members were fre-quent. A National Peace Accord reached in September 1991 achieved virtu-ally nothing.

By mid-1992, however, the pattern began to change. The government, still that of President De Klerk, saw more clearly that it needed the ANC, just as the ANC needed the government, for any smooth transition; some of the more brutal of the security forces' units were disbanded and open support for the IFP decreased. The fighting nevertheless continued, and in one bloody fortnight in July 1993 220 people were killed. With the approach of South Africa's first universal franchise election, set for April 1994, violence escalated. The ANC, whose experience of the recent years included political and at times brutal GDR and Soviet training, spawned affiliated groups and organizations as brutal as any of the IFP. One of these was the ANC's attempts, not wholly successful, to create Self Defence Units (SDUs), arming them with AK-47s. In some areas the SDUs openly took over from the police, ignoring pleas for restraint from Mandela. Each side extended no-go zones, the IFP running a "lives for votes" campaign. In March–April over 600 died in violence in the Durban area and Zulu rural areas; it was estimated that some 10,000 people had been killed in the four years between De Klerk's February 1990 speech and the election.

The IFP was not the only military worry of the South African government. In 1992 the Ciskei's defence force, the gendarmerie raised by the government of one of the Black client mini-states created by grand apartheid, opened fire on an ANC demonstration killing 24, and in the following year it became necessary to blockade another of the mini-states, the Transkei, to contain armed *Umkhonto* and PAC groups which had been attacking local whites. White extremists in their turn launched a small and ineffectual bomb campaign in 1994, many being later arrested.

For the final stages of the transition and the election the South African government's Transitional Executive Council mounted a 10,000-strong National Peace-Keeping Force. A special unit of this force had to be sent to cope with hostel versus squatter camp warfare in three East Rand townships of Kathelong, Thokoza and Vosloorus, achieving only little success; the violence ended with the usual depressing result of vandalized homes, empty schools, piles of rubbish and choked sewers. Just before the actual election itself tension was greatly reduced by an unexpected announcement by Buthelezi, dropping his objections to it. The respite, and Buthelezi's declining personal popularity, led to a gradual fall in the level of IFP violence; over 1,000 people were killed in the 12 months after the election, but with numbers falling thereafter. There was nevertheless a particularly violent IFP massacre of 18 ANC members which occurred as late as Christmas Day in 1995 – the murderers in fact being convicted in 1997.

The legacy of the Inkatha and the whole culture of violence in South Africa over four decades was one of violent crime, almost uncontrollable on account of the easy availability of weapons, in particular the AK-47, imported from Mozambique and elsewhere. In 1992 the police seized 891 AK-47s but admitted this was only a small proportion of all such weapons in a country still torn by "the culture of the gun".

Angola and Mozambique 1990–7

Although South Africa had withdrawn from direct involvement in the affairs of the two civil war-ridden states, the momentum of the conflicts which Pretoria had supported continued, America more than replacing South Africa as the major supplier for UNITA for two years, though covert and probably unauthorized local SADF help continued also for a while.[5]

In Angola a ceasefire agreed in June 1989 broke down almost immediately with fighting renewed. Early 1990 saw a weighty Angolan government offensive against UNITA, the main aim of which was an attempt to take Mavinga. Both sides took heavy casualties, and the fighting continued until May 1991, each side seeking to strengthen its position at international level negotiations. These talks led to a further ceasefire agreement, which also provided for the fusion of the two forces into one army and elections in September 1992, all with supervision by the UN, the USA and the Soviet Union. In 1992 it appeared there were dissensions within the UNITA camp, two senior officers defecting, but there was a return to insurgency by FLEC-R (*Frente de Libertacão do Enclave Cabinda – Renovada)*, the most effective of three separatist insurgent groups in the Cabinda enclave. In March the demobilization of both armies was, ostensibly, begun, but the international supervisory force was inadequate and its mandate overoptimistic. The whole ceasefire settlement collapsed when Savimbi rejected the September election result. His control of some two-thirds of the terrain of Angola had failed to secure him an electoral win against the MPLA's holding of the more populous one-third, and in the winner-takes-all loser-loses-all nature of most African elections the result was explosive. Savimbi's disavowal led to revenge attacks on UNITA members lawfully in the capital, and in one of these UNITA's Vice-President Chitunda was killed.

Fighting resumed at the end of October with a disastrous UNITA attempt to take Luanda which was foiled by MPLA's Spanish-trained gendarmerie. Some of the most violent warfare of the whole era followed in areas as far apart as Lubango, Benguela and Cuito Cuanavale. The government army took time to recover from premature demobilizations and the loss of its Soviet and Cuban advisers but were able to recapture several large towns including Lubito, Caxito, Namibe and Benguela, and briefly also Huambo, to which Savimbi had moved his headquarters. In Huambo, however, the government forces found themselves invested by UNITA which, although bombarded by heavy artillery and MiG-23 air-to-ground strikes, once again displayed its remarkable powers of resistance and eventually retook the city. Also in the southeast and east UNITA was active in the Luanda area with the aid of Zairean soldiers and mercenaries, UNITA occupied Soyo in the northwest. It was only restrained from taking control of Cabinda by the United States which had begun to change its pro-UNITA policy, stopping military aid. The Luanda government, using a private military company, hired British and South African ex-soldiers and with their aid temporarily recaptured Soyo.

Against a background of fruitless negotiations the war lapsed into one of attrition, though UNITA succeeded in retaking Soyo. UNITA's army now totalled some 60,000, its arsenal included 107 mm multiple rocket launchers and heat-seeking missiles, and the UNITA military units still retained their excellent discipline and control.

But the American change of policy reflected an increasingly critical international view of UNITA, seen as pursuing an unnecessary war against a government in Luanda that had won an election and was modifying its former rigid Marxism. Despite a massive, and in the end after nine months unsuccessful, assault on Cuito, UNITA, faced with a UN oil and arms embargo, agreed in 1994 to accept the September 1992 election result and withdraw from all the areas it had occupied since October 1992. A peace process was set in motion providing again for demobilization, military integration, power-sharing and national reconciliation, with a more effective 6,000-strong UN force.[6] UNITA made a point of hindering the work of the UN troops when they arrived, and whenever possible they stole UN equipment. The military situation, however, turned in favour of the government whose troops were by now better trained and equipped.[7] After heavy fighting in the first half of 1994 in the northwest and west-central provinces of Angola, UNITA was driven out. On 9 November their stronghold of Huambo was lost to them. The Angolan army was not able to turn this success to full account. On the advance to Huambo they lived off the land, which was not possible in UNITA country, and their logistic arrangements were still very weak. Once again UNITA recovered, and by late November was attacking in the north and northeast. Apart from the determination of the ethnicities of eastern Angola, in particular the Ovimbundu, UNITA's sustainability was a result of illegal diamond sales and the ongoing support of President Mobutu in Zaire.

The demobilization and integration process hardly moved forward in 1996–7, the difficulties of quartering and livelihood being immense, and given an absence of goodwill on the part of UNITA which still retained control over almost two-thirds of the country with its own capital at Bailundo. There were signs of disagreement in the UNITA command, Savimbi refusing to participate in the peace process and ensuring he still retained an army, some of which was even despatched to Zaire to try to support the Mobutu regime. FLEC insurgent groups again reappeared in Cabinda.

The collapse of the Mobutu regime in May 1997 and the difficulties the collapse presented UNITA had by July led to renewed fighting. The Angolan government which appeared to think that the situation presented an opportunity to crush UNITA once and for all opened attacks on UNITA positions in the northeast and on the UNITA force returning from Zaire. UNITA's response was an indication of the failure of the peace process – firm resistance to the government attacks in the north and the reopening of guerrilla strikes, mining and sabotage throughout eastern and southern Angola and in Cabinda. It was estimated that UNITA still controlled over 35,000 men, many of whom had been quartered for resettlement or who had deserted rejoining and with remnants of Mobutu's army providing additional manpower. Most of UNITA's infantry and artillery weapons had not been handed in. UNITA's force structure of battalions, columns, special force platoons, motorized anti-aircraft sub-units and engineer platoons still existed, and were distributed with 9,000 men in the north, 11,000 in the east, 11,000 in central Angola and 4,000 in the south. Fresh weapons and ammunition were said to be reaching UNITA from Bulgaria through Mozambique and Congo-Brazzaville, some being dropped to forward units from aircraft with no marking while the bulk was flown in on a diamonds-for-weapons basis at UNITA's two main airfields, Luzamba in the northeast and Andulo, not far from Bailundo. In effect, the country was partitioned in a military confrontation.

No accurate figures exist for the total casualties in the Angolan civil war. The lowest estimate is 500,000 but the reality may be much higher. The country was devastated and at least 2 million people lost their homes. Once flourishing town populations were reduced to miserable groups of thin, bent people, dressed in rags with many blind, lame or with limbs amputated as a result of mines, all struggling to survive amid the ruins of the devastated towns and villages. Estimates of unrecorded mines still *in situ* range from 9 million to 20 million. No country in Africa has suffered so much as Angola from its 32-year-long civil war.

Some of the differences between UNITA with its strong ethnic and regional firm bases and RENAMO have already been suggested. RENAMO was nevertheless to fight with ferocity, causing the immense economic and social damage which was the aim of its campaigns.[8] An element of resentment against South Africa, after the more publicized than real disengagement following the 1984 Pretoria Declaration, led RENAMO to target installations such as electric pylons linking power from the Cabora Bassa dam to South Africa. The FRELIMO government's difficulties were increased when, following an earlier appeal made by President Machel to President Banda of Malawi to end Malawi support for RENAMO, Banda reacted by expelling many hundreds of RENAMO fighters into Mozambique where they posed the threat of splitting the country. RENAMO's power and FRELIMO weakness led the Mozambique government into an abortive attempt to negotiate with RENAMO using South Africa as a go-between. Predictably, in view of South Africa's parallel policies of covertly helping RENAMO while overtly observing the Nkomati Accord, this failed; for military help the FRELIMO government in January 1987 turned again to Zimbabwe. Mixed FRELIMO and Zimbabwean forces then set in hand a series of slow-moving attacks in February, recapturing a number of the northern towns lost previously. In May South African special forces carried out another raid in Maputo looking for ANC supporters, and in so doing they effectively ended the Nkomati Accord. Unofficial South African help for RENAMO was then increased. May and July saw RENAMO reprisal attacks across the Zimbabwe border, over 350 being mounted in the period January 1987 to June 1988. RENAMO also raided into Zambia, which led to hot pursuit operations by the Zambian army and the destruction of two RENAMO camps in 1988. In December 1987 an amnesty offer made to RENAMO produced only a small number of men willing to surrender.

Despite recurrent sharp internal divisions within such leadership as it possessed, RENAMO went on to launch powerful attacks in Mozambique's southern provinces. In one town RENAMO massacred over 400 people. The RENAMO military aim was to cut off Maputo, and they succeeded in mounting two very bloody ambushes on roads north of Maputo; in one, in October, they killed 270 and in the second, in November, 63. FRELIMO's convoy guards were badly trained and badly motivated – only when stiffened by Zimbabwean troops could FRELIMO launch effective attacks on RENAMO.

By 1988 despite some Western military and economic aid, the Mozambique government's dependence on the 10,000 or so British-trained Zimbabwean troops in the centre and south and 3,000 of the less capable Tanzanians in the north was almost total. The Soviet Union started to withdraw its 750-strong mission and with them went the smaller number of East Germans; the withdrawal of the latter was the cue for the Tanzanians to announce that they too would withdraw.

Meanwhile RENAMO continued to attack road and rail links, in particular the Maputo–Zimbabwe line. RENAMO attacks reflected the looseness and indiscipline of the movement, now estimated to be some 18,000 but of these only 50 per cent were in controlled units. Major attacks on important targets would be mounted with an effective command and plan by up to 600 men. Smaller groups, out of central control, would be more concerned with pillage, massacre or, more simply, food. Identification between RENAMO, the government forces or plain bandits was often difficult – RENAMO quite often wore captured uniforms, the government could not always afford uniforms for its soldiers, while the bandits might wear uniform or plain clothes.

The refugee problem, internal and external, of the thousands fleeing across the borders of Mozambique reached new dimensions, particularly after a largely ineffective offensive against RENAMO in June. The scale of the violence and the refugee problem and a report on the subject written by a US State Department consultant led to a fall in international, particularly American and Portuguese right wing, support for RENAMO. This change in international opinion, the clear indication of the ending of Soviet support and consequentially any hope of a FRELIMO military victory, the approach of change in South Africa and the continuing poor response to the amnesty offer, all enabled Western countries to put pressure on Machel's successor, Chissano, to pursue more liberal domestic policies and seek a political accord. Two years of talks and negotiations followed.

In April 1989 RENAMO agreed to a one-month ceasefire to allow food and help to reach the internal refugees, estimated at 1 person in 12; for the rest of the year fighting was at a rather lower intensity. In early 1990 Chissano announced a programme of reform that met many of RENAMO's ostensible demands. Fighting, including on 15 February a violent attack on a train arriving in Mozambique from South Africa in which over 75 people were killed, nevertheless continued for most of the year. It was widely held that Chissano personally directed his military not to encircle one RENAMO base where Dhlakama was believed to be present in order not to prejudice negotiations. A ceasefire was agreed in December, RENAMO securing an undertaking that operations by Zimbabwean troops would be limited to the protection of railway lines. The ceasefire was short-lived with a resumption by RENAMO early in 1991 of attacks on the roads to Malawi with, later, attacks which succeeded in again cutting the Cabora Bassa power lines and railway link. After much further negotiation, in October 1992 a fresh ceasefire was brokered in Rome between Chissano and Dhlakama, each now war-weary and aware that outright victory was not possible. Both sides agreed to withdraw their forces to assembly areas for demobilization. In December the UN agreed to provide a 7,500-strong peacekeeping contingent, ONUMOZ (United Nations Operation in Mozambique), to supervise demobilization, integration of the two forces into one army and an election.[5] Although the arrival of this force was considerably delayed and there were initial clashes between units of the newly integrated national army and RENAMO in the north and elsewhere, by early 1994, though, the security problem had become one of local frictions and banditry rather than full civil war. RENAMO, however, retained its own control over several groups of armed supporters and after the departure in February of the last of the "Blue Helmets" it continued to pose a threat to the country's stability.

The banditry was fuelled by the huge quantities of weaponry in the territory. ONUMOZ, reasonably efficient in demobilization, failed badly in disarmament. Weapons were concealed by both sides in a variety of improbable locations – on one occasion, for example, three lorries worth of ammunition was found in a hospital outbuilding. The government's weaponry included on paper the full range of tanks, armoured personnel carriers, field and anti-aircraft artillery and logistic support vehicles found in Soviet army motor rifle divisions in the 1970s (except for FROG missile launchers), together with MiG-17 and MiG-21 aircraft, transport aircraft and helicopters, and a few of the powerful Mi-24 gunship helicopters. The Soviet Union had, however, refused to supply Mozambique with the costly SU-25 aircraft, despite requests. Much of this sophisticated equipment was so poorly maintained that in any case it could not be used, and almost all of it was unsuitable for containing RENAMO. More significantly, the government distributed 1.5 million AK-47 rifles to the civil population during the war. The total of AK-47 rifles sent to Mozambique may well have been 6 million. At this time the Soviet army was introducing a new lighter rifle, the AK-74, to its own regiments. There were in consequence huge quantities of surplus AK-47 rifles.

RENAMO's armoury was limited to small arms, grenades and mines captured or supplied by South Africa from supplies taken in Angola. RENAMO also possessed a few artillery pieces, displayed for propaganda purposes but little used, and exceedingly efficient computerized signals equipment provided by South Africa, both for its own use for command and for interception. RENAMO relied on porters for transport.

Although 80,000 weapons were surrendered to the UN by September 1994 thousands more were sold, very often by RENAMO or Mozambique army officers, to dealers in South Africa via Komati Poort or Swaziland. The war also left a serious mine problem, though not on the same scale as that in Angola.

Continuous warfare since 1984 had reduced Mozambique to being one of the poorest countries in the world, though it was better placed to recover than the more badly devastated Angola. Total deaths are impossible to assess precisely. It was estimated that 100,000 civilians had been killed by 1988; to this figure must be added others killed between 1988 and 1993, and many thousands more who died from war-related disease or famine. At least a million and a quarter Mozambicans fled across borders to neighbouring countries as refugees.

As in South Africa the more lasting legacy of the wars remains that of unrest in the military and a general culture of corruption and crime.

Chapter Seven

Wars of integration and disintegration II: 1980 to 1997

The last two decades of the twentieth century were to see further African wars of integration and disintegration. Pressures and tensions were heightened by worsening economic conditions, accelerating population growth and social frustration in many countries, leading on to collapsed or failed states within which genocidal epidemics of the mind prevailed. World interest was elsewhere, on changes in Europe and events in the Middle East. In the African conflicts several new features appeared that made warfare in this period even more repellent than before.[1]

The first of these features was the easy availability of light weaponry. The numbers available from Mozambique were noted in the previous chapter. Other sources were war-weary UNITA and PLAN soldiers, and dubious conduits from the constituent republics of the former Soviet Union. These light weapons, in particular the AK-47 rifle and the RPG-7 grenade launcher, were robust, needed no infrastructure to maintain and few spare parts, were simple to learn and were easy to conceal in caches or to smuggle. Any form of effective control of the proliferation of light weapons is exceedingly difficult; in Africa all control was lost, and some countries also developed the capability to manufacture ammunition if not the weapons. The collapse of USA–USSR bipolarity deprived a few countries of a protective superpower patronage, making them a tempting target for a faction equipped with light weapons. While no all-inclusive answer can be given to the question as to whether weapons create conflict, there is no doubt that easy availability affects the course of any conflict.

A second feature was the appearance in Africa of European, American, Israeli and South African companies describing themselves as security firms or military consultants. Until the 1980s large commercial interests may have funded one faction or another in a conflict. In the 1980s and 1990s commercial involvement became more direct. Companies, often of former soldiers,

155

would assume specific security commitments thereby acquiring a corporate identity. Some of the companies were of good repute with commendable aims, but others fed on conflict, on occasions offering their services before a conflict opened as a proposal and advertising their success in any previous operation. The worst connived, admittedly sometimes under duress, with factions to exploit the resources of an area held by that faction in arms-for-product deals.

The third and perhaps the most repulsive of the new features, already mentioned in the case of RENAMO, was the appearance in many wars – Uganda, Somalia, Liberia, Sudan – of juvenile and child soldiers, some as young as seven.[2] For faction leaders child soldiers, often homeless or orphans as a result of local fighting, possessed many advantages. They were easy to manipulate and could be made to offer total loyalty free from the pursuit of women or riches. Many in several of the conflicts were volunteers while others were forced into joining by threats against themselves or their families. Alcohol, drugs and promises of attractive consumer goods such as radios or bicycles were further pull factors. Push factors included frustration, lack of education or employment prospects, in some countries a video culture of violent films, or sometimes quite simply food or a desire to avenge the death of relatives. In some cases juveniles would be subjected to traumatic initiation rites, perhaps the public killing of a captive or even a neighbour, which like the Mau Mau oath of the 1950s set a person apart. Juveniles and child soldiers were put to a variety of tasks: some in combat groups, others gathering intelligence or manning check points from which they could loot or kill; others simply carried stores. Training was generally crude and discipline severe – beatings or worse. Homosexuality featured noticeably and independent observers detected stress symptoms – sleeplessness, nightmares, incontinence.[3]

These three features all served the interests of a new generation of faction leaders and militia warlords. These by the 1990s came to recruit and act in new ways; some would recruit regardless of ethnicity and fight across and disregarding international boundaries. These frontiers were in any case so increasingly disregarded by large-scale smuggling and refugee movements as to appear irrelevant. In a number of territories faction fighting had, by 1997, produced "no war no peace" situations, in which peace processes might be under way but, as in Angola, the reality remained, a reality in which large areas of a territory would remain under the control of one or more factions who with armament not surrendered would continue to defend local frontiers.

It is perhaps more clear when setting out the events to consider the northern African territories first, with black Africa to follow, rather than adhere to a strictly chronological sequence.

Ethiopia 1980–93: Eritrea

In the 1980s Ethiopia continued to be beset by internal revolts. One of these, in Eritrea, was to succeed and result in full independence for the region, the first boundary change from a liberation campaign on the map of Africa.

The EPLF, which by the end of 1981 had succeeded in driving its rival, the ELF, completely out of Eritrea, continued its struggle against the government of Colonel Mengistu Hailemariam. In 1982 Mengistu attempted a hearts and minds programme of economic reconstruction and development for Eritrea, but it made little appeal and, turning to fierce repression, Mengistu launched an eight division strong military offensive directed by himself with a successful commander from the Ogaden war, General Gebre Kidan, in the field. His aim was to reoccupy the northeastern Nakfa area which was under EPLF control. The assault largely failed, the Ethiopians suffering several thousand casualties, while the EPLF still retained control over large areas of the north and northwest.

In 1984 the war developed to a new intensity, with initial EPLF successes – the capture of Tessenai, the defeat of a powerful Ethiopian force at Mersa Teklai and in the following year the capture of Barentu. Success was, however, followed by setback. A massive Ethiopian counter-offensive recaptured almost all the lost territory including Barentu, Mersa Teklai and the Red Sea coast. But the cost to the Ethiopians, both in actual casualties and war-weariness, coupled with growing resentment against the oppressive regime of Mengistu, reduced these successes to Pyrrhic victory; the Ethiopian army lost motivation while the EPLF remained undismayed, and this was reflected in continuing attacks which were growing in effectiveness, always tightly disciplined and often based on small 12-man strike groups.

In December 1987 the EPLF was in a position to launch a major offensive which could now combine conventional forces, some 18,000 strong in 12 brigades, using captured Ethiopian tanks and guns and supported by 20,000 regional militia, with sustained guerrilla operations. Their first success was the reoccupation of Nakfar, followed in March 1988 by a spectacular military victory, annihilating three Ethiopian divisions at Afabet which had been the Ethiopian army's regional headquarters. The EPLF effectively smashed the Ethiopian army in the area, capturing quantities of tanks, guns and missile launchers, and obliging Mengistu to withdraw troops from the Ogaden; his difficulties were compounded by attacks by the Tigré People's Liberation Front (TPLF) on his logistic convoys throughout 1989 and the withdrawal of Soviet support following the political developments in Moscow.

In February 1990 the EPLF occupied Massawa. The Ethiopians' subsequent attempts to recapture the city, including random massive napalm bombing, all failed and incurred wide international criticism. Discontent within Ethiopia itself had led to the formation of the Ethiopian People's Revolutionary Democratic Front (EPRDF) which, with logistic support and some reinforcement from the EPLF, opened a new military revolt against the regime.

By early 1991 the EPLF had surrounded Asmara, controlling the airfield, and was reasserting control of the Red Sea coast, including the Ethiopians' last remaining outlet to the outside world, the port of Assab. The EPRDF moved successively into Gondar, Gojjam and then Shewa provinces, so threatening Addis Ababa. The end came in May with the flight into exile of Mengistu, the capture of Addis Ababa by the EPRDF, the capture of Asmara by the EPLF and the formal surrender of Ethiopian forces in Eritrea.

A useful contributor to the success of the EPLF, and later the EPRDF, had once again been the TPLF which early in the decade extended its control over large areas of the province, despite the presence of a 40,000-man Ethiopian force, including special mountain units, and heavy air strikes by Soviet Mi-24 helicopter gunships and MiG-21 and MiG-23 air-to-ground strikes. The TPLF, operating in small units, were able very successfully to harass the Ethiopian army's lines of communication to Eritrea, killing or wounding some 4,000 troops in 1980 alone. In 1984 some 200,000 Tigrayans were moved out of the province into Sudan. The move appears to have been organized by the TPLF to attract international sympathy; as such it was a failure and the Tigrayans were returned. The move, further, led to friction with the EPLF, the friction turning to clashes with casualties on both sides. As a consequence and also as a result of ongoing divisions in the TPLF leadership, the Ethiopian army achieved some success in ejecting the TPLF from much of east and central Tigré and cutting the TPLF's communications with the EPLF.

Fighting, sometimes sharp, continued for the next three years. The Ethiopian army appeared to be gaining control, launching continuous aircraft and helicopter strikes, while the EPLF and TPLF remained at loggerheads. Change began in the early months of 1988 when the Ethiopian army was obliged to redeploy troops from Tigré after the loss of Afabet and forced to withdraw, often following the overrunning of weak garrisons from north Tigré. The TPLF and EPLF resumed co-ordination of their activities, so enabling the TPLF to develop its actions in south Tigré where in May 1988 they took a garrison town, Maychew, so compelling the Ethiopian army to retreat southward, in the process suffering a further defeat at Amba Alagi. But although now capable of putting at least 20,000 men in the field, the TPLF still attracted the priority attention of the Mengistu regime, which succeeded in forcing them out of the main urban centres they had taken. However, as the regime crumbled the TPLF recovered and by May 1990 had won a series of conventional warfare battles against the demoralized, hurriedly-drafted conscripts of the Ethiopian army, so leading the EPRDF forces on the road to Addis Ababa. One dimension of the war in which both sides were very actively engaged was food deprivation, particularly in drought-stricken areas. The TPLF in 1988 captured two major food distribution centres, while the riposte of the Mengistu regime was the bombing of both EPLF and TPLF food-growing areas and supply centres, causing numerous deaths. Famine added to the death totals, particularly among civilians. The OLF, despite divisions in its leadership, maintained a state of lawlessness rather than insurgency in Oromo province; only in 1982 and 1988 did this result in any serious clashes.

After the collapse of the Mengistu regime and the installation of an interim government in Addis Ababa in which Tigrayans figured prominently, the country returned to some semblance of stability. A referendum was held in Eritrea in April 1993 as a result of which Addis Ababa conceded independence.

The numbers of people killed in these protracted conflicts cannot even be satisfactorily estimated. All the combatants exaggerated figures for propaganda reasons. Several hundred thousand refugees fled from Eritrea into Sudan, and in 1988 about a quarter of a million were receiving famine relief, mostly from Western Christian agencies but some from the Ethiopian government.

Chad 1980–97

The exclusion by Oueddai, supported by a new small Libyan-backed faction, the *Conseil Démocratique de la Révolution* (CDR), of Habré from the government, occurring at the same time as renewed sparring between their respective forces, led to a resumption of full civil war between the factions in March 1980. Oueddai drew on Libyan support to defeat Habré and a several thousand strong Libyan garrison arrived in the country. In the following year Oueddai was himself challenged by a FROLINAT breakaway faction which led to a bloody clash involving Libyan troops at Abeche. In arrangements brokered by the French and capitalizing on Oueddai's growing distrust of Gadaffi, the Libyans were persuaded to withdraw, to be replaced by an Organization of African Unity sponsored Inter-African Force (IAF).

The departure of the Libyans provided Habré with a new opportunity, and despite OAU efforts to mediate, he slowly extended his faction's authority southwards, from northern towns taken in December 1981 and January 1982 to the occupation of N'Djamena in June. Oueddai was forced to flee and what was left of the GUNT disintegrated. Habré then moved on into the south overcoming both Kamougué and the CDR. He became president and the AIF was withdrawn. This success, however, served only to set the stage for the next round of fighting in 1983, when Oueddai with Libyan support reoccupied much of the north. Habré's difficulties were compounded by splits within his own faction but he received support from the south, where many of Kamougué's followers united with his FAN to form a united *Forces Armeés Nationale Tchadiennes* (FANT). In June Oueddai's forces under General Djogo occupied Faya-Largeau and the remainder of the north. With the aid of American weaponry including Redeye and Stinger anti-aircraft missiles and a Zairean army contingent of 2,500 backed by Mirage air-to-ground strike aircraft and Aermacchi liaison machines, Habré's FANT recaptured Faya-Largeau in July.

This recapture led to a massive Libyan offensive in the following month. Advance intelligence of the Libyan moves was gathered by United States Boeing E3-A reconnaissance aircraft which, with an F-15 fighter escort, appears to have been in the area. The French estimated the Libyan force to total 6,000 men. In its 3,000-strong first echelon in the Faya-Largeau area preparing to move towards N'Djamena were some 30 armoured reconnaissance vehicles, 80 armoured personnel carriers, 15 BM-21 multiple-barrelled rocket launchers and 20 122 mm howitzers. Air support included Sukhoi SU-7 and Tupolev 28-P aircraft used for bombing. This threat met an immediate French response, the largest French military deployment in Africa since the end of the Algerian war.[4] The French despatched from France, staging in Bangui, a force of 2,800 men with 450 vehicles including armoured cars, Crotale anti-tank missiles, 105 mm guns and heavy mortars. Air support included Gazelle helicopters and Jaguar aircraft with 30 mm cannons and HOT anti-tank missiles, Mirages IIIs equipped with cannons and Magic missiles, and two navy Breguet electronic surveillance aircraft. In the event, although little of this force was directly committed, its deterrent effect was nevertheless considerable. The operation also gave the French army field trials opportunities for the Crotale missiles, the electronic fire control for heavy mortars, the counter-bombardment surveillance equipment and the new signals systems.

The Libyans moved according to Soviet European battlefield doctrine and training, expecting to deploy from the protection of their armoured vehicles before a clear target or objective. They were not well trained, and were slow in movement and unimaginative in tactics. Under a measure of French direction, FANT light vehicles with anti-tank rocket launchers and mortars moving very much faster were able to shoot the Libyan armour to pieces. The Libyan casualties were very severe. The French–FANT success established a line across Chad, between Salal and Arada across which France made it clear that she would not permit any Libyan or Oueddai incursions. By September fighting had ended and the bulk of the French force had returned home.

Attempted crossing of the line by Oueddai units in January 1984 led to French air-to-ground strikes, the French losing an aircraft, and the extension northwards of the French protected zone to the 16th parallel. Trouble, however, was to break out next in the south where in August 1984 a southern faction, the *commandos rouge* or *codos* led by Colonel Kotiga, opened an insurgency against the Habré government. By November it was evident that this campaign was failing, and a substantial percentage of the *codos* joined the Habré forces. These were to be strengthened further by splintering within the Oueddai movement, several small factions transferring their allegiance to Habré.

Libyan ambitions remained unsatisfied. Despite a 1984 Franco-Libyan agreement providing for the withdrawal from Chad of the forces of both countries, an agreement adhered to by France, a further massive build-up of some 4,000 troops in northern Chad followed in late 1985. These supported Oueddai's troops who crossed the interdiction line, but were checked by FANT forces supported by French air-to-ground strikes from Bouar, an airfield in the Central African Republic. The check was followed by the defection to Habré of further small factions, sometimes after shoot-outs and clashes within the Oueddai camp; these clashes extended to Oueddai's own *Forces Armeés Populaires* (FAP), Oueddai himself being wounded, probably by Libyans in circumstances never adequately explained. The new-style French intervention, Operation *Epervier* (Sparrow Hawk), was to be the first of several, an interesting case of the use of air power in support of a regime, the task falling on Mirage and Jaguar fighters, KC-135 in-flight refuellers and observation aircraft.

These conditions, in which the FAP were now fighting their former Libyan backers, enabled Habré's FANT to reoccupy much of the north in March 1987. In a brief but remarkable campaign known as the Toyota war, led by Colonel Deby, the FANT's light overland vehicles with MILAN anti-tank missiles, cannons and machine-guns moving at speed, destroyed the Libyans' dug-in defensive positions and slowly moving tanks, in particular at Fada and along the Ouadi Doum, killing and capturing over 3,000 elite "deterrent unit" Libyan troops and destroying their tanks and aircraft. A Libyan attack on a southern town led to further French intervention in the form of air-to-ground attacks. After clearing most of the north FANT forces re-entered Aozou, but were forced to withdraw following Libyan air attacks; they then invaded southeastern Libya, but their momentum could not be sustained. In September the OAU mediated a ceasefire. This ceasefire was, however, not strictly observed. Libyan forces, some based in Niger, others supporting a new "Islamic Legion" based in Sudan, caused clashes later in 1987 and in early 1988.

Habré appeared to be strengthening his political position along with his military security, reaching a *modus vivendi* with Libya in July 1988 and including Kotiga, Kamougué, FAP figures and Ouman, the leader of the fresh breakaway from Oueddai, in a reconstituted government. Signs of further troubles to come, however, soon appeared with the defection of the Chad armed forces commander Hassan Djamous, and his predecessor, Colonel Idriss Deby, to Sudan, a defection caused by Habré's victimization of the Zaghawa clan, Djamous being killed a little later. Clashes on the Sudan border followed, turning to a full-scale invasion by Deby, also a Zaghawa, and his new faction, the *Movement Patriotique du Salut* (MPS), in March 1990. The French moved troops and aircraft to the area, in the face of which the MPS withdrew. In November Deby's MPS, some 2,000 strong, launched a further invasion. This time the French, by now disillusioned with Habré, stood by as the MPS quickly occupied first Abéché and then N'Djamena, killing several hundred of Habré's troops. Habré himself fled into exile and Oueddai indicated that his faction might support the MPS.

Chad's military situation in the next six years remained on the borderline between civil disorders and civil war. In September 1991 attacks thought to have been the work of Habré supporters were launched against garrisons in Tibesti. In the following month a dissident ethnic group attacked N'Djamena airfield, but the assault was put down with French aid. In December a new faction, the *Mouvement pour la Démocratie et le Développement* (MDD), composed of former Habré supporters, mounted attacks in the western Lake Chad area, enjoying some success until they were checked by French air strikes and 400 ground troops. This uprising led to severe repression and pogrom treatment of southerners. In February 1992 another new faction which included discontented military personnel, the *Comité de Sursaut National pour la Paix et la Démocratie* (CSNPD), made an unsuccessful coup attempt in the capital. In May the MDD faction returned to attacks in the Lake Chad area, taking advantage of operating from within Nigeria; government forces put down the uprising, but two others followed in October and November, both also being put down. In January 1993 Habré followers staged a coup attempt which was easily suppressed. In February the Chad government faced two local rebellions, one of the MDD in the Lake Chad area and one of the CSNPD in the south. Both were put down, the latter with massacres of southern civilians. The rest of 1993 saw several local ethnic and social clashes, to be followed in 1994 by the first attacks against the government of two new factions, one a Sudan-based *Front National du Tchad* (FNT), whose uprising was put down in January, and the second a new southern faction, the *Forces Armeés pour la République Féderale,* whose uprising received the same treatment in August.

162

The Chad government, under Deby's presidency, continually sought to devise constitutional arrangements that would provide a national consensus, but ministerial quarrels and the short lives of ceasefire agreements reached with one faction or another remained indicators of the fundamental instability of the country. The Deby government's major success was to secure the withdrawal of the Libyans from Aozou following an International Court of Justice ruling in Chad's favour, in May 1994. A small French Foreign Legion detachment remained. By mid-1997 most of Chad was tranquil but a small number of secessionists operating across Niger from Benin were still active in the south, and Oueddai was leading a part-Toubou insurgent force that occasionally launched small-scale raids into Chad, also from Niger.

Western Sahara 1976–97

The second, post-independence, phase of warfare in Western Sahara stretches back before 1980 to 1976. Immediately after formal independence, Morocco and Mauritania by secret agreement partitioned the territory, two-thirds in the north going to Morocco, one-third in the south to Mauritania. The occupying troops from both countries very soon afterwards found themselves under heavy attack from the Polisario, some 10,000 strong.

The Polisario at the time possessed several assets to make it an effective guerrilla force: politically they were well-directed and united with a strong ethnic consciousness, free at least at first from internal faction fighting; they had sanctuary in Algeria where they could recruit, train, organize and deploy; they knew their own terrain; they could choose when and where to strike, forcing their opponents to be prepared to defend a huge area; their members were accustomed to the severity of the climate and the harshness of the terrain. They received a wide range of equipment – AK-47 rifles, machine-guns, mines, mortars, multiple rocket launchers, a few BMP armoured personnel carriers, and T-55 and T-62 tanks – from Algeria, Libya and possibly also direct from the Soviet Union. The Polisario had, in addition, in Mauritania one weak opponent, and one in which many people from the Reguibat, Tuareg and Izarguen peoples were sympathetic to them, while the Mauritanian army, perforce drawn from black Africans in the country's south, lacked motivation.

Early attacks therefore concentrated on the Mauritanian held area, motorized columns of 100 or more rebels raiding from Algeria deep into Mauritania. Many of these raids were successful, but one in June 1976, however, over-reached itself. A 600-strong column in a hundred vehicles led by Polisario's Secretary-General Ahmed el Wali attempted to invest Mauritania's capital,

Nouakchott, in the hope of sparking off a revolution. Although the force actually shelled the presidential palace the attempt failed. Much of the column was cut off and destroyed on its way back, el Wali being killed.

After a period of recovery, fresh Polisario assaults were launched in 1977, one on 1 May achieving a striking success when the insurgents briefly occupied the mining town of Zoueraté, the Mauritanian garrison offering no resistance. Six French technicians were kidnapped, a mistake to cost the Polisario severely. Moroccan troops were flown into the town and, under a co-operation agreement, to other areas of Mauritania as well; French advisers also arrived. The presence of the Moroccans, however, did not stop Polisario raiding columns which mounted several more attacks during the year, targeting mining centres, railway lines and military bases. In December French air force Jaguar air-to-ground strike aircraft and Breguet Atlantique reconnaissance aircraft, together with an increased number of advisers, all arrived to supplement the Moroccans, by then some 10,000 men with a squadron of F-5 air-to-ground fighter-bombers deployed in the field.

This powerful mix of reconnaissance, air-to-ground strikes and effective ground troops held the Polisario in check, two of their columns being severely mauled, mainly by Jaguar air strikes. Nevertheless the devastating economic effect of the campaigning, and the Mauritanian resentment against the presence, by now everywhere in the country, of Moroccan troops led to a coup in Nouakchott in July 1978. The Polisario decided to offer a ceasefire to Mauritania and cease operations against Mauritanian forces, while Morocco extended its claims to include the former Mauritanian zone.

In January 1979 the Polisario launched a major offensive, Operation *Houari Boumedienne*. Over the next two years constant attacks were launched against Moroccan positions in Western Sahara, with occasional raids into southern Morocco itself. Fast-moving columns or *Katibas* of 400 to 600 light vehicles, some now armed with 90 mm cannon, carrying 2,000 to 4,000, on occasions 5,000 men, fought pitched battles with even larger, ponderous Moroccan columns of over 1,000 vehicles, tanks, armoured-cars and light artillery. These proved too unwieldy for efficient command. Isolated Moroccan garrisons were cut off and had to be supplied by air, and casualties were often heavy. One notable attack, specifically designed to frighten Moroccan public opinion, took place in January 1979 against the south Moroccan town of Tan Tan, when the insurgents took a number of school students as hostages. The town was attacked twice more during the year.

The insurgents, however, suffered from only limited anti-aircraft protection. They managed to bring down a few Moroccan F-5 aircraft and a Hercules transport, using either SAM-6 or SAM-8 missiles (which may have been fired by East Germans or Cubans), but by 1981 their weakness forced a change of tactics to one of smaller columns attacking by night. To counter these attacks, also in 1981, the Moroccans turned to a new strategy, the construction of a two-metre high defensive *berm* or wall, supplemented by minefields, sophisticated electronic surveillance systems and strong points, with OV-10 Bronco counter-insurgency aircraft and helicopter gunships in support. Starting at the eastern edge of the Saharan territory in 1982 to allow the reopening of the phosphate conveyor, by 1987 a 2,700 km long wall of sand, rock and reinforced concrete had been completed in a strategy reminiscent of the French in the Algerian war. In addition the Moroccan military had become better trained, local commanders being given more discretion, were better equipped and had been brought up to a total of over 150,000 troops in huge garrisons. Equipment by 1990 included over 300 American or French tanks, over 250 field and medium artillery guns, and 40 multiple-rocket launchers. The war for "greater Morocco" had become a nationalist crusade. Fighting was reduced to Polisario hit-and-run attacks along the *berm* using Soviet BMP-1 armoured vehicles but only occasionally penetrating deep into Morocco. The Moroccans pursued and harassed these raids from the air by attack helicopters. In these clashes some 40 to 100 men on both sides would be killed and each side would proclaim a victory. Fighting was particularly severe in 1987, just before the arrival of a UN mission. Claims and counter-claims of military success were made by each side.

The strength of the Moroccan defence, and declining support for the Polisario from Algeria and the Soviet Union, both preoccupied with domestic concerns, together with the inability of the Polisario to maintain the equipment that they possessed and the defection of some of its senior personnel, all served by 1991 to produce a military stalemate. A UN-brokered peace plan providing for a ceasefire, force reductions and a referendum to determine the territory's future had been agreed in 1988 but the mission was continually harassed by the Moroccans and broke down with again a resumption of heavy fighting in September and October 1989 and in August 1991. The ceasefire, patrolled by a UN observer force, was eventually implemented in September 1991.[5]

Conditions for the referendum had, however, not been agreed by July 1997, the issues being the voting eligibility or otherwise of the original inhabitants living as refugees in Algeria, and some or all of the Moroccan settlers from the first and a later smaller second Green March.

Sudan 1983–97

The settlement of 1972 and the subsequent atmosphere of reconciliation between the Moslem north of Sudan and the Christian south were to prove short-lived; in fact, a pattern of small-scale southern guerrilla activity never really ceased. The government of President Nimeiry, under mounting political, economic and social pressures, gave way to Moslem hardliners. The autonomy given to the south was broken by a division of the south into three regions, and in September 1983 Moslem law, *sharia,* was introduced; almost immediately alcohol drinking, a Dinka custom, was punished by flogging and scores of men lost hands or feet for petty thefts. The result was an exodus of refugees to Ethiopia and renewed full rebellion.[6]

The most active ethnicity of the new rebel army, the Sudan People's Liberation Army (SPLA), remained the Dinka, who deserted in large numbers with their weapons from the Sudan army, in particular the 105th Battalion of southern soldiers who in January 1983 refused an order to move to the north. Other factors enabled the SPLA soon to become one of Africa's most powerful guerrilla armies. Several of its field commanders, including its leader, the American university educated Colonel Garang, had served in the Anya-Nya and later in the southern units of the Sudan army. Weaponry and training facilities were provided by Ethiopia; by late 1983 formed and trained units, several hundred strong, were taking the field.

The Dinka predominance, however, aroused resentment in some areas. As in the 1960s these areas, in response, produced recruits for pro-government militias. These unpaid militias or *murahadin* were increasingly to form the bulk of the government's forces, as Khartoum never dared impose conscription on the Arab north. They were drawn from a variety of ethnicities opposed to those in the SPLA for local reasons; economic frustration was also a recruitment factor. One militia raised among the Nuer called itself Anya-Nya II and fought for Khartoum until 1987 when most of it changed sides to join the SPLA.

Despite these problems, the SPLA quickly succeeded in bringing to a halt construction work on two major development projects that were perceived as being built to help the north more than the south, the Jonglei canal and the Bentiu oil wells, as well as generally dominating the rural areas of two of the south's provinces, Bahr el Ghazal and Upper Nile. The strategy, as in the 1960s, was to overrun police and military outposts and harass communications, including food distribution into towns, while not occupying any outpost or town for any length of time. The SPLA, too, formed its own small local militias. Their need to survive for operations in the rural areas led both the government militias and the SPLA to coerce villagers into providing food and recruits. The resulting famine situation greatly worsened the refugee problem. Facing disaster, Nimeiry rescinded his division of the south and, in theory also, the imposition of the *sharia,* but he was himself overthrown in a military coup in April 1985.

His successor, General Swar ad Dahab, promised reform and the SPLA called a ceasefire. But the reforms did not meet the SPLA's demands and the *sharia* law remained; fighting resumed. Swar ad Dahab's attempt at a return to constitutional government was largely negated by the fact that elections held in 1986 could not take place in the south because of the fighting. The largest party elected, the Umma, returned Sadik al Mahdi to power, but he was under constant pressure from northern Islamic militants, in particular the National Islamic Front (NIF) headed by Hassan al Turabi, and all the numerous attempts to reach a political settlement failed.

In the field conditions steadily worsened. The SPLA captured the town of Rumbek in early 1986 and shot down a Sudan Airways aircraft in August. Nearly a million people faced starvation and the fighting intensified with ever increasing ferocity. April and August 1987 saw two particularly brutal massacres of Dinka people, over 1,000 being killed in the first and 300 in the second. In reply the SPLA, supported by Ethiopia, began to strike into Central (Blue Nile) province. The SPLA maintained its grip in the south, reducing the Sudan army to beleaguered garrisons supplied by air. The government also armed northern and eastern Arabs in militias; these would raid into the south. In one clash in March 1987 the SPLA inflicted heavy casualties on one of these, a Rizeigat militia. In revenge the Rizeigat killed over 1,000 Dinka, mostly by burning them alive in railway carriages. Others, women and children, were forced to become slaves.

The year 1988 saw no improvement. The Islamic pressure on Sadik sharpened. The SPLA, now estimated to be at least 25,000 in strength following the inclusion of Nuer personnel from Anya-Nya II and other smaller ethnicities and including at least 2,000 children, repeatedly attacked food convoys sent from Kenya and Uganda. Thousands of refugees streamed into Khartoum where they were attacked in the streets by northern Moslem militants; others fled to Ethiopia, either to find food or to escape conscription into the SPLA, hundreds dying on the way. The country as a whole was bankrupt. To facilitate peace talks the SPLA called a ceasefire in May but the talks broke down.

In 1989 political turmoil, with two unsuccessful coup attempts in Khartoum, continued. The SPLA's attacks became even more effective as they now possessed light artillery. The northern borders of the old Southern region of Sudan had been secured, units were operating in Kordofan and Blue Nile and much of the Ethiopian borderland was under SPLA control. The town of Torit was captured. A brief ceasefire for the supply of food to the south only temporarily alleviated the famine. In June the Sadiq government was overthrown by a military coup which placed its leader, General al Bashir, in titular control but the real power lay with Turabi and the NIF. Negotiations between Bashir and Garang achieved nothing, the lull in the fighting ending in October.

Rebel successes continued in 1990, the southern capital, Juba, being placed under siege, and convoys carrying supplies to other urban garrisons being ambushed. The Khartoum government's difficulties were increased by the failure of all mediation efforts and the suspension of support from other Arab countries as a consequence of Khartoum's support for Iraq and the formation of an opposition government-in-exile in January 1991. The insurgents, however, suffered a setback in 1991 following the ending of the Eritrean war of independence. The Khartoum government had supported the Eritreans who, on gaining their independence, expelled Sudanese refugees and SPLA members, so worsening the already desperate refugee problem. Massacres of several hundred in the Nuba mountains were reported, while Bashir also began to receive military assistance from Iran.

The conflict had now taken on a new religious and ideological ferocity, a result of the influence of Turabi and the NIF on Bashir. The struggle against the south was seen to be a holy war. The paranoiac Arab north seemed determined to be more Arab and more strictly Moslem than the rest of the Arab world. Its militancy, enforced by a secret police at home, was also for export abroad, with efforts at destabilizing the regimes of neighbours and, ultimately, of making Africa a Moslem continent. Iran sponsored a branch of Hezbollah in Khartoum, where other Islamic militant organizations also congregated. The regime's practices included torture, summary execution, slavery for captured SPLA prisoners and forced conversion to Islam for southern children. A Popular Defence Force of "volunteers" was formed to support the army.

The renewed pressures on the SPLA brought simmering internal disputes into open conflict, three largely Nuer groups merging to form a United Democratic Salvation Front faction headed by Riek Mashar. These took to the field against Garang and his predominantly Dinka following; in the fighting several thousand were killed. The rebel cause was further weakened, the miseries of the population worsened and the government army, in offensives mounted in early 1992, was able to recapture or relieve large areas that it had lost. In June government forces reopened a river passage to Juba and the railway line to Wau. In July they briefly captured Garang's headquarters at Torit. The SPLA, however, recovered from these blows and by the end of 1992 had returned to its earlier strategy of harassing the government forces' lines of communication to the southern towns. Except for a brief ceasefire during a period of international diplomacy aimed at ending the conflict, fighting continued throughout 1993, the government forces, backed by Libyan-piloted aircraft bombing, inflicting heavy casualties on the SPLA in a major offensive in August. Further major government attacks were launched in January 1994. Thousands of troops, armoured vehicles and guns were transported by barge up the Nile and thereafter along roads to the border towns through which the SPLA crossed into Sudan from assembly areas in Uganda and Zaire. These attacks achieved some local successes, two reasons being ammunition shortages and faction divisions within the SPLA, two breakaway factions signing a peace accord with Khartoum. These, however, fell out among themselves and in the internecine fighting involving the factions and the main SPLA several hundred more people were killed. Despite these difficulties, the SPLA's overall hold on many smaller towns, villages and the rural areas generally remained unbroken. A further government forces offensive in October was a clear failure. The SPLA, having received further supplies of light weapons and ammunition probably from Israel or the USA, was able to inflict defeats and heavy casualties on the government forces in both the Juba and Torit areas. In the east Mashar's breakaway faction resumed fighting against the government, first capturing an armoured column and then effecting a reconciliation with Garang and the SPLA in April 1995.

A new ceasefire was brokered by the former US president Carter in March 1995, but violations by both sides followed. Khartoum's acceptance of the ceasefire may only have been to impress the outside world at a time when usually reliable sources were reporting two mustard gas attacks on the SPLA. The gas, provided by Iraq, was dropped in canisters from aircraft, on both occasions wide of the target zone. The SPLA remained in control of much of the south. In the east, brokered by goodwill from Eritrea, whose government despite Khartoum's support still harboured resentment over Sudan's earlier aid for the ELF against the EPLF, a new co-ordinated Sudanese National Democratic Alliance (NDA), was formed from three groups. These agreed to form a military wing, National Alliance Forces (NAF), of Moslems opposed to the Khartoum government, to continue operations from Eritrea.

The ceasefire had provided the SPLA with an opportunity to regroup both in the south and in Uganda, and to prepare further attacks. In response, the fighting spilled over into Uganda as the NIF backed the Lord's Resistance Army (LRA), an anti-government resistance movement (see p. 177). The reinvigorated SPLA, under its new field commander, Oyay Deng Ajak, and backed by 130 mm field artillery from Uganda, mounted a campaign designed to pre-empt an expected Sudan army offensive in October 1995. The campaign brought the SPLA back to the Juba area. Ugandan personnel, it is thought, fired the howitzers and possibly provided other support while Ugandan units followed their own agenda against the LRA.

The SPLA's successes continued in 1996, once again placing southern towns under siege and occupying one on the Aswa river. They captured a few T-55 tanks, armoured vehicles, artillery pieces and mortar, and routed the Sudan government forces in the area. These, however, retaliated with an offensive, attempting to drive south. They were met with a renewed SPLA onslaught supported by Uganda. Khartoum's difficulties were compounded by an Eritrean supported NDA attack in the eastern Kassala area, and by a renewal of Ethiopian support for the SPLA, Addis Ababa resenting NIF support for Oromo secessionists.

The NDA and SPLA, although poorly co-ordinated, secured a number of successes in the first half of 1997. The NDA mounted two attacks, one in the north aimed at cutting the road and rail links to Port Sudan, and one in the east aimed at Damazine, the source of electric power for Khartoum. In the south one SPLA column occupied Yei, the second largest town, and other smaller towns. Another column advanced on Kaya in the Torit area, and Juba was under threat from three directions. The SPLA had recruited and trained some 15,000 new recruits. With aircraft chartered with Eritrean help, the SPLA was able to transport tanks and men across the Nile at will. The Khartoum government was reported to be reduced to the forcible recruitment of schoolboys who received a scanty 15 days' training, a plastic-covered page of the Koran to ward off infidel bullets and a key to unlock the gates of heaven should they be struck down. Defection of officers and soldiers to the rebels increased, but conflict between the insurgent factions also continued, with fighting between different groups now including six breakaway factions, the most important being Mashar's UDSF. The NIF offered a "peace charter", a move almost certainly intended to legitimize a return of Mashar's UDSF to the Khartoum government camp so that it could become a militia guarding Bentiu and the Upper Nile. In April 1997 a peace accord was signed in Khartoum between the NIF, the UDSF and the splinter factions of the SPLA. The accord was rejected by Garang who with the main SPLA continued vigorous campaigning in the south, threatening Juba; the NDA maintained its threat to Port Sudan.

In July 1997 the position was one in which effectively Sudan was divided into three. Both the NIF and the SPLA claimed that ultimately victory would be theirs, but although each had the capacity to win local successes neither had the capacity to achieve total victory. The important differences between the 1960s civil war and the 1980–90s conflict are that in the former the majority, but not all, of the insurgents sought total secession while in the latter a majority, but again not all, sought full autonomy, and that Turabi's NIF sees militant Islam as an international crusade, justifying attempts to assassinate the presidents of Egypt and Eritrea, bombings in New York and other wider terrorist activities.

While it does not seem that either side deliberately planned mass genocidal famine, the nature of the war produced this result. Khartoum would play down the seriousness of famine situations or just ignore them. Other contributing factors were the fact that the militias of both sides were unpaid, living by requisitioning or plain looting of settled areas or famine migrants, while the

SPLA's blockading of the southern towns was met by the army's creation of free-fire zones involving the prohibition of the growing of any crops which could provide concealment for insurgents. Both sides would deliberately obstruct famine relief in the interests of some local advantage with indifference to consequences. The total number of deaths from war, starvation and starvation-related disease from 1983 onwards can only be estimated to be at least 1,250,000.

Algeria 1992–7

Algeria's first war against the French saw the victory of the FLN, a nationalist movement divided into factions, in part a reflection of the FLN's lack of any ideology. Its bureaucratic and military leaders aimed to create a generally Western-patterned infrastructure. In this frame Islam became, under the 1976 constitution, the state religion but not the ruling authority. The FLN, however, continued to fall into faction feuding, its leading figures became corrupt, leading lavish lifestyles, and the country fell into serious economic decline. The government, despite a burst of vigorous leadership under Colonel Boumedienne between 1965 and 1978, after 1980 proved at a political level incapable of mediating the conflicts between interests, rural traditions of village self-government, ideology and unmodernized religion, and at a day-to-day level it seemed incapable of solving the country's problems – rapidly rising population and dissatisfaction over continuing and worsening poverty, highlighted by a drift to the towns. Strikes and riots gave warning of the troubles to come. Resentment turned popular feeling against concepts of a Western-patterned infrastructure and towards an Islamic state on the Iranian pattern. Fundamentalist groups formed and were indoctrinated in the mosques and Koranic schooling, their teachings harking back to the Algeria of Ottoman days before 1830. The violence that followed was, therefore, in many respects a second phase of an ongoing struggle begun in 1954: what was Algeria to be?

The killings began in 1992. They were the result of the decision by the government of President Chadli Benjedid, terrified by the sweeping success of the FIS, an umbrella organization of fundamentalist groups, in the first round of elections held in December 1991, not to hold the second round due early in 1992 at all, even though it had engaged in some gerrymandering of constituencies in its favour. Following this decision a state of emergency was declared, Chadli was forced to resign, and a High State Council was set up by the army which invited Boudiaf, one of the *neuf historiques* of 1954, to return from exile and become head of state. The FIS was banned, its leaders and

9,000 of its members placed in detention. The ban led to fragmentation and factions.

The insurgency opened with attacks on the security forces, barracks, police and gendarmerie posts, state institutions, political figures and intellectuals. Boudiaf himself was assassinated in June 1992. The methods were the same as those of the FLN in the war against the French – ear to ear throat slitting, disembowelling, castration and torture. As was to continue throughout the war, the attacks were generally medium-scale in size, groups ranging from 30 to 150 men who would split up and disappear after their attack had taken place. The security forces, as always in such circumstances, found few opportunities to bring a group into battle. The increasing number of these attacks and killings very quickly amounted to civil war. In areas terrorized by these activities women were forced into full Moslem concealment robing and kept largely in their homes and many hundreds, including young girls who refused to conform, were killed off, all in the name of applying the precepts of pure Islam. Government forces replied with equal ferocity, their operations repeating the methods of the French security forces – pursuit groups modelled on Challe's *commandos de chasse* and the extensive use of helicopters. These, in turn, achieved small-scale successes, 20 to 40 rebels being hunted down and killed in a number of operations. Prisoners were only rarely taken. Occasionally large-scale cordon and search operations would yield larger numbers of suspects, many hundreds being detained without trial.

In June 1992 the FIS turned its attention to foreigners, a number being killed, some painfully, obliging foreign governments to advise their nationals to leave Algeria. Later in 1992 the most powerful of the fundamentalist groups, the *Groupe Islamique Armée* (GIA), ordered all foreigners to leave Algeria on pain of death. In February 1993 the FIS declared the conflict to be a holy war against the infidel state and its fighters, *mujahideen*, or holy warriors. Neither side in the conflict was totally united. The GIA was challenged by the *Armée Islamique du Salut* (AIS), a challenge adding numbers to the death totals. Within the regime factions and clans jostled for power and authority.

In 1994 the violence reached new heights, over 300 people, including 60 soldiers, being killed in one week in January. The newly appointed head of state, Zeroual, proved no more capable of ending the violence than his predecessors. The next year, 1995, saw a car bomb attack on a police headquarters in which 45 people were killed. Shortly afterwards government helicopter gunships destroyed a village alleged to be sheltering rebels, killing over 150 people. In March the government claimed that troops under General Bey killed over 600 GIA members in a large-scale ambush at Ain Defla, near Blida; it would appear that the GIA had been attempting to follow the pattern of the 1955 FLN Soummam Valley conference but was taken by surprise. The infrastructure of the state suffered increasingly with telephone poles hacked down, schools including girls or those teaching any subject in French burnt down, houses, farms and forests destroyed and vehicles booby-trapped. The government raised a new force of local militias to supplement the 125,000-strong army gendarmerie and other security units, and was able to draw on substantial French financial and technical military support.

The conflict again spilled over into France where fundamentalists among the 900,000 Algerians living in France, in revenge for the French aid to the government, mounted several bomb attacks in Paris. A project in December 1994 to hijack an airliner and crash it in the centre of Paris was thwarted by French security forces who captured the aircraft at Marseilles.

The events of 1996 and early 1997 suggested several new developments. The first was mounting evidence of abuses of power by the government forces, with captives suffering blow-torching on the chest and genitals during interrogation. Some evidence suggested that certain local massacres might have been the work of government forces, either as recrimination or as provocation, or as an attempt, in disguise, to secure world opinion, rather than being the work of fundamentalists. Another issue was that the Algerian army, based largely on conscripts, included some sympathizers with the fundamentalists; these aided, or simply passed on intelligence, to the insurgent groups and officers may well have been afraid of ordering them into the field. Criminal gangs masquerading as fundamentalist groups appeared to worsen the situation. The fundamentalists themselves remained fragmented – even the GIA lacked a unified command structure though groups communicated with each other. Names of leaders – Mansouri Melini, its founder, who was executed in 1993, Djamel Zitouni, Farid Hamani and Antar Zouabri – occasionally appeared. The threats to kill foreigners were extended to Saharan oilfield personnel. The number of incidents of bombings and massacres which had fallen slightly in early 1996 rose again. Among the most horrific was the killing of the French Archbishop of Oran who had been a supporter of the FLN in the 1950s and 1960s. GIA leaders claimed the massacres were entirely justified – women, children and the aged living in areas under the authority of Algiers had surrendered to the government and were therefore enemies, in the eyes of God deserving of death. Any innocent among them could be considered a martyr, their soul having been saved from corruption.

To try and secure a legitimacy and marginalize the fundamentalists the government held an election in June 1997, predictably winning a majority but amid numerous allegations of malpractices. The result failed to secure any respite from the daily pattern of bombings and killings. GIA insurgents used armoured lorries to crash through village road blocks before massacring the inhabitants. Over 500 people were killed by insurgents in the first six weeks after the election, mostly in the Algiers–Blida area. Estimates suggest that since the civil war began at least 80,000 people had been killed by one side or the other by July 1997.

Zimbabwe 1980–8

The elections provided for in the December 1979 ceasefire agreement were held in the following year, amid sharpening tension between supporters of Mugabe's largely Shona ZANU party and its rival, Nkomo's Ndebele-based ZAPU. ZANU emerged as the winner but in an effort to secure national unity Mugabe gave ministerial posts to Nkomo and three other ZAPU leaders.

The atmosphere, however, remained uncertain and unstable. Mugabe distrusted some of the white political figures of the former regime whom he suspected of retaining contacts with South Africa. He was also apprehensive over power-sharing with ZAPU, which had affinities with the Zulu in South Africa, and he personally found it difficult to work with Nkomo. Above all he was concerned that Zimbabwe should not follow Angola and Mozambique into protracted general civil war. At the same time ZAPU felt that it had been denied its fair share of the rewards of victory, and additionally, Ndebele land was suffering severely from land shortage and drought.

Friction began within the process of the integration of the insurgent forces into the new Zimbabwean army.[7] Violence spread to Bulawayo and the Ndebele rural areas in August and September 1980, at which point the Mugabe government deployed Shona units of the army and extra police. By the end of the year over 60 people had been killed, mostly in Bulawayo. The violence worsened in 1981 with clashes in Bulawayo and Gwelo, and ZIPRA insurgents who had not given up their weapons at the ceasefire emerged from the bush. While no definite connection between the ZAPU party as a whole and the insurgents was ever established, there is no doubt that many local ZAPU officials and former ZIPRA personnel were involved. The government held ZAPU to blame, and alleged covert South African support. In response to the violence the regime formed what was in effect a "small private political army", the 5th Brigade, all ZANU Shona trained by North Koreans and wearing a distinctive red beret, for the purpose of asserting its control against what it referred to as "dissidents". The 5th Brigade only appeared on public parade once and was little publicized. It was referred to as the *gukurahundi* in Shona, a word whose usual meaning was the separation of wheat from chaff.

In 1982, after several open political differences, Mugabe dismissed Nkomo and the ZAPU ministers, alleging they were involved in a conspiracy. Caches of arms were discovered, training camps were alleged to have been found, and a number of white and Ndebele officers, including General Lookout Masuku, the former ZIPRA commander, were arrested. Ndebele soldiers deserted from the new army and in a spectacular raid on Thornhill airfield 13 fighters of the country's new air force were destroyed. In June the government mounted the first of a series of operations involving curfews, control of movement, the closure of shops and cordons and searches in Ndebeleland, but the violence continued with at the end of the year insurgent attacks on buses, cars and trains.

The next year, 1983, saw a few insurgent attacks on white farms, with farmers and their families being brutally killed. In response the 5th Brigade sweeps became the more brutal. They would generally arrive in lightly armoured trucks in an area with a list of wanted men, known ZAPU officials, whom, together with young men of military age, they would arrest. If they felt that the area was hostile, some or all of those arrested would be shot immediately, the villagers being ordered to prepare communal graves. People in an area would be ordered to a rally where they would be obliged to chant ZANU slogans for several hours. Any appearing to lack enthusiasm would be beaten up or removed for subsequent interrogation under torture. Only a few survived for eventual release from prison. Where specific insurgent units in the bush could be identified and located, parachute troops, using the former Rhodesian army fire-force tactics, were dropped.

In March 1983 Nkomo fled to Britain, though he returned to Zimbabwe later in the year. The insurgency continued throughout 1983 and 1984; the country's general election in 1985 was accompanied by riots, assassinations, street clashes in Bulawayo and harassment of ZAPU candidates. After the election, in which ZAPU lost heavily, the regime turned to a new strategy, of carrot and goad, to last for two years. Talks about unity were opened and on occasions detainees released; at the same time sweeps and mass arrests would also be launched to demonstrate the strength of the regime. The 5th Brigade was broken up, its work accomplished. Finally in December 1987, after an especially bloody massacre in the previous month, the two parties agreed to unite; new power-sharing arrangements followed. A little later an amnesty was announced, the offer being taken up by the majority of the Ndebeleland bush insurgents.

The total number of dead in this conflict is impossible to ascertain. A minimum of 3,000 seems certain, though church leaders have put forward at least 7,000. The price paid for national unity, however, was infinitely less than that in Angola and Mozambique.

Uganda 1980–8

Uganda's troubles in its first 20 years of independence were primarily domestic, or the products of Amin's aggressive ambitions. The country's next series of problems, of which the refugees in the 1960s were a forewarning, were to extend the consequences of Uganda's singular strategic situation. The country lies astride the headwaters of the Nile and adjoins territories torn by civil conflicts that carried implications for Uganda's own stability, sometimes through cross-border ethnic linkages, sometimes for wider political or religious reasons.

The fall of Amin did not bring political normality.[8] The presence of Tanzanian troops working to a Tanzanian agenda brought about the downfall of Lule, the first post-Amin president; a second, Binaisa, was removed by the military. A military commission then paved the way for the return, supported by the north, of the former president, Obote, who won an election in December 1980. The country nevertheless remained unstable with the army looting and pillaging, fighting over famine relief convoys in Karamoja, residual resistance from armed former soldiers of Amin's army in the northwest and an anti-Obote guerrilla campaign striking at military posts and police posts. The leading role in this campaign was taken by a group called the Peoples Resistance Army, led by Museveni and at the outset operating in six groups in the Luwero district of Buganda. The groups quickly gained followers, over 4,000 by March 1981. They were able to mount 300-strong attacks on local army barracks but were unable to break out more widely, their operations being checked by Tanzanian troops still in the country. The regime's largely Acholi UNLA army, recruited from the urban unemployed, indisciplined and ill-trained, became increasingly repressive as the pressures upon it mounted. The anarchy worsened in 1983; in 1984 a revived and expanded Museveni-led National Resistance Army (NRA) now appeared. It included some 1,500 Rwanda refugees, a number of young men from Toro as well as a large number of Buganda, both areas traditionally hostile to Obote, and some 3,000 juvenile or child soldiers, some under 12 and including a number of girls, mostly orphans whose parents were killed in the Obote era. Overall, this new NRA was in effect a coalition of the south, hostile to the northerner Obote. It was equipped with a small number of rifles and grenade launchers supplied by Libya. The NRA opened increasingly effective operations in the southwest of the country. Obote was overthrown in a military coup in July, but the policies of the Acholi coup leaders, General Tito Okello and Colonel Basileo Okello, were not acceptable to the NRA. Following mediation by the president of Kenya, political agreement between the Okellos and the NRA was negotiated but this soon afterwards collapsed. The NRA resumed its campaigning against the UNLA in a conflict that was partly ethnic, Okello's Acholi fighting to protect their homes. Museveni soon cleared the southwest and used profits from coffee sales to finance further operations. His army was now over 9,000 strong organized in 1,000-men battalions, well equipped with weaponry captured in successful attacks on barracks at Masindi and Kabamba. After heavy fighting Museveni's NRA entered Kampala in January 1986, but over two years more of fighting were to follow, the chief sufferers being the civilian population. The NRA pursued and scattered the UNLA, who, after sacking Kampala had fled northward, pillaging and looting as they went. They were finally destroyed after a three-day battle involving heavy artillery near Gulu in March 1986. Other groups, the most dangerous being a "Uganda People's Democratic Army" (UPDA) opposed to Museveni had also to be contained; in 1987 a new threat, in the form of a 6,000-strong militant religious sect armed mostly with spears, the Holy Spirit Movement, appeared, to be defeated in a bloody encounter, over a thousand being killed by the NRA. Early 1988 saw occasional insurgent raids and ambushes but by the end of the year Museveni had come to terms with the UPDA and secured control over almost all of the country. His government estimated that at least 800,000 people had been killed in the years 1970–86.

Museveni had made a great appeal for national unity, portraying both Obote and the Okellos as a return to northern domination. Generally the discipline of his NRA supported this, though there had been excesses in the NRA's operations against the former Amin soldiers in the northwest and also in the final 1986–7 operations. Some of the excesses may have been the work of other factions, two of which were allied with the NRA. Museveni's appreciation of the need for discipline stemmed from his experience as Defence Minister under Binaisa, and his own beliefs in a politicized national army and people's militia.

When in power Museveni, faced with the problems arising from Uganda's strategic situation, sought to secure his position through the creation of friendly regimes on his borders, a policy much influenced by refugee problems and leading him into involvements, sometimes willingly, sometimes perforce, in the internal affairs of others. The consequences in the case of Sudan have already been outlined; other consequences in respect of Rwanda, Burundi and Zaire follow. But, as the reverse side of the coin, dissident movements in neighbouring countries came to support anti-Museveni movements. As already noted, Sudan, incensed by Museveni's support for the anti-Moslem fundamentalist insurgency in the south, in 1996 backed the extreme Christian group, the 1,000 strong Lord's Resistance Army, in the hope of destabilizing Museveni, killing more civilians than Ugandan soldiers and abducting hundreds of children. A West Bank Nile Front rebel group based in Zaire was also active in north Uganda. In mid-1997 dispossessed Hutu from both Rwanda and Burundi and escapees from Mobutu's defeated army were operating with Ugandan dissidents in a movement named the Allied Democratic Forces National Army for Liberation of Uganda in western Uganda; these required a 3,000-strong NRA military presence to contain them. Sudan-based rebels were continuing to harass areas in north Uganda, the LRA drawing on former UNLA personnel and developing terror tactics of mutilation and child abuse.

Somalia 1987–97

Unlike other African states with frontiers drawn in the last years of the nineteenth century, the people living in the republic of Somalia possessed a common language, religion and culture. The bitterness and ferocity of the civil war into which the Somali state collapsed in 1988–9 is therefore all the more difficult to explain. Neither the traditional land and natural resources rivalries with their concomitant structural instability between the major clans, the Samaal group of Dir, Darod, Isaq and Hawiyah, and the Saab group of Rahanweyn and Digil, and all their sub-clans that form Somalia, nor any "first image" generalization of an innate turbulence of character, nor legacies from the partitions of Somalia in the colonial era, are sufficient, though all set the stage for factional warlordism. Weaponry was available in quantity, from old Soviet and recent massive US military aid, in local barracks all over the country.

The motivation of the actors was set off in the years following the disastrous Ogaden war, from which the country's president, Barré, a member of the Marehan sub-clan of the Darod, emerged with much diminished legitimacy. To try and secure himself Barré had for some time previously manipulated clan politics in divide and rule actions, some involving the collective killings of professional men of opposing clans, most notably the northern Isaq against whom he had a personal family vendetta. Isaq soldiers in reprisal and together with activists from the Mijerteen sub-clan of the Darod, attempted a coup against Barré in 1978. The attempt failed and its leader fled to Britain where he and his followers formed a resistance group, the Somali National Movement (SNM), which led an uprising. The Barré government then launched punitive air and artillery strikes against the northern Isaq civilian population.

Barré's style of government inevitably produced the destruction of the state as rival generals proceeded to recruit and arm men from their own clans. Somali society, already based on the clan and sub-clan social network divisions, now found these divisions heavily armed, with warlords heading militias replacing clan elders and councils, the militias being funded from profits in the local qat drug trade.

Supported by Ethiopia, the SNM continued a campaign of minor guerrilla attacks, sometimes supported by T-54 tanks, against the government in the early 1980s. Another smaller group in the east, the Democratic Front for the Salvation of Somalia (SSDF), of Darod Mijerteen, also opened small-scale insurgency from 1981 but achieved little due to internal divisions. The fighting included mining, the slaughter of opponents' stock and the poisoning of wells.

In 1987 the conflict sharpened to rebellion when the SNM launched effective attacks, twice cutting off Hargeisa and the links to Djibouti, and successfully engaging in a pitched battle with government forces using tanks near Burao. The following year saw heavy fighting in the north. The claims and counter-claims are confusing but it would appear the SNM briefly occupied all the northern towns before being bombed, shelled and eventually, after extreme brutality by the government forces, driven out. The government forces were led by Barré's son-in-law, General Mohamed Siad Hersi "Morgan". Some Somali airmen refused to fly against their own people; they were replaced by mercenaries from South Africa and Zimbabwe using aircraft loaned by Arab states. Some 50,000 people were killed and several hundred thousand refugees made homeless in the devastated towns. The SNM then reverted to rural guerrilla fighting.

The next two years, 1989 and 1990, saw the rapid erosion of Barré's authority. The SNM continued to harass and virtually control all the routes to the northern towns, though they took casualties from the extensive minefields laid by General Morgan. In the centre of the country the newly formed United Somali Congress (USC) under the formidable Italian-trained General Mohamed Aideed, a member of the Habr Gedir sub-clan of the Hawiyah, began to threaten Mogadishu, entering the suburbs. In the south a Somali Patriotic Movement (SPM) of Ogaden Darod was also in revolt. The country was in anarchy, the capital terrorized by gangs with guns. Barré unwisely gave out quantities of weapons to men he thought he could trust.

In January 1991 Barré fled into exile, to return in an attempt to retake Mogadishu three months later. This attempt was foiled by Aideed in a brief but destructive campaign. Aideed apparently received some aid from South Africa, probably non-governmental. While these operations were in progress a leading figure in another Hawiyah sub-clan, the Abgal, Ali Mahdi, proclaimed himself as interim USC president with a former Barré political leader as prime minister. This was unacceptable to Aideed and an inter-Hawiyah sub-clan fight broke out to last between December 1991 and March 1992, devastating Mogadishu. The chaos worsened in 1992 when Barré's forces, allegedly aided by Italy, made two attempts to return, one in April and one in

September. After the defeat of the first at the battle of Afgoi, the aged Barré departed into exile, but his son-in-law Morgan and Darod Marehan clansmen fought on in the Jubaland south around Kismayu until early 1993, at times in violent conflict with the SPM now led by Colonel Jess and linked with Aideed's USC.

By the end of 1992 all six major factions were in action, with sometimes elements of one in loose partnerships, for one limited purpose, with another to attack a third or one or other of the several lesser local clan or sub-clan factions. The fighting and famine conditions were estimated to have already killed 350,000. The Aideed United Somali Congress/Somali National Alliance which included the USC, a faction of the SPM, a faction of the SDM and the non-Darod southern Somali National Movement could field between 5,000 and 10,000 men. It certainly possessed light weapons and appears also to have acquired some field and anti-aircraft artillery and light armoured vehicles. Jess's majority SPM, its southern ally, was a few hundred men strong with a handful of armoured vehicles and artillery pieces. Their main opponent in the south was Morgan's Somali National Front (SNF) with rather greater numbers of men and artillery. In the centre Ali Mahdi's USC fielded some 3,000 to 4,000 men with again, a few armoured vehicles. Further north along the coast, the SSDF, now reinvigorated and led by General Abshir Musa, was of approximately similar strength and equipment. The most powerful of the factions on paper, though its 6,000-strong men, armour and artillery was spread among several local militias, was the northern SNM, though already internal sub-clan frictions were appearing. Several factions, most notably Aideed's USC, included juvenile and child soldiers. None of the factions at this stage sought a permanent break-up of the Somali state – all sought to preserve local resources for their own use, and if feasible to secure control of the whole.[9] Later, as the conflicts worsened, the Isaq-dominated north was to declare independence in May 1991, but this may only have been a distancing rather than a permanent move.

The violence of the fighting in the Mogadishu area and the failure of several attempts to broker a peaceful solution eventually led to international military intervention, initially in the form of UNOSOM I, a largely Pakistani military force intended to escort food relief convoys which arrived in August 1992. Inadequate in size, it was increased to over 4,500 but all their efforts were thwarted by the faction warlords, in particular Aideed. In December the UN authorized intervention without consent in the form of the Unified Task Force (UNITAF) under American command and eventually to total, at the height of its deployment, 37,000 troops from 21 nations. These were posted out to nine Humanitarian Relief Sectors in convoys escorted by armoured vehicles. The intention was that as soon as the force had secured order sufficient for humanitarian work, UNITAF would subsume to a projected

32,000-strong UNOSOM II, which after some delay took place in May 1993. The lead for this force was 28,000 American marines, the American public being shocked by television pictures of the fighting and famine but at the same time convinced of their military invincibility following the Gulf War. The US president, Bush, also hoped for election advantage. It was never made clear whether the force was simply for humanitarian relief or to impose a settlement, and the American force commander, General Robert Johnson, was ill-chosen. The UN mandate envisaged disarmament of the factions, by force if necessary; the Americans were at the outset unwilling to implement disarmament, fearing casualties at the hands of the "technicals" as the faction fighters' light lorries with heavy machine-guns mounted on them were described. In the meantime Aideed united several factions in a coalition, Somali National Alliance (SNA), with his USC.

On 9 December 1992 the US marines made a theatrical beach landing at Mogadishu, the object of much sardonic comment, and proceeded to occupy the airfields. Immediate reinforcements, 10,000 strong, were flown in from the USA together with a French Foreign Legion unit from Djibouti; other units were deployed to the Kismayu area. Initially this mass of force secured a respite, the USC/SNA factions agreeing not to oppose it. In the south the US forces at the outset opposed Morgan's SNF in favour of Aideed's ally Jess, but they soon changed policy to one of supporting Morgan against Aideed, to the latter's disgust. The apparent initial success of the force was followed by the withdrawal of part of the US contingent, UNITAF thereby becoming UNOSOM II under the command of a Turkish general, Bir, its numbers totally inadequate for any peace enforcement by disarmament, even though 17,000 American troops also remained in the country but not as part of the UNOSOM force.

While the UN force succeeded in saving a number of lives by the provision of food it was, however, soon to become a disaster, the prime causes being the ambiguity of its mission coupled with the failure of American intelligence accurately to evaluate the Somali scene. Part of the United States' own Operation *Restore Hope*'s hidden agenda was the elimination of Aideed, long suspected of pro-Soviet sympathies, and in operations aimed at disarming factions and capturing their stocks, Aideed's faction was particularly targeted. Somalis of several factions accordingly began to view UNOSOM II as one more faction, an invader, and faction leaders' promises to disarm became meaningless. The two USC groups reconciled their differences to present a common front while Aideed's financier, Ato, profited vastly from the building of camps for the UN troops. Stoning of the UN force soon turned to sniping, followed by shelling of UN compounds and ambushing of convoys. In June Aideed took advantage of the US partial withdrawal to attack a Pakistani patrol engaged in disarmament work, killing 24 and mutilating their corpses.

Some UN soldiers from the Italian, Belgian and Canadian contingents committed atrocities in reprisal. In total four UN civilians and 151 soldiers were killed in this period.

Most contributing countries directed their troops to remain neutral in the faction fighting. A Belgian unit moved from a peacekeeping to a peace-enforcing area found itself unable to cope; one reason for the death of the Pakistanis was the hesitation of forces from other countries over intervening to save them. Both these events stemmed ultimately from the lack of clear mission definition. A little later four American servicemen were killed in an ambush.

The different contingents began to pursue their own paths. The Pakistanis, mauled, adopted a bunker mentality so giving Aideed a free hand in their area of Mogadishu. The Italians opened contacts with Aideed to which the American government tacitly acquiesced – almost certainly because they were at the time seeking Italian airfields for use for operations in Bosnia. The Belgians also tended to pursue their own interests. In a series of abortive operations, US forces, authorized by the UN Secretary-General following the death of the Pakistanis, tried to capture Aideed. In one attempt in October 1993 a US Delta special forces unit using AC-130 aircraft armed with cannons, helicopters and 105 mm guns was trapped, losing two helicopters and 18 soldiers, the corpse of one being dragged through the streets. The American reaction to the trapping of their force was an indiscriminate machine-gun and cannon helicopter strike on the area in which several hundred people were killed. The event represented a serious reverse for UNOSOM II, a reverse followed three days later by a mortar-attack on Mogadishu airport in which 13 American soldiers were injured. The American preference for operations conducted from the air rather than on the ground led to friction, the Italians in particular protesting against the bloody attack on what was assumed to be – but probably was not – a USC/SNA headquarters in July. The Italians were then moved out of Mogadishu. The only fully successful disarmament operations were those carried out, with considerable tact and skill, by an Australian battalion in the Baidoa region.

American public opinion was not capable of accepting their forces' death rate and US troops were withdrawn by March 1994. The reduced UNOSOM force abandoned the search for Aideed but was incapable of any effective action. In November the UN voted for its withdrawal, effected over beaches guarded by US and Italian marines in February 1994. The country and its capital were left to the rival factions. Amid renewed clan fighting a split between Aideed and his backer Ato occurred, bringing further fighting to Mogadishu. A grouping of pro-Aideed factions proclaimed him president in June 1995, but in August 1996 Aideed, who faced internal dissension within his own USC faction, died following injuries received in fighting against Ali

Mahdi; his son Hussein Aideed continued to lead the faction. In the north, small rebel factions, largely from the Gahardji clan but including some Isaq opposed to the north's declaration of independence, opened insurgency in late 1994, developing into more serious fighting in 1995 and 1996. In 1997 there was fighting in southwest Somalia where Ethiopia was supporting local factions opposed to the younger Aideed, and the Bay-Bakool region where a new faction, the Rahanweyn Resistance Army (RRA) had emerged.

By mid-1997 no agreement had been reached between the faction war-lords, now over 25 in total, and both the country and its capital remained in a state of anarchy, with exchanges of small-arms and artillery fire in several areas, most notably the capital Mogadishu. A conservative estimate puts a total of 250,000 deaths as a result of the fighting in the period 1991–7.

Burundi and Rwanda 1988–97

The ethnic tensions in Burundi and Rwanda were in the 1980s and 1990s to flare into new dimensions of genocidal horror only equalled in this century by the Nazi Holocaust of European Jews or the butchery of Pol Pot in Cambodia. Later, extension of the conflict into the neighbouring state of Zaire was to bring about the expulsion of President Mobutu in 1997.

The start of the decade was deceptive. It had seemed that in Rwanda the 1973 military coup of General Juvenal Habanyirama had opened a new, non-conflictual style of politics. The government was largely Hutu, mostly from the north; politics, in so far as they were tolerated at all, were conducted between Hutu factions within the government and southern Hutus allied with moderate Tutsis. In Burundi it had also seemed that the 1976 overthrow of the Micombero regime and the limited reforms of the regime's successor, that of Colonel Jean-Baptiste Bagaza, had suggested a promise of new eras of compromise and consensus. Not unreasonably, as it appeared, the French government sold weaponry to both governments. While Mobutu in Kinshasa was proven yearly to be more corrupt and incompetent, he continued to be regarded by the West as a solid Cold War ally whose removal would be likely to allow in a regime sympathetic to Moscow. The French again funded and trained certain key units of Mobutu's army, and as already noted helped to preserve the regime in 1977 and 1978.

Warnings that the basic problems were in fact still unresolved were evident in the animosities occasioned by the refugee problems. Some 45,000 mostly Tutsi refugees from the wars of the 1960s were, after persecution, forced to return to Rwanda from Uganda in the mid-1980s. In 1987 Bagaza was overthrown in a military coup by Major Pierre Buyoya, whose reconstituted administration continued to reflect Tutsi domination. Renewed violence in consequence erupted in August 1988 in northern towns. Hutu, alleging Tutsi persecution, massacred several hundred Tutsi. The regime's response was swift and savage, the Tutsi-dominated army killing an estimated 20,000 Hutu and forcing some 100,000 refugees to flee into Rwanda and Zaire. In tense conditions complicated by several unsuccessful coup attempts and a small-scale Hutu uprising at the end of 1991 in which some 500 people died, Buyoya then introduced a series of reforms. These permitted an ethnic parity "shared power" system, and admitted Hutus into politics and the government. In elections in June 1993 a Hutu, Melchior Ndadye, was elected president but in October 1993 he was murdered by Tutsi soldiers whose leader was later arrested. At the same time ferocious ethnic violence reopened. Tutsis started mass killings of Hutus near the Rwanda border. Hutus killed several hundred Tutsis east of Bujumbura; in the north Hutus burnt a hundred women and children alive in one town, killing 400 in another. A death total of 150,000 is estimated for this post-presidential assassination period. Again, hundreds of thousands of refugees fled, hundreds dying from malnutrition or disease. Following a decision that the legislature could choose the president, another Hutu, Cyprien Ntaryamina, was elected in January 1994.

Meanwhile in Rwanda, suffering severely from population pressure, crop disease and the slump in world coffee prices, an even worse situation was developing, a renewed Tutsi challenge to the Habyarimana, northern Hutu-dominated government. In October 1990 the Rwandese Patriotic Front (RPF – referred to in French as the *Front Patriotique Rwandais* (FPR) and locally as the *Inkotanyi*), a largely Tutsi organization that had formed in Uganda, launched a 10,000-strong insurgent force across the northern border, occupying several towns. President Obote had opposed Rwandans living in Uganda and countenanced their harassment to the extent of some 100 dead in 1982. His successor, Museveni, had links, including long-standing friendships, with the future RPF commanders Fred Rwigyema and Paul Kagame. Without necessarily conniving at the assault the Ugandan government appears to have turned a blind eye towards the preparations; it may also have assessed that any move to prevent it would be dangerous for Uganda. The force included a number of disaffected Ugandan soldiers and was initially led by General Rwigyema who had been a Ugandan deputy defence minister. Its equipment included some light artillery and a few BM-21 multiple rocket launchers, but the bulk of the weaponry was limited to machine-guns, mortars and grenade rocket launchers.

Belgium and France sent troops to Rwanda to protect expatriates, but they were not committed against the RPF. French Foreign Legion parachute troops guarded the airport against which some sort of fake attack was launched, the noisy pyrotechnics being reported by the French as justification for their presence. In fact that presence had more to do with French suspicions that anglophone Africa, backed by the United States and in the person of Museveni, was trying to take over a francophone land.

A Zairean contingent assisted Habyarimana's 5,000-strong army, equipped with field guns, Panhard armoured cars and a few helicopters, in defeating the RPF insurgents and pushing them back into Uganda, General Rwigyema being killed in action. From there the RPF turned to guerrilla warfare and cross-border raids; a line-up began to emerge of French and Zairean support for the Habyarimana Hutu regime against the support of Uganda's President Museveni for the Tutsi cause, at this stage still only covertly opposed to the Mobutu regime in Zaire.

Low-intensity guerrilla warfare with occasional daring RPF raids continued for the rest of 1990 and 1991. The Rwanda army was stiffened with French weaponry and assisted by French officers experienced in counter-insurgency. At local levels RPF raids aroused small-scale reprisal massacres, the numbers of victims ranging from a dozen to 60. In July 1992 a ceasefire was agreed. The ceasefire was to be monitored by a military observer group from several African countries, make provision for a neutral zone and start an integration of the RPF with the Rwandan army. The ceasefire soon broke down with serious violence in February 1993 when the RPF made a ruthless but successful raid threatening the capital, Kigali. Over a million refugees fled to Tanzania or Uganda. New ceasefire arrangements, this time to be monitored by a UN observer mission (the UN Observer Mission Uganda–Rwanda (UNOMUR) consisted of 105 observers and officials), were negotiated. These provided a temporary relief, culminating in the Arusha Accords peace agreement of August 1993 signed by Habyarimana and the RPF leader Colonel Alexis Kanyarengwa. The RPF was permitted training and logistic bases both in Rwanda and in Uganda and Zaire. This dangerous arrangement in effect provided Rwanda with two armies – the government army commanded by the hardline General Bizimana and the RPF army under General Paul Kagame. In October 1993 a further UN Assistance Mission for Rwanda (UNAMIR) was approved and over 2,000 troops deployed, the largest contingents coming from Bangladesh, Belgium and Ghana.

The settlement fell apart on 6 April 1994 when an aircraft carrying both President Habyarimana of Rwanda and President Ntaryamina of Burundi, returning from further peace negotiations in Tanzania, was shot down at Kigali, both presidents being killed. The target was undoubtedly Habyarimana rather than Ntaryamina. The missile used was of Soviet manufacture supplied by the French who had captured it in Iraq. The shooting down was almost certainly the work of hardline Hutu members of the presidential guard resentful of the concessions made to the RPF, though wild rumours suggested the RPF or even the French. The event sparked off one of the most frenzied manifestations of "epidemic of the mind" of the twentieth century. Both sides were locked into their history and new myths of their own recent creation. To the regime, the RPF were evil exiles stirring up a minority within the population that they, the regime, had succeeded in pacifying and satisfying. To the RPF the regime had a usurped authority which it had misused and abused so deserving destruction.

Hutu hardliners in the Rwanda military, notably Colonel Théoneste Bagosora and General Augustin Bizimana, became an effective ruling elite that carefully organized and directed the genocide that followed. The Kigali urban Hutu turned on the Tutsi, and also on moderate Hutu, whom they immediately blamed for Habyarimana's murder. The presidential guard killed the prime minister and her Belgian personal guard before hacking scores to death. The government radio and press urged on the "destruction of opponents", a code term for mass killing which rapidly became nationwide. The aim was quite simply to exterminate the entire Tutsi people.[10] The principal executioners were the unpaid, over-expanded and untrained 50,000-strong Rwanda government army, the gendarmerie and the 30,000 or so *interahamwe* Hutu militia, raised by Habyarimana in 1992; in some towns the unemployed poor joined in. Often Hutus were forced under pain of death to murder Tutsis or other Hutu with whom they had been friendly neighbours. The killings were generally brutal, effected by matchet slashing, mutilation or slow dismemberment, usually of the reproductive organs, and the burning of houses and compounds, together with their inhabitants. Peasants were cajoled into the work of killing by local activists who mixed a rhetoric of a need to purge an area of enemies of the people with exculpatory euphemisms such as "bush clearing". New frontiers were to be created by ethnic cleansing. By the end of July an estimated 800,000 people – men, women, children, babies, mostly Tutsi but also some Hutu unwilling to join in the massacring – had been killed.

The RPF began to move in from its northern bases in mid-April. It had acquired funds from exiles and weapons from friends in Uganda, the world arms traders and supplies coming from the collapsed Soviet Union. Its strength was well over 20,000. The two armies met in a war largely of grenades, mortars and small arms. Only in the Kigali area did the government forces fight with any resolution. The massacres and fighting came effectively to an end in July when Kigali fell to the RPF. The success, accompanied by some retributive genocidal carnage, was followed by RPF advances on two axes to the south and to the west. By 18 July the RPF was in control of most of the country and the Hutu government had fled. However, some 25,000 Rwanda Hutu government troops, gendarmerie and *interahamwe* had fled with their weapons and their command structure into Zaire where they deliberately concealed themselves in the refugee camps across the border.

The Belgians quickly withdrew their contingent from UNAMIR. The French sought, in vain, for an "international police force" and were generally regarded as having provided covert support for the Hutu government. The key to the French government's attitude appears to lie in the Sudan. It was again argued in Paris that the United States was supporting Museveni as a bastion against Islamic fundamentalism, this support, including acquiescence in alleged Museveni designs on francophone lands, was unacceptable to France. Ordered not to intervene, French troops were frequent spectators at scenes of massacre.

As the Rwanda government began to collapse, French troops, secured by a UN resolution, were ordered to occupy the western town of Cyangugu to provide a safe zone for refugees; other French detachments secured Tutsi communities under threat elsewhere. The refugee problem, now one of Hutu fleeing from the RPF, overwhelmed relief agencies by its size – a million wretched, sick and terrified people streaming into Zaire, with another million fleeing into Tanzania, Uganda and Burundi.

By the time the new RPF government, headed by a Hutu but with real power in the hands of Kagame, had installed itself in Kigali, the country had been devastated and looted. Thousands of its women were pregnant following rape; 30 per cent of the population were living in exile while those remaining in Rwanda were in a state of collective shock. Tutsis who had lived in exile abroad returned to grab Hutu land and property, usually vacated but, if not, then seized at the point of a machete. The French deployed into Zaire (in hired Russian aircraft), their main concern being the Goma refugee camp. Cholera then broke out in the Zaire refugee camps killing 30,000, and French troops with large bulldozers buried the dead in mass graves.

The French then withdrew, as a stronger UN force, UNAMIR II, was despatched, comprised of units drawn from a number of African countries with technological and medical units from Britain and Canada. The United States provided a separate humanitarian relief force. A certain amount of medical, food and water supply and transport repair work was accomplished but some of the units were particularly cautious in their involvement and overall the force achieved only limited initial success.

The inability of a peacekeeping force to keep peace when one or both sides do not want peace was highlighted in April 1995 by attacks upon the 200,000 Hutu refugees who had sought safety in camps under UN protection in Rwanda. Within the camps, inevitably, were a large number of former *interahamwe*. The RPF government requested the UN to return these refugees home, a request followed by the surrounding of the camps by RPF troops who brushed the UN protection soldiers aside and began a clearance of the camps. In one camp near the Burundi border *interahamwe* forced ordinary Hutu to try and break through the RPF troop cordon as a human shield for themselves, slashing with machetes those that refused. The RPF troops replied with machine-gun fire and grenades launched against those that had succeeded in rushing the cordon – 2,000 dead remains the lowest estimate.

Despite the international revulsion, or more likely because of the absence of any effective international intervention, the ethnic war between Tutsi and Hutu continued in both countries and increasingly in Zaire in 1995 and 1996. Tutsi soldiers massacred Hutu at a Rwanda camp early in 1995 and elsewhere Hutu "disappeared". In Burundi, Ntaryamina's successor, Sylvestre Ntibantunganya, a Hutu, appealed for ethnic reconciliation but proved unable to control, or secure international help to control, covert small-scale ethnic warfare. The 18,000-strong largely Tutsi Burundi army, funded on heroin and gold smuggling operations, massacred 250 Hutus in October 1995, and each week more murders were reported – usually of Hutu, both educated elite and peasant, but sometimes Tutsi soldiers in reprisals. One estimate, perhaps only slightly exaggerated, suggested a death total of 3,000 a month in 1995–6. Both Tutsi and Hutu "militias" appeared, and unpaid soldiers and militia took to looting. To the north Hutu rebels, with help from Hutus of the former Rwanda army, successfully sabotaged roads and burnt houses. In the capital Bujumbura, Tutsi militia groups cleared several suburbs of Hutu in 1995 and in mid-1996 the Burundi army began to expel the Rwandan Hutu refugees from the north – back into Rwanda where any suspected of *interahamwe* activity met short shrift. In July a military coup reinstated the former more moderate military leader, Buyoya, almost certainly in an effort to prevent the hardliner Bagaza from seizing power.

By early 1997 it appeared that both governments had reasserted only limited control. Drawn from the one million Hutu refugees repatriated from Zaire, armed bands of former *interahamwe* or Rwanda army still roamed certain areas in Rwanda killing and burning; in Burundi Hutu militia were reopening guerrilla war with mining and shooting, and two rival Hutu factions, the Party for the Liberation of the Hutu People (Palipehutu) and the Forces for the Defence of Democracy (FDD), were engaged in bitter fighting against each other. In both countries the Tutsi regimes' forces were exacting reprisals in no-war-no-peace situations.

Zaire 1996–7

The eastern regions of Zaire, being a fringe of the interlacustrine zone, included a substantial Tutsi population who were referred to locally as the *banyamulenge*; as a result of discrimination they had mounted small revolts in 1984 and 1990. The consequence of the events in Rwanda and Burundi, the arrival in these regions of Zaire of thousands of Hutu refugees and *interahamwe*, had the effect of aligning the Zairean Tutsis with their fellows, in turn leading the Zaire government to reject the Zairean Tutsis as legitimate citizens of Zaire.

A combination of the Tutsi ascendancy in both Rwanda and Burundi and the intense unpopularity of the grossly corrupt, bankrupt and feeble Zaire government of President Mobutu, led to the formation in 1996 of an Alliance of Democratic Forces for the Liberation of Congo-Zaire (ADFL). The French title was *Alliance des Forces Démocratiques pour la Libération du Congo-Zaire* (AFDL-CZ). As well as its Tutsi military leaders and Shaba insurgents the coalition also included a number of Lumumbists from the Kisangani area. The ADFL leader, Laurent Kabila, was a Luba, a veteran of the 1977 and 1978 Shaba attempts to overthrow Mobutu. The ADFL's military commanders were mostly Tutsi, and received direct support from within Rwanda and Uganda, both anxious to drive potential unrest away from their borders, with indirect support from Ethiopia. The men who joined and were to join the ADFL's army as it moved into Zaire in 1997 were not only Tutsi but were drawn from a number of ethnicities. A few fighters from Belgium and Ethiopia were also included, as were elderly Shaba veterans of the 1960s and 1970s. As they advanced ADFL units were able to recruit from discontented soldiers of Zaire's army who joined up with their rifles, tying a white band round their heads. Some ADFL men received a good American-style combat kit with boots, others the combat kit but no boots, yet others no uniform at all. Some, but not all, received training from Ugandans, Angolans or Tanzanians. Discipline varied but although the ADFL had to live off the land they occupied there were few reports of excesses once into central and western Zaire. In eastern Zaire excesses against the Hutu refugees were as appalling as any of the events of the three previous years. Among the most brutal were boy soldiers. The ADFL's weaponry extended to a few light artillery pieces but was otherwise limited to rifles and rocket grenade launchers. Opposed to them was the rabble – there can be no other term – of the Zairean army, unpaid, demoralized and whose activities, with only a few exceptions, were limited to rape, looting, killing – a particular target being followers of the Kibangui breakaway Christian church – and then running away. To stiffen this useless body of men Mobutu tried to repeat the recipe of Tshombe by hiring mercenaries, some 300, mostly Bosnian Serbs totally inexperienced in Africa together with a few Frenchmen and Belgians. These were recruited by private French and South African security consultancy companies. The French and Belgians flew three ex-Yugoslav aircraft, and four Mi-24 Soviet-built helicopter gunships were hired, probably from Ukraine. The mercenaries themselves were equipped with rifles that had once been Yugoslav army equipment. These had limited value as ammunition and spare parts soon ran out. Other aircraft at the mercenaries' disposal included a few light Puma and Gazelle helicopters, and a few Yugoslav air-to-ground strike aircraft. The Zairean air force's machines were all unusable. The mercenaries themselves were equipped with SAM-14 ground-to-air missiles of no use since the ADFL had no combat aircraft, and former Yugoslav army rifles, 60 mm mortars, machine-guns and rocket grenade launchers.

Later, as the ADFL army penetrated further into Zaire, UNITA, anxious to secure the route for the export of minerals from the area of Angola that it controlled, also contributed two well-equipped units to try to stiffen Mobutu's troops. In response the MPLA provided light armoured vehicles and some personnel to the ADFL in both the Kisangani and Kinshasa areas. The ADFL claimed that France had tried to support the Mobutu regime but no evidence of direct French government military help appeared.

The ADFL's operational art was one of bold advances by groups of varying size, sometimes on foot, sometimes by lorry, light vehicles or river barge – a rain-forest version of the Toyota war. Important towns such as Kisangani were surrounded by a "tourniquet" of groups, cutting the supply lines of the government forces. The style's success was due to the virtual lack of effective opposition, the enthusiastic welcome given to them in areas that they occupied and efficient control and communications, reported to be South African signals equipment obtained via Uganda. To have crossed so quickly from east to west Zaire in difficult bush and jungle terrain with poor roads was a remarkable achievement. In their favour was the ineptitude of the Zairean army, which failed to demolish bridges or ordnance parks. Nevertheless many men died on the march from malaria or dysentery, and often soldiers had only a few biscuits as a daily ration.

The ADFL forces first overran the Zairean government's eastern Kivu province bases, in the process stampeding at least 50,000 Hutu refugees into the jungle where hundreds were to die from starvation and disease. The ADFL then advanced south, north and west, in this process cornering and killing former Rwanda Hutu soldiers, gendarmes and militia. The killings extended to wives, women and children, lured out of the bush by promises of Western aid. Local villagers were encouraged to join in the slaughter, described as "slow extermination" by the UN Secretary-General. Surviving refugees were transported back to Rwanda by the UN and other agencies where thousands were detained.

The Zaire government's mercenary-backed counter-attack using the helicopter gunships only momentarily checked the advance of the ADFL army, estimated to be 10,000 strong, to the despair of Zaire's one competent general, Mahele Bokunu, who was French-trained and had distinguished himself commanding the Zairean army battalion which secured the Kolwezi airstrip in 1978. Kisangani fell to the ADFL on 15 March, the Zairean army troops attempting to flee and being shot at by the mercenaries who then themselves departed in the helicopters. In early April Zaire's second city, Lubumbashi, also fell. International attempts to broker a ceasefire and settlement all failed and by late April ADFL units had moved through Angola to the west of Kinshasa severing the link with the capital's port, Matadi. On 17 May, by now invested by some 5,000 ADFL, the city fell. Mobutu, whose Presidential Guard had refused to fight, fled to Morocco. General Mahele was murdered by his own men, and the victorious ADFL army killed off several hundred soldiers and supporters of the defeated regime. At the same time, two insurgent groups opposed to the ADFL opened fresh guerilla campaigns, in north Kivu armed bands known as Mai-Mai, and further south a Babende faction.

The collapse of the Mobutu regime marked a complete reordering of the balance of power across central Africa and was a severe blow to French influence and patronage.

Liberia 1989–97

The civil war in the small West African republic of Liberia was unexpected, both as an event and in its protracted ferocity.[11] Until 1980 the country had been dominated by a coastal Baptist Masonic elite referred to as Americo-Liberian, a description reflecting the origins of the Liberian state, freed American slaves. This elite had co-opted a limited number of indigenous peoples, established itself in plantations and small businesses, and from the 1880s onwards governed the territory through its own political party, the True Whig Party (TWP). The country had lacked the beneficial infrastructure side of colonial rule while the hinterland peoples had been used as cheap labour and deprived of social services. The instruction of the young generation, except for the privileged, had been limited to American videos of violence which formed the revolutionary literature of the pre-literate.

In 1980 this established order was overthrown, and the last TWP president brutally murdered in a coup led by Master-Sergeant Samuel Doe. The new regime quickly proved itself very much more oppressive and bloody than its predecessors. Doe and a small group of fellow conspirators, mostly from the small Krahn ethnic group, enriched themselves, murdered their opponents, including several hundred after an unsuccessful counter-coup attempt, and managed an election in which they could appear as the winners. At the same time the economy declined, unemployment rose and the United States drastically reduced its aid.

On 24 December 1989 a force, mounted with some covert francophone African support and styled the National Patriotic Front of Liberia (NPFL), entered Liberia from the Ivory Coast intending to overthrow Doe. Its leader was an Americo-Liberian, Charles Taylor. It quickly gathered much initial support from several ethnicities, in particular the Gio and Mano, but very soon turned to pillage. The Armed Forces of Liberia (AFL), poorly trained and incompetent and as prone to brutal massacres as the NPFL, were unable to stop the NPFL advance which reached the suburbs of Liberia's capital, Monrovia; there a small faction broke away from the NPFL to call itself the Independent National Patriotic Front of Liberia (INPFL).

The three-sided fighting, massacres and destruction led the Economic Co-operation Organization of West African States (ECOWAS), to send in a military peacekeeping force, the ECOWAS Monitoring Group ECOMOG. The force, at the outset mainly Nigerian and Ghanaian troops, was approved by the AFL and INPFL but not by Taylor's NPFL to which the anglophone countries, particularly Nigeria, were strongly opposed. ECOMOG's first commander, a Ghanaian General Quainoo, proved incompetent. He was unable, despite the firepower of the several thousand strong force's light artillery, machine-guns and mortars, to impose order or to prevent the killing – by slow torture carefully recorded on television – of Doe by the INPFL. Quainoo was then replaced by a succession of Nigerian generals, Dogonyaro, Bakut and Olurin, who until 1965 kept ECOMOG, in which the largest component was always Nigerian, working to a Nigerian agenda – a part of the problem rather than its solution.

For the next four years fighting continued. The NPFL remained the strongest of the factions, controlling large areas of the country, establishing its own "parliament", radio station and administration, and through exploitation of the economic resources of the areas it occupied in co-operation with expatriate companies, purchasing weapons. The NPFL was, however, never strong enough to take Monrovia – a major offensive in October 1992 using field artillery captured from the AFL was beaten off by ECOMOG with air-to-ground strikes. ECOMOG, however, took heavy casualties. Reinforcements for ECOMOG were hurriedly brought in, raising its total to over 14,500 men, so enabling it to retain its hold on Monrovia with a sponsored interim government. But ECOWAS decided against an advance into the NPFL's northern strongholds as being likely to drive the NPFL into a guerrilla war. The INPFL faded away but other factions emerged to challenge Taylor's NPFL. The most important of these was the United Liberian Movement for Democracy in Liberia (ULIMO), which scored some initial successes against the NPFL until it split into a largely Krahn ULIMO-J and a largely Mandingo ULIMO-K. A little later the NPFL also sustained a split, a Central Revolutionary Council-NPFL appearing and, probably with the support of ULIMO-K and yet one further faction, a southern-based breakaway from the AFL, the Liberian Peace Council, temporarily occupying Taylor's capital Gbarnga. The final total of armed factions reached eight. Throughout the four years ECOWAS convened a series of meetings attempting to broker a ceasefire and a peace process. These all came to nothing, usually as a result of the intransigence of Taylor.

By mid-1995, however, conditions were changing. Both Nigeria and Ghana for their own internal domestic reasons wanted a settlement and General Sani Abacha, the Nigerian head of government, dropped his opposition to the NPFL. Although the NPFL had recovered much of the territory it had lost, it was affected by the general war-weariness and ECOMOG had lost the services of East African battalions, their governments being exasperated. A conference convened in Abuja in August set in motion a peace process providing for a ceasefire, a transitional government including representatives from all the major factions, the disarming of the factions and eventual elections.

The process did not unfold smoothly. ECOMOG was not sufficiently strong to enforce order in areas vacated by faction forces, and funds were insufficient to cover the costs of disarming and resettling the faction fighters. Violent fighting broke out in Monrovia in April 1996 when the NPFL allied with ULIMO-K to savage ULIMO-J, later joined by the AFL and LPC. So violent was the fighting that many ECOMOG soldiers simply ran away. The fighting spread to other areas but was brought to a halt in May. Political pressures and a reinforced ECOMOG under two more Nigerian generals, John Inienger and the notably able Victor Malu, working to a much more impartial agenda, eventually restored order. To stamp out corruption, Malu dressed himself in civilian shirt and jeans and offered bribes to soldiers on ECOMOG road blocks; those accepting were immediately arrested. The peace process was resumed and disarmament speeded up. In July 1997, under ECOWAS supervision, Taylor won a general election, but his critics claimed his methods had lacked scruple: he himself had said that if he did not win he would recommence fighting.

The war was characterized by a number of distinctive features. The fighting styles of the various factions was poor. A visitor to NPFL headquarters at Gbarnga noted that he saw ten lieutenant-generals and hundreds of colonels, mostly illiterate. Men joined the factions for a mix of ethnic, personal and local economic reasons such as the protection and exploitation of a local asset for their own gain. While some factions such as the largely Krahn AFL were based on ethnicity, others, notably the NPFL, drew recruits from many groups. The NPFL ran several training camps where recruits received rudimentary instruction. A few of the more skilled received signals and vehicle training. Women served alongside the men.

The factions' fighting methods were often based on terror and fantasy; faction fighters wore bizarre costumes such as shower caps, carnival masks, Rambo shirts, women's wigs and plastic pseudo spacemen helmets. ULIMO-J fielded a "Butt-Naked Brigade". Legends such as "Here comes dead body trouble" were scrawled on the side of vehicles. Checkpoints would be adorned with skulls, and killing was often deliberate slow cruelty. Lucky charms and symbols adorned trucks, while rape and looting were more evident than military skill. Weaponry remained essentially automatic rifles from a variety of sources but mostly AK-47s, RPG-7 grenade launchers and machine-guns, with a few cannons mounted on trucks. The AFL and Taylor's NPFL also possessed some light artillery. Killings were often totally random, the wearing of a neat suit being seen as evidence of membership of Doe's former rule and, *ipso facto*, a death warrant, or victims, even women and babies, being from another ethnicity.

Child soldiers figured in all factions, at least 40,000 under 15 with many much younger in the field. In addition to the push and pull factors already noted other causes may be suggested. Particularly important in Liberia were the initiation rites for the children; these, it has been argued, were a debased and repulsive form of traditional puberty initiation rites sometimes involving cannibalism, designed to secure control through fear. Also evident was the attraction of the "weapons effect" – the display of guns heightening desensitization and deindividualization, the desire to follow and merge with the herd, and the effect of the violence shown on videos. Drawings of the scenes of the war by Liberian schoolchildren often included a television set among the weapons, reflecting a youth culture of violence.[12] ECOMOG is significant as the world's first regional peacekeeping force not sponsored by the UN. In its service in Liberia it came to draw on francophone and East African nation units; the large preponderance, however, always remained Nigerian. On the credit side ECOMOG without doubt saved a large number of lives in areas it controlled. In operations, though, it was prone to overkill with excessive use of fire or air-to-ground strike power, or on the streets excessive manhandling and shooting, often a result of the absence of any peacekeeping training. Its worst feature was that of general, almost institutionalized, looting and rape, "Every Commodity or Movable Object Gone" in Liberian views. A UN military observer mission UNOMIL was also present in Liberia, and its work may have contributed to curtailing the Nigerian agenda of ECOMOG.

Notable also in the Liberian war was the linkages between factions and commercial companies. Taylor's NPFL, controlling for most of the war large areas of the country including access to the outside world, was able to coerce expatriate iron ore and timber companies into making substantial "arms for resources" payments. The NPFL's massive but ultimately unsuccessful 1992 attempt to take Monrovia was prepared and launched from the Firestone rubber company's Harbel plantation. The capture by ECOMOG of the port of Buchanan in 1994 was a severe blow to the NPFL. ULIMO-K drew support from mining companies in western Liberia and the LPC from timber trading on the Ivory Coast border. In some areas ECOMOG's Nigerian officers ensured themselves a cut of the commercial profits, or used their force to sell off equipment to their personal profit. In the last years of the war the major factions spawned off local small factions so that they could appear clean while in practice retaining control of an economic asset.

In considering the aims of the Liberian factions, however, it does at least appear that none of them contemplated an actual break up of the Liberian state. They fought and exploited either to control the country or to ensure a voice in its government.[13]

In terms of human suffering a 1997 estimate suggested a death total, including those from starvation and war-related disease, of 200,000; 1,500 died in the April 1996 fighting in Monrovia alone. At least 800,000 refugees fled across the country's borders and another 1.25 million were displaced internally. Huge areas of the country were devastated and much of its limited infrastructure was destroyed. An estimated 18,000 landmines remain to be cleared.

Sierra Leone 1991–7

The post-independence years in Sierra Leone saw political turbulence, military coups, a one-party state and rapid economic decline, with concomitant riots over food prices and student unrest in the early 1980s. As in Liberia, a major social and political cause of Sierra Leone's troubles was the structural imbalance between the coastal Creole elite and the hinterland peoples, in particular the northern Temne and the southern Mende.

The creator of the one-party state system, President Siaka Stevens, who during the period of his rule had twice had to be buttressed by Guinean troops, retired in 1985 and was succeeded as president by General Joseph Momoh, who had been the army commander. Momoh proved unable to arrest the economic decline or curb mounting corruption and was overthrown in a military coup led by Captain Valentine Strasser in April 1992; the coup was followed by a brief conflict in which Guinean troops attempted to restore Momoh, without success.

The country was, however, already suffering from the overspill of the Liberian civil war. Over 100,000 refugees had arrived in 1990 and, more seriously, Liberian rebels of Taylor's NPFL had launched border clashes with the aim of forcing Sierra Leone to withdraw its contingent from ECOMOG and close ECOMOG's Freetown base. The Sierra Leone government replied with the deployment of 2,000 troops and hot pursuit raids into Liberia, but further developments were to involve Sierra Leone itself in civil war and warlordism. An insurgency movement, the Revolutionary United Front (RUF), led by Corporal Feday Sankoh and including a number of student radicals, supported by Taylor's NPFL, opened attacks on the government in July 1991, capturing several towns in the south and east. Taylor's aim was quoted as that of "doing a RENAMO" on Sierra Leone. The Sierra Leone army (SLA), with the help of additional forces from Guinea and Nigeria, a 1,000-strong contingent of the former Liberian army that had sought refuge in Sierra Leone and some British and United States logistic support, regained most of the territory that had been occupied by the RUF, without, however, destroying the RUF movement. The Liberian war continued to overspill, with ULIMO forces using Sierra Leone territory as a base for attacks on the NPFL despite the posting, in May 1992, of ECOMOG troops along the border.

The RUF's campaigning in 1992 was limited to asset-stripping in the areas, most notably in the diamond mining town of Koindu, that it controlled, together with scrapping with the SLA and Guinean troops in the Liberian border area villages. In early 1993 government forces retook Koindu, and a little later and, with the assistance of Liberian ULIMO fighters, much of the border area that had been held by the RUF. For the remainder of 1993 and for early 1994, the SLA, now with Israeli-trained units, retained the initiative, extending control in the border areas, taking an RUF base in the north and reoccupying towns in the east. It also began to follow the example of the RUF in asset-stripping to pay for its operations. Its rapid expansion to a total of over 14,000 was beyond the resources of the state to cover adequately.

In late 1994 the RUF was able to intensify its operations, being reinforced by a small group of mercenaries recruited in Burkina Faso and a larger number of trained but disaffected soldiers that had deserted from the SLA. No clear ethnic linkage characterized the RUF, though northerners were conspicuous. The RUF style of campaigning was based on rapid movement along forest tracks, equipment being carried by porters coerced into support. ULIMO-K also maintained a measure of support in the border areas. The RUF, unusually for African warfare, developed effective operational public relations, Sankoh having been trained as an SLA photographer. As in Liberia, the RUF also manipulated local grievances and traditional ethnic initiation customs together with videos of violence to motivate their adult and traumatize their child soldiers. Some of these had only wooden replicas of guns.

RUF groups intermittently cut off the southeastern town of Kenema, and in November opened harassment of the approach roads to the northeastern town of Kabala. It financed its operations by means of looting and profit extracted from diamonds in areas that it controlled, a procedure developed further when in January 1995 the RUF, now active in the entire hinterland, occupied the mines owned by two large mining companies, though one was recaptured by the SLA a little later. Three other notable RUF attacks were one on Bo in December 1994 and one on Kambia in January 1995; neither of these succeeded in occupying the towns, though a third attack, on Marampa, only 100 km from Freetown, was briefly successful. In addition to a strategy of terror, the RUF began the deliberate taking of hostages, expatriate and local, threatening to kill them unless particular demands were met.

As in Liberia the chief sufferers in the fighting were the civilian populations, a number being killed or manhandled. It was estimated that over three-quarters of a million people were on the move, either to neighbouring territories or to the area around the capital. The war produced a new name for a familiar practice, the "sobel", a soldier by day and a rebel bandit by night. Lawlessness, indiscipline and looting of aid agencies' food supplies characterized both sides in the conflict.

The RUF lost much of the general popular support it had at the outset through the violence of its methods, especially the enforced recruiting of young men. In the case of the attack on Bo, when the populace realized that many of the attackers had only replica guns they rose to expel or kill the attackers. Villages organized home guard groups based on Poro society structures, and traditional Mende hunters known as Kamajors also fought the RUF.

The government, unable to cope with its own resources, turned to the outside world for help. It first enlisted 58 Gurkhas who had previously served in the British army. These were ambushed by the RUF and their commander, a Canadian, was killed; the survivors left Sierra Leone. Of more immediate value were two Guinean army contingents provided by Conakry and a Nigerian garrison unit in Freetown.

Later in 1995 and using the offices of a Pretoria-based company, Executive Outcomes, financed it was said by the De Beers group of mining companies which had interests in Sierra Leone, the Sierra Leone government next acquired a new mercenary force recruited in South Africa, some black, some white and a number from the Angola border war special units, 32 Battalion and the Koevoet. Also from South Africa came pilots for Russian troop-carrying helicopters. Other assets, which a rescheduling of foreign debts enabled the Sierra Leone government to acquire, were two Russian Mi-24 helicopter gunships flown by Ukrainians, with cover provided by Nigerian air force Alpha interceptors.

With these assets the government was able in 1995 gradually to reassert some measure of control over much of the country, first recapturing Marampa and a major mining installation and then in July reoccupying a number of smaller towns including Koindu and, with the help of particularly brutal Liberian ULIMO-K fighters, clearing much of the area around Bo. Under intense international humanitarian pressure the RUF progressively released its expatriate and some of its local hostages but, although weakened by its reverses, it still remained active in several areas. It had received new supplies of AK-47 rifles and RPG-7 rocket launchers from Taylor's NPFL in Liberia, provided in exchange for diamonds, but SLA signals interception of traffic between the RUF and the NPFL led to the destruction of RUF bases. Desertions from the rebel camp increased internal faction tensions.

This stalemate situation also led to friction in the SLA, a first coup attempt being foiled in October 1995, but a second led by Brigadier Maada-Bio proved successful in ousting Strasser in January 1996. Maada-Bio secured a truce with the RUF in November and made arrangements for a general election in which the victor was a Mende, Tejan Kabbah, heading an eastern–southern coalition. To this point, it was estimated 15,000 people had been killed.

Kabbah's government was not to survive long. A military faction headed by Major Johnny Paul Koromah seized power, probably to pre-empt an RUF coup, on 25 May 1997, proclaiming an Armed Forces Revolutionary Council (AFRC), as the ruling authority. The Council included RUF leaders, the most important being Colonel "Leather Boots". Sankoh himself, arrested in Nigeria, was not able to join. The ECOMOG garrison in Freetown, preponderantly Nigerian but including Ghanaian and Guinean detachments, embarked on an attempt to break Koromah and his council. This external intervention served to unite the SLA and RUC in opposition to the Nigerians and fighting erupted in the streets of Freetown. A Nigerian warship bombarded from the sea, but was in turn attacked by the rebels. Nigerian troops seized the airport. Law and order collapsed in the city with widespread looting.

Nigeria's motives in leading the ECOMOG action were criticized as a renewed hegemonic ambition and an attempt to impress the West. But a wider and more justifiable motive was a concern, felt also by other West African leaders, and a fear of the spread of the mindless anomic violence, mainly of youth, that had characterized the Liberian conflict. Evidence of this was increasingly to be seen in Freetown as the RUF arrived in the suburbs in strength, over 6,000. The faction's headquarters were guarded by the members – some only seven years old, others 14-year-old "veterans" of the Liberian civil war – of its SBU or Small Boys Unit. RUF fighters in the streets wore ragged dress and were often high on drugs; a number were former members of Taylor's NPFL.

The Nigerians sustained a number of casualties and found themselves less and less able to cope with urban street fighting, more of gangland style than professional soldiering. Air or ground firepower had few targets to pinpoint. Unfortunate Nigerians or Sierra Leone opponents of the AFRC taken prisoner suffered dismemberment by castration, or excision of the heart for later consumption by the captors, or simple beheading. RUF brutality was at least equalled by the SLA who were responsible for some of the most bestial of the excesses. The only group to support the ousted Kabbah were the Mende hunter Kamajors, some 5,000 strong and now effectively a militia who opened attacks on the SLA in the south, hoping to capture diamond producing areas. At the same time a northern Temne faction, the Kapras, came to the support of the SLA.

By mid-July the military situation had reached a stalemate. After some sharp fighting in which over 100 people were killed, the Nigerians lost control of the airport but still controlled areas of Freetown and its suburbs. On the Liberian border the SLA had inflicted heavy casualties on a several hundred strong Kamajor attack, but the AFRC were beginning to experience the serious effects of the ECOWAS countries' economic sanctions.

Small wars, domestic conflicts and foreign interventions

Since the end of the civil war Nigeria has experienced both local unrest amounting in some cases almost to local civil war and a border dispute that on several occasions led to exchange of fire. In December 1980 a populist militant Moslem movement sparked off rioting in Kano. The rioting was suppressed ruthlessly, the movement leader Muhammad Maitatsine being killed. The movement erupted again in October 1982 with serious rioting in three north Nigerian cities. Several hundred people were killed before the rioting was ended and the movement banned. The Abacha regime also embarked on a violent vendetta against the southeastern Ogoni people, one of whose leaders, Ken Saro-Wiwa, a distinguished writer, was arrested and later executed in 1995. The occasion appears to have been Ogoni resentment against the circumstance of oil exploitation in their territory. The frontier dispute concerns the Bakassi Peninsula on the border with Cameroun, said to have potential oil and fisheries wealth. At present partitioned, the peninsula first saw fighting between Nigeria and Cameroun with border clashes and Nigerian air strikes in 1978–9. These recurred intermittently in the 1980s and early 1990s with more serious engagements in 1993, despite an earlier cease-fire agreement, in which field artillery and helicopter gunships were committed and a number of casualties suffered by both sides. Each country blamed the other. The quarrel tends to intensify, as a xenophobic distraction, at times of political difficulties in Nigeria.

In December 1995 a long-standing border dispute between Burkina Faso and Mali over the ownership of an area known as the Agacher Strip led to a five-day war. In the course of this conflict Burkina Faso claimed to have routed a small force of Mali tanks and infantry, but Mali troops nevertheless moved some way into Burkina Faso. Burkina Faso aircraft bombed Sikasso in Mali, and Mali aircraft bombed Ouahigouya in Burkina Faso. Under international pressure the fighting, which had cost each side some 300 dead, was ended and troops withdrawn from the Strip. Later an International Court judgment partitioned the area between the two countries. The war only demonstrated the incapacity of the armies of impoverished African states to achieve a decisive success.

A similar border conflict, again inconclusive as neither side could wage warfare any further, occurred between Mauritania and Senegal in 1990–1, following the arbitrary and brutal expulsion of a large percentage of its black population by Mauritania. Artillery shots were exchanged.

France continued to intervene in African countries in the 1980s and 1990s. In West Africa French *Troupes de Marine*, with a small Zairean contingent in support for political reasons, intervened in 1986 to buttress the authority of President Eyadama of Togo. In 1991–3, *Marine* and Legion troops helped the Djibouti government of the Territory of Afars and Issas in its conflict with the Afars, and in 1995 the French navy intervened to end a brief local conflict between Yemen and Eritrea over possession of the Kanish Islands in the Red Sea.

More complex were operations in the Central African Republic (CAR), the Comores and Congo-Brazzaville. The removal of "Emperor" Bokassa had not secured political stability in the CAR and a coup in 1981 installed a military government which under French pressure held elections in 1993. However, a military mutiny led by a sergeant broke out in May 1996, the cause being a move to withdraw heavy weaponry. The mutineers fought with the Presidential Guard, disorder extending to looting and beatings. The 1,400 French garrison had to be reinforced by a further 600 troops, mainly Foreign Legion, flown in from elsewhere in Africa, to protect expatriates and secure the authority of the country's president, Ange-Félix Patassé. An armoured squadron and combat helicopters were used against the rebels, who surrendered at the end of the month.

A second mutiny occurred in December 1996, progressing to a ten-week uprising. An ethnic dimension emerged more clearly, the mutineers being southern Yahomo while units loyal to Patassé were, like himself, northern Baya. The French did not intervene politically but they mounted a helicopter gunship shoot against the mutineers in reprisal for the death of two French soldiers. A settlement, the Bangui Accord, was brokered by the presidents of Chad and Gabon, and an African monitoring force (MISAB – the Inter African Mission to Monitor the Bangui Accord – consisting of units from Chad, Gabon, Mali, Senegal and Burkina Faso), with French logistic support, was set up to supervise the agreement.

A further mutiny erupted in June 1997, monitoring force units being attacked and in reply taking control of the areas with some severity. The fighting rose to the level of exchange of mortar and machine-gun fire by both sides, some 100 people being killed. A ceasefire was agreed at the end of the month.

The inhabitants of the Comores voted for independence in 1975, but a majority on the largest island, Mayotte, later voted for continuing French rule. A former Katanga mercenary, Bob Denard, became commander of the Comores presidential guard in a period of complex domestic turmoil. Using this authority and after a "conversion" to Islam, he began to threaten expatriates. In a swift surgical intervention by a Foreign Legion detachment based in Mayotte he was removed in October 1995. A separatist revolt broke out in July 1997 on Anjouan, one of the component islands of independent Comores.

Most serious of these three larger-scale operations was that in 1997 in Congo-Brazzaville. The country had had a turbulent political history since independence in 1960. Political rule ended when a Marxist military government took power for a time, supported by Cuban troops. In 1992 a restored civilian government permitted a multi-party system. Parties were, however, ethnically based and formed their own militias. These engaged in a year of street skirmishes between July 1993 and July 1994, over 2,000 people being killed. A truce in 1995 was supposed to have provided for the disarmament of the militias, but most kept their arms hidden in ethnic ghettos among Brazzaville's shanty townships. The 1997 civil war broke out following the attempt on 5 June by the former military ruler of the state, General Denis Sassou Nguesso, at the head of his militia faction named "Cobra", to eject the elected president, Pascal Lissouba. Earlier events in Kinshasa across the Congo river had served to whet political and more carnal desires, and destructive political activity prior to a presidential election scheduled for July had heightened tensions. The Cobra faction held that France had been supportive of Lissouba, who had been purging the army of followers of Nguesso so making it a partisan force. The 6,000 or more expatriates became a target for attack, a number taking refuge in two large hotels. The French troops already in Brazzaville were inadequate in number and France despatched further Foreign Legion troops from elsewhere in Africa as reinforcement. Some were dropped by parachute while others were flown in at the airport, bringing with them light armoured vehicles. The total of Legion and *Marine* troops had reached over 1,200 by the end of June.

The Cobra militia brushed aside efforts by the government army, known as the "Zulus", to disarm them and occupied half the city, some of their men, like the Liberian faction fighters, being dressed in women's clothes and wearing wigs. The army, which had had some training provided by Lav-Dan, a private Israeli security company, replied with rocket, machine-gun and 120 mm mortar fire. Other smaller militias appeared. One, headed by the mayor of Brazzaville, Bernard Kolelas, and named the "Ninjas", attempted to mediate in vain, in a mounting orgy of looting, butchery and rape, several thousand people being killed. The ethnic dimension of the fighting increased the ferocity, Lissouba's Zulus being mainly southern Congo Kouyou, while Nguesso's Cobras were northern Mbochi together with some former soldiers of Mobutu's army. The mayor's Ninjas were Bakongo, neutral in this dispute, although they had been among the worst of the factions in 1993. As in Liberia and Sierra Leone, clothing and slogan names were fashioned to strike terror. The authority of the state collapsed amid successive broken ceasefire agreements and renewed heavy daily exchanges of light artillery and mortar fire. By mid-July the French, further reinforced by big six-wheeled armoured cars equipped with 90 mm guns, "heavy metal peacekeeping" in the words of one observer, had evacuated nearly 5,000 expatriates. A ceasefire was negotiated in July, by which time over 1,000 people had been killed, but the truce collapsed when UNITA faction fighters entered the conflict to secure their diamond export routes in favour of Lissouba, and Angolan troops moved in to support Nguesso.

The costs of French military interventions and the setbacks suffered by France in Africa prompted a reappraisal of French policies in July 1997, and reductions in French garrisons were announced. Nevertheless an account of warfare should recognize the efficiency of the French military in Africa in the 1980s and 1990s. At the top there was clear political control, and with the regiments of *Troupes de Marine* and the Foreign Legion France possessed units free of NATO commitments and which were trained, equipped and psychologically and medically prepared for Third World intervention operations. Companies and squadrons from different regiments would be drawn from garrisons all over Africa to meet particular needs, Bouar in the CAR being the pivotal staging-post.

There was only one direct British military intervention, that in Gambia, when in 1981 a British special forces detachment rescued the wife of the president of Gambia, held captive in a coup attempt. The president, Jawara, later enlisted the help of Senegalese soldiers and after a week of fighting the rebels were crushed. A very heavy death toll, over 1,000, was the result of looting and banditry by prisoners released from gaol.

On the night of 14–15 April 1986 the United States took military action against Libyan territory, action that amounted to an act of war. The United States had long been irritated by the policies of Libya's leader, Colonel Gadaffi. In March Libya fired several Soviet-made SAM-5 anti-aircraft missiles at American naval aircraft flying from aircraft carriers. American aircraft and missile cruisers fired missiles at the Libyan missile sites and at Libyan missile corvettes, sinking at least one. The killing, by a bomb, of an American serviceman in Berlin brought matters to a head. Eighteen F-111 aircraft, operating by permission of the Prime Minister Mrs Thatcher from bases in Britain, together with naval aircraft, bombed specific targets in Libya's two most important cities, Tripoli and Benghazi. Some of the bombing went wide and civilians were killed, among them an adopted daughter of Gadaffi. Reports, never confirmed or denied, claimed that a Soviet destroyer was sunk in the operation and that the American attack followed earlier French air strikes.

The effect of the air attacks was largely the reverse of that intended. Gadaffi, whose domestic position had been weak, was able to recoup sympathy and support both within Libya and the wider world.

In several African countries local regional unrest has led to localized warfare. In southern Senegal a Movement of Casamance Democratic Forces, with a military wing *Attika* centred on the Christian and non-Moslem peoples of the Ziguinchor area, opened an intermittent secessionist insurgency campaign in 1981. This campaign in 1986, 1990–1, 1993, 1995 and 1997 required Senegalese government military forces to contain it. In Ghana chieftaincy and land disputes in the north between Konkombas and Nanumbas, and their respective Dagomba and Conja allies, cost over 2,000 lives in 1994, with further clashes and deaths in 1995. In Kenya periodic ethnic clashes between Kikuyu and Kalenjin peoples in the Rift Valley reflected the desire to acquire new lands driven by the Kikuyu population increase. A Tuareg uprising, styled the Democratic Revival Front, broke out in Niger in 1994. A peace accord was agreed in April 1995, but small-scale clashes with Niger government forces were continuing in 1997. There had also been earlier a very localized Tuareg uprising in Mali.

These conflicts, albeit small, possess significance as many of them complement at parochial level, and so illuminate, the causes of the larger conflicts already examined – those of communities seeking to extend the boundaries of land or economic assets that they control, believing extension to be essential for survival.

Chapter Eight

Conclusion

This work has surveyed what might initially appear to be an unwieldy variety of wars with no common themes – anti-colonial liberation wars, inter-nation wars, civil wars and ethnic secessionist or purely factional uprisings. Only a few approximate to accepted Western concepts of war, that is, warfare between armies of nation states or European civil war, generally tidy, organized wars with front lines and structured, uniformed armies. In fewer still have generally agreed Western "principles of war" – a strategy directed towards a clear objective, the offensive, overall unity of command, mass and concentration of forces, manoeuvre, surprise, security, simplicity and administration/logistics – played the guiding parts. The European conceptual distinction between conventional war and low-intensity warfare with lower casualty rates is also inappropriate in African conditions, as the events set out in the last chapter showed. The warfare in Liberia, Rwanda, Burundi, Zaire and elsewhere was low-intensity in terms of the numbers actually engaged in the fighting and the simplicity of their weaponry; the death totals are those of conventional war. African warfare also is generally a much more improvised business, as previous chapters have set out. The "strike where we can with what we can" approach of ZANLA, for example, was much more effective than the Soviet-style strategy of ZIPRA. Terror and massacre have been major, psychological warfare, weapons carried to extremes even exceeding those of the Nazis or Stalin's Soviet Union. Professional soldiers in armies have become factions and have been supplanted or challenged by ill-disciplined militias who have no respect for rules or laws governing the conduct of war. Only the Nigerian civil war, the Uganda–Tanzania war and South Africa's warfare in Angola at all resemble the wars of Europe.

The conflicts have removed or destroyed the economic and social mechanisms that support life, creating vast refugee and environmental pollution problems. Humanitarian operations have failed more often than they have succeeded, either because they are too little and too late, or because they are seen as a threat and attacked, or because they become the captives of one faction or another relying on them for protection in order to deliver relief.

Can any common theme or themes for twentieth-century warfare in Africa be discerned? Despite the very wide differences, consideration can perhaps be given to two themes, one for the Maghreb and one for sub-Saharan Africa. In the case of the Maghreb, in particular, as suggested earlier, Algeria, and arguably in the formative last years as a French protectorate Tunisia also, a quest for communal or national identity seems to emerge. The French found the labelling of Algerian insurgents very difficult, often using the term HLL – *hors la loi* or outside the law. Post-independence Algeria is fighting over the question of what law – modern or medieval Islamic. In Western Sahara a Moroccan identity is being sought by a Stalinist physical movement of people to assert claims thereby, it is hoped, made politically correct.

In the case of sub-Saharan Africa, below the surface of political rhetoric, not far removed from most of the anti-colonial insurgency movements and in almost all of the civil war or ethnic secession conflicts, it can be suggested that there lies a quest for land, *lebensraum,* or in a few cases the energy, industrial or other economic potential of an area of land. South Africa's apartheid, both in its horizontal or vertical forms, had the same aim. Factions have fought to try to acquire such assets, and often but by no means always have the factions been formed from one particular ethnic group. The fighting has been dismissed by many, including some historians, as "tribal" and the conflicts' causes as "tribalism", aiming unreasonably to break up a new nation state when they should be applying their efforts to development within existing frontiers.

This perception is based on an incorrect interpretation of the past and too loose a study of the circumstances in which peoples come to identify them-selves as members of ethnicities or other labelled collective groups. The point already made in the introductory chapter needs re-emphasis. The ethnic affiliations of African peoples were at least in part the result of the clash of interests between the need of the colonial power to govern in tidy manageable units and the generally passive resistance of African peoples to division for this purpose. Certainly, also, colonial rule enhanced ethnic awareness as much in the eyes of the colonizer as the colonized. Secession from the colonial created state was therefore seen by the colonial or ex-colonial power as contumacious, a heresy.

Such secessionist aims were, however, the case in the conflicts of the 1960s, notably in Katanga, Biafra, Chad, Eritrea and Sudan. In the case of Chad, Sudan and Eritrea the ethnic, religious, historic and cultural gaps are so great that secession in some form is still sought, with Eritrea successfully gained. But elsewhere, whether the dissent be Tutsi versus Hutu in Rwanda and Burundi,

Inkatha in KwaZulu/Natal or the various factions in Angola, Liberia or Sierra Leone, there seems no expressed direct deliberate desire to break the colonial frontiers, only to secure assets within them. In Shaba (Katanga) secessionism quickly lost majority support; in Iboland, formerly Biafra, secessionism appears dead. Nor are any of the ethnicities divided by colonial frontiers fighting for reunification as their major aim. Secessionist or regional dissent is nevertheless presented in the West as "tribalism" or in Somalia as "clan feuds" – in postmodernist terms a new "other" – a denigration for Africans comparable with the Orientalism "other" denigrating Asia. This construct, being in large part consciously or unconsciously both a product of the past and racial, obscures understanding of the real issues.

The insurgent movements of the late twentieth century and the violence they brought are, then, increasingly concerned with local land, local plantations, a local mine or, as in South African urban areas, job opportunities, because these are seen as the only form of local economic security. Some movements always remained ethnic-based; others are based on a religious faction or a former pre-colonial kingdom; while yet others appear as a new version of the pre-colonial *ruga ruga,* armed bands in quest of a fiefdom, on occasion in partnership with unscrupulous European or American business interests. In several countries which are apparently stable the quest for personal or group security is limited to lawlessness and banditry with government authority effective only by day or only in certain areas. But all are primarily concerned with, in Joyce Cary's words written in the early 1950s, "the will to live" perceived as the possession of land or another economic asset. It is this will to live that is challenging, in some cases superseding, the Western-style nation, though not doing so deliberately. It was not the main aim of, for example, the movements of refugees cutting across existing formal national frontiers to bring down those frontiers to which they were largely indifferent. As noted earlier, in his reference to pre-colonial Africa, Illiffe described Africans as frontiersmen with innumerable and informal local frontiers. Africans of the late twentieth century think and fight in the same way. They, too, are frontiersmen seeking or defending frontiers to be shaped formally or informally, in accord with their energies, aspirations and above all the will to survive, the official national frontiers serving as the arenas in which the conflicts take place.

In such conditions, consideration of questions such as whether war is a cultural, political or ideological phenomenon, whether or not human nature is essentially aggressive, or whether any distinction could be made between legitimate and unacceptable uses of force, had by the 1990s become in the African context irrelevant. In the destruction and death comparisons can be made, to a certain level, with Europe's Middle Ages or the seventeenth-century Thirty Years' War. But poverty in Africa is more widespread than in medieval or early modern Europe. While economies remain or become impoverished, warfare in Africa will return increasingly to its endemic pre-colonial mode, with outbreaks of peace ever more temporary, the spoils of a war required more than a military victory in Darwinian struggles for human survival.

Appendix: technical note

A summary of the characteristics of six major insurgency weapons may be useful.

1. AK–47: Kalashnikov assault rifle (Avtomat Kalashnikova) designed in 1947:

Calibre:	7.62 mm
Weight:	4.3 kg (more with magazine loaded)
Effective range:	300 m (sight range 100–800 m)
Magazine:	30 rounds: rate of fire (sustained) – 600 rds per minute

   Improved versions were manufactured by the USSR with reduced weight and increased sight range and also a folding stock, and by the GDR, Poland, Romania, Czechoslovakia, Hungary and China. The Polish version provided for rifle-grenade equipment.

2. RPG–7: rocket-propelled grenade launcher (Reaktivniy Protivatankovyi Granatomet 7):

Calibre:	Tube 40 mm
	Grenade 80 mm
Weight:	Tube 6.5 kg
	Grenade 2.5 kg
Velocity:	120 metres per second
Effective range:	300 m

   The weapon was designed for infantry anti-tank protection. Its capabilities for wider use were soon recognized by insurgency movements.

3. SAM–7: surface-to-air missile (NATO code name GRAIL; Soviet designation STRELA – Arrow):

Guidance system:	Infrared homing
Propulsion:	Solid fuel
Diameter:	70 mm
Range:	Horizontal 3.6 km; vertical 1.5 km

4. PMN-1: Soviet pressure operated anti-personnel mine:

Weight:	550 g; bakelite body with a black rubber pressure plate
Explosive weight:	240 g
Explosive:	TNT
Diameter:	112 mm
Height:	56 mm
Operating pressure:	8–25 kg

5. TM-46: Soviet metal-cast anti-tank blast mine:

Weight:	8.6 kg
Explosive weight:	5.7 kg
Explosive:	TNT
Diameter:	305 mm
Height:	108 mm
Detonating pressure:	120–400 kg

6. SPM: Soviet limpet mine used for demolition or sabotage:

Weight:	2.5 kg
Explosive weight:	9.5 kg
Explosive:	TNT
Length:	267 mm
Width:	115 mm
Height:	58 mm
Detonating pressure:	120–400 kg

The wide variety of mines supplied to African armies and to insurgency movements came not only from the Soviet Union but also from Belgium, China, Czechoslovakia, France, Italy, Portugal and South Africa.

Notes

Chapter One

1. In his introduction to his *Africa: the history of a continent*, John Illiffe offers the useful concepts of "frontiersman" and "innumerable local frontiers".
2. Ali A. Mazrui (ed.), in *The warrior tradition in modern Africa*, provides a useful introduction to the study of pre-colonial warriors though some of the argument is overstated.
3. Some examples of soldiers' songs appear in Anthony Clayton, *Communication for new loyalties: African soldiers' songs*.
4. The phrase "epidemic of the mind" was first used by Albert Einstein when describing German nationalism in 1917.

Chapter Two

1. Of especial value as an overview of all these campaigns is Ian Beckett and John Pimlott, *Armed forces and modern counter-insurgency*.
2. More has been written about Mau Mau than any other anti-colonial campaign; a selection of titles appears in the bibliography. The best single account is Wunyabari O. Maloba, *Mau Mau and Kenya: an analysis of a peasant revolt*. Also of specialist value is this author's *Counter-insurgency in Kenya, 1952–60* and, for purely British military operations, Gregory Blaxland's *The regiments depart*. This work also includes some description of the Canal Zone conflict.
3. Most of the literature concerning the French North African campaigns is in French; the most important items are listed in the bibliography. The only English text in respect of Tunisia and Morocco is this author's chapter in his *The wars of French decolonization*. This latter work also covers the Algerian campaign of which the fullest and most detailed account remains Alistair Horne, *A savage war of peace: Algeria 1954–62*. Also useful are Alf Andrew Heggoy, *Insurgency and counter-insurgency in Algeria*; Charles Robert Ageron, *Modern Algeria*, and François Portheu de la Morandière, *Soldats du Djebel* (French text).

4. In respect of Cameroun, this author's *The wars of French decolonization* and Guy Arnold's *Wars in the Third World since 1945* both provide short accounts.

5. Although the death toll, on both sides, in the Angolan 1961 uprising was much greater than in Kenya, the literature concerning this uprising is limited. The fullest account is that of W. S. van der Waals, *Portugal's war in Angola*; also useful are John A. Marcum, *The Angolan revolution* (two volumes) and D. M. Abshire and M. A. Samuels, *Portuguese Africa, a handbook*.

Chapter Three

1. The most informative works in respect of Angola are John A. Marcum, *The Angolan revolution* (two volumes) and W. S. van der Waals, *Portugal's war in Angola*, which work also includes some useful material on Mozambique, Portuguese Guinea and Portugal itself. Eduardo Mondlane's *The struggle for Mozambique* covers events until 1969, while for the later years B. Munslow's *Mozambique: the revolution and its origins* and Father Adrian Hastings' *Wiriyamu* are important. A valuable short guide to the campaign, also by Hastings, also appears as an article entitled "Some reflections upon the war in Mozambique", in *African Affairs*, December 1974. The most detailed military account of the campaign in Portuguese Guinea is provided by Al J. Ventner in his *Report on Portugal's war in Guiné-Bissau*. Barbara Cornwall, *The bush rebels*, offers an eye-witness account of Mozambique and Guinea in the late 1960s.

2. For all three campaigns, Ian Beckett and John Pimlott, in *Armed forces and modern counter-insurgency*, provide a useful one-chapter overview.

3. In March 1975 General Spinola led an attempt to remove the left-wing officers that succeeded him. The attempt failed and Spinola was forced into exile. When the leftist groups were put down by moderate officers Spinola returned to Portugal. He was made a Marshal in 1981 and died in 1996. His last public appearance was in March 1995 when, in hospital, he welcomed his former PAIGC opponent, President Nuno Vieira of Guinea-Bissau, visiting as a gesture of respect for Spinola's conduct of the campaign.

4. A considerable body of literature about the Rhodesia–Zimbabwe war has appeared. Of especial value are D. Martin and P. Johnson, *The struggle for Zimbabwe*; Ngwabi Bhebe and Terence Ranger, *Soldiers in Zimbabwe's liberation war*; Ken Flower, *Serving secretly: Rhodesia into Zimbabwe 1964–1981*; Paul I. Moorcraft and Peter McLaughlin, *Chimurenga! The war in Rhodesia, 1965–1980*; David Lan, *Guns and rain: guerillas and spirit mediums in Zimbabwe*; and Terence Ranger, *Peasant consciousness and guerilla war in Zimbabwe*.

5. The most useful texts on the subject of the Western Sahara are Maurice Berbier, *Le Conflit du Sahara Occidental* (French text), and Tony Hodges, *Western Sahara: the roots of a desert war*.

Chapter Four

1. The names of territories, provinces and places used in this chapter are those that were in use at the time of the events.

2. For general coverage of events in the Congo at the time of independence, Catherine Hoskyns, *The Congo since independence, January 1960–December 1961*, although written from an extreme nationalist perspective, still remains the most useful work. Georges Abi-Saab, *The United Nations operation in the Congo 1960–1964*, sets out the political background to ONUC's military operations and offers a brief outline of the events. Some illuminating detail appears in General Carl von Horn, *Soldiering for peace.*

3. A United States Army paper, *Dragon operations: hostage rescue in the Congo 1964–65*, by Major Thomas P. Odom, and David Reed, *111 days in Stanleyville*, provide accounts of the Simba uprising and events in Stanleyville. The account of the commander of the 2ème Régiment Etranger de Parachutistes, Colonel Philippe Erulin, *Zaire: sauver Kolwezi*, provides a full coverage of this operation.

4. For Rwanda, Gerard Prunier's *The Rwanda crisis 1959–1994: history of a genocide* is of especial value.

5. Such detail of the fighting in Sudan as is available is set out in Edgar O'Ballance, *The secret war in the Sudan.*

6. In respect of Eritrea, Ruth Iyob, *The Eritrean struggle for independence: domination, resistance, nationalism, 1941–1993*, and Haggai Erlich, *The struggle over Eritrea 1962–78: war and revolution in the Horn of Africa*, are both valuable.

7. A library of books about the Nigerian civil war exists. Pre-eminent, and indispensable, is John de St. J. Jorré, *The Nigerian civil war*. Useful military detail appears in General Obesanjo, *My command*; Fola Oyewole, *Reluctant rebel;* Elechi Amadi, *Reminiscences*. Works that consider wider international and political issues arising from the war cannot be considered here, but Jorré's work provides a valuable introductory reading list.

8. An invaluable military account of the Ethiopia–Somalia war is provided in an article "Soviet intervention and the Ogaden counter-offensive of 1978" by Mark Urban, published in *The Journal of the Royal United Service Institution for Defence Studies (RUSI)* **128**, June 1983.

9. In view of Russian military weakness after the collapse of the Soviet Union in 1991, it is salutary to recall Soviet military capabilities when the USSR was at the height of its military power, at about this period.

10. The most informative account of the Tanzania–Uganda war appears in Amii Omara-Otunnu, *Politics and the military in Uganda 1980–1985*. S. M. Mmbando's *The Tanzania–Uganda war in pictures* contains some interesting detail. The Tanzanian government's official publication, *Tanzania and the war against Amin's Uganda*, notes the initial limits set in the original plan.

11. The British press at the time published photographs of Soviet assault bridge-laying tanks on their way from Mombasa to Uganda. These were wrongly captioned as surface-to-surface missile carriers on account of the superficially similar shape of the covered-over equipment to that of rockets.

12. Sections of John Keegan (ed.), *World armies*, provide material on military operations in North Africa in the 1970s.

13. For the events within and after the Zanzibar revolution, this author's *The Zanzibar revolution and its aftermath* may be found useful. Blaxland's *The regiments depart* sets out the events following the mutinies of the Eastern African armies. I am grateful to several British retired officers for material concerning the Shifta operations. A chapter by Martin R. Doorabos, "Kumanyara and Rwenzuraru, two responses to ethnic inequality", in Robert I. Rotberg and Ali A. Mazrui (eds), *Protest and power in Black Africa*, sets out the violence in Toro.

NOTES

Chapter Five

1. There are particular difficulties in assessing events of the Namibia–Angola border war. The South Africans were generally uncommunicative during the war though they openly admitted white casualties. The Angola-Cuban side exaggerated for propaganda purposes. The most reliable accounts, drawing on interviews conducted after the end of the war and incorporating useful criticism and judgements, are, in respect of South Africa, Willem Steenkamp, *South Africa's border war*, and in respect of Namibia, Colin Leys and John Saul, *Namibia's liberation struggle*. Valuable chapters on Angola–Namibia and on Mozambique appear in Karl P. Magyar and Constantine P. Danopoulos (eds), *Prolonged wars: a post-nuclear challenge*. Also informative is Daniel Spikes, *Angola and the politics of intervention*.
2. The two most useful works on RENAMO are Alex Vines, *Renamo: terrorism in Mozambique*, and Eric Berman's United Nations Disarmament Project paper, *Managing arms in peace processes: Mozambique*. A French text, Christan Geffray, *La Cause des armes au Mozambique*, is also instructive on RENAMO, as is an article by Paul Fauvet, "Roots of counter-revolution: the Mozambique National Resistance", in the *Review of African Political Economy* **29**, 1984. For UNITA, Fred Bridgland's *Jonas Savimbi* is useful although journalistic.

   In considering sources it can often be useful to look at lacunae. In the case of the border war, and the earlier sizeable Cuban intervention in the Ogaden war, only the briefest and most perfunctory references appear in the Soviet literature of the time, though more generous recognition began to appear after the collapse of the Soviet Union.
3. "Shoshorona" is an onomatopoeic word, the sound of footsteps among leaves.

Chapter Six

1. The semantics are interesting. The State Security Council used words such as "elimineer" (eliminate), "uitwis" (wipe out) and "uit die sameling verwyder" (remove from society) in instructions issued to security forces. These drew their own conclusions as to the action required. *The Times* of 23 October 1996 records the proceedings of the Truth and Reconciliation Commissions in which President Botha's complicity in the Khotsio House bombing was alleged by the Police Commissioner at the time. *The Economist* of 18 October 1997, quoting from proceedings of the Commission, provides the semantic details.
2. The texts referred to in the notes of the previous chapter remain the most useful basic works for the border war. Further detail concerning the last stages of the Angolan operations appears in Helmoed-Romer Heitman, *War in Angola: the final South African phase*.
3. The Angolan and Cuban regiments were organized on the lines of a Soviet motor-rifle regiment, 1,500–2,000 men in three battalions, each of some 300, with supporting armour and artillery. South African writing uses the term "brigade" for these regiments. The Angolan regiments included Cuban cadres.
4. The pre-1990 years of the Inkatha war are well described and analyzed in Matthew Kentridge, *An unofficial war: inside the conflict in Pietermaritzburg*. Further developments are summarized in Chapter 4, "Violence on the Reef 1990–91", of Duncan Innes, Matthew Kentridge and Helena Perold, *Power and profit: politics, labour and business in South Africa*. Also instructive are John Kane-Berman, *Political violence in South Africa*, and Martin J. Murray, *The revolution deferred: the painful birth of post-apartheid South Africa*.

5. Developments in the mid-1990s are generally too recent to appear in academic writing. This chapter has drawn on periodicals, in particular *Africa Confidential* and *The Economist*, for material.

6. UNAVEM III – United Nations Angola Verification Mission III. The bulk of the force was composed of troops from Brazil, India, Romania, Pakistan, Uruguay and Zimbabwe. Britain and Portugal provided specialist logistics and communications personnel.

7. *Jane's intelligence review* of June 1993 includes an article on "The resumption of civil war in Angola", by Dr M. Berdal, which was followed by an article in *Jane's intelligence review yearbook: the world in conflict 1994/95* on events in Angola in 1994 by Dr A. Aloa. Both are useful.

8. Eric Berman's UN publication *Managing arms in peace processes: Mozambique* gives an excellent summary and analysis of events in the country; Alex Vine's *Renamo: terrorism in Mozambique* is also valuable.

Chapter Seven

1. Material for the years 1955 to 1997 has been culled from issues of *The Times, The Independent, The Economist, Le Figaro*, the BBC *Summary of World Broadcasts, West Africa, Képi Blanc, Africa Confidential, Jane's Intelligence Review Pointers* and the *Revue Historique des Armées*.

2. Child soldiers are, of course, not a purely African phenomenon. In the last quarter of the twentieth century they have also been evident in Afghanistan, Yemen, El Salvador, Sri Lanka, Nicaragua, Jerusalem and Honduras. Earlier, Hitler's Germany recruited child soldiers in the last months of the Second World War.

3. The patterns seem to bear out much child psychology theory: the "weapons effect" and "aggressive cues" acting as catalysts for desensitization and deindividualization; the loss of a sense of personal identity and responsibility when in such situations so that individuals merge within a group; the way in which juveniles followed the examples of elders to violence; the effect of sustained media exposure to violence and the lengths to which people will act aggressively when commanded to do so; and the way of some, when captured, of exposing their vulnerability but continuing to boast of kills in a form of animal ritualization. Some child soldiers remained in fugue states unable to recall traumatic events.

4. A French text, *Tchad 1983, Operation Manta*, by Eric Lefèvre, offers an account of this remarkable long-distance intervention. Also useful is Raymond W. Copson's *Africa's wars and prospects for peace*.

5. MINURSO – the United Nations Mission for the Referendum in Western Sahara – has included officers from a number of countries. It was originally intended to be 1,700 strong, including 550 observers and a 700-strong infantry battalion, logistic support and an air unit, but these force levels could not be maintained as time progressed.

6. Sudan's second civil war is covered in J. Millar Burr and Robert O. Collins, *Requiem for the Sudan: war drought and disaster relief on the Nile*, and M. W. Daly and Ahmad Alawad Sikainga (eds), *Civil war in the Sudan*.

7. Peter Godwin's *Mukiwa, a white boy in Africa* includes descriptions of Zimbabwe's local civil war. The phrase "a small private political army" was that used by Mussolini's Foreign Minister Ciano to express his admiration for Hitler's SS.

8. Uganda's post-Amin history is recorded in Kenneth Ingham, *Obote, a political biography*, and in a valuable Edinburgh University Occasional Paper, *Breaking with the past? A consideration of Yoweri Museveni's National Resistance Movement, and of social and political action in Uganda during its government* by Justin McKenzie Smith. Museveni's own account appears in his *Sowing the mustard seed*.

9. Comparison may be made with England's Wars of the Roses. ". . . No question of principle or even class interest was involved . . . It was a faction fight . . . contending for power and wealth and ultimately the possession of the Crown": G. M. Trevelyan, *A history of England*, pp. 262–3.

10. Another code term was an instruction to "cut down trees", a reference to the tall stature of the Tutsis. A later broadcast ran: "The baskets are only half full. Fill them to the brim."

11. An overview of Liberia's civil war to September 1995 is provided in the author's *Factions, foreigners and fantasies*. Three further works of especial value merit mention: Clement Adibe's UN paper, *Managing arms in peace processes: Liberia*; Stephen Ellis's illuminating article, "Liberia 1989–1994, a study of ethnic and spiritual values", in *African Affairs*, April 1995; and William Rend's article, "The business of war in Liberia", in *Current History*, May 1996.

12. Liberia's strangely distorted version of the English language acquired a new verb, "debede", an onomatopoeic word reflecting self-loading rifle power. "He debede that man" simply means "he shot that man."

13. Again a comparison with England's Wars of the Roses is illuminating. G. M. Trevelyan, after noting Fortescue's analysis of the cause of the wars as "lack of government", wrote: ". . . rival kingmakers did not seek to divide or destroy the royal authority but to control and exploit it" (*History of England*, p. 255).

Chronology

1951

October	Egypt	Guerrilla attacks on British in Suez Canal zone begin, to continue until 1952.

1952

September	Kenya	Mau Mau insurrection opens.

1953

March	Kenya	Lari massacre.
August	Morocco	Sultan Mohamed deposed.
October	Morocco	Terrorist attacks on French in Morocco begin, to continue until 1956.

1954

January	Tunisia	Insurgency opens to continue until 1956.
November	Algeria	FLN commence war against France.

1955

August	Morocco	Massacre of French in Middle Atlas.
	Algeria	Philippeville massacre.

October	Morocco	Insurgency opens in Rif and Middle Atlas.
November	Morocco	Sultan Mohamed restored.

1956

March	Morocco	Independence.
	Tunisia	Independence.
May	Algeria	Massacre of French conscripts at Palestro.
August	Algeria	Soummam Valley conference of FLN.
September	Algeria	FLN bombings open Battle of Algiers.
October	Kenya	Capture of Dedan Kimathi, effective end of Mau Mau campaign.
	Algeria	Ben Bella and others hijacked by the French.
November	Egypt	Anglo-French attack upon Suez.

1957

January	Algeria	Massu appointed to command in Algiers.
September	Algeria	Battle of Algiers ends.

1958

February	Tunisia	French aircraft bomb Sakiet.
April	Algeria	Street demonstrations in Algiers.
May	France	De Gaulle invited to form government.

1959

February	Algeria	Challe launches the first of his series of offensives.
November	Rwanda	Hutu killing of Tutsis begins.

1960

January	Algeria	Barricades Week.
March	South Africa	Sharpeville shooting opens internal conflict in South Africa.

June	Mozambique	Portuguese police and troops kill over 500 at a nationalist demonstration.
July	Congo	Independence. United Nations Force authorized.
August	Congo	Massacre of Luba in Kasai province.

1961

March	Angola	Insurgency against Portuguese opens, to continue until 1975.
April	Algeria	Abortive coup attempt by four generals.
August	Guinea-Bissau	PAIGC opens armed struggle against Portuguese, to continue until 1974.
	Congo	First UN operation in Katanga province.
September	Congo	Second UN operation in Katanga province.
	Ethiopia	Insurgency opens in Eritrea.

1962

March	Algeria	Ceasefire.
July	Algeria	Independence.
November	Ethiopia	Eritrea incorporated into Ethiopian empire. Insurgency opens.
December	Congo	Third UN operation in Katanga province.

1963

January	Congo	Katanga secession ended.
	Portuguese Guinea	PAIGC insurgency campaign develops.
September	Sudan	Southern insurgency opens, the first phase to continue until 1972.
December	Rwanda	Tutsi *inyezi* attack launched, repulsed and followed by massacre.
	Kenya	Somali *shifta* war leads to declaration of emergency.

1964

January	Zanzibar	Revolution and killing and expulsion of a large number of Arabs.
	Tanganyika	Army mutiny; British intervention.
	Kenya	Army mutiny; British intervention.
	Uganda	Army mutiny; British intervention.
August	Congo	Simba rebels occupy Stanleyville.
September	Mozambique	FRELIMO insurgency campaign opens.
November	Congo	United States and Belgian rescue operation, Stanleyville.

1965

June	Chad	FROLINAT formed.
November	Zimbabwe	Rhodesian declaration of independence.

1966

February	Namibia	First PLAN military assault.
April	Zimbabwe	Insurgency campaign against Rhodesian government opens, to continue until 1979.
May	Uganda	Ugandan army enforces deposition of Kabaka of Buganda.

1967

July	Nigeria	Civil war opens.
October	Nigeria	Federal army occupies Enugu.
	Kenya	Somali *shifta* war ends.

1968

May	Nigeria	Federal army takes Port Harcourt.
August	Chad	FROLINAT opens insurgency.

1969

February	Mozambique	Assassination (in Tanzania) of Mondlane.
April	Chad	French intervention force despatched.

1970

January	Nigeria	Biafran surrender, end of Nigerian civil war.
February	Lesotho	Rebellion opens, to continue until April.

1971

November	Eritrea	Splits open in ELF.

1972

March	Sudan	Ceasefire negotiated.
April	Burundi	Hutu uprising, followed by retributive massacre of Hutu.
December	Mozambique	Wiriyamu massacre.

1973

May	Western Sahara	Polisario formed.

1974

April	Portugal	Revolution in Lisbon begins; end of Estada Nova.
	Namibia	South Africa transfers control of forces from police to military.
September	Guinea-Bissau	Independence.

1975

June	Mozambique	Independence.
August	Angola	South African forces occupy Ruacana Falls and Calueque power station.
November	Angola	Independence.
		Failure of FNLA to take Luanda.
	Western Sahara	"Green March" of Moroccans.
December	Angola	First appearance of Cuban ground force units with Angolan MPLA troops.

1976

February	Western Sahara	Independence.
June	South Africa	Soweto uprising.
August	Uganda and Tanzania	Border clashes.

1977

January	Ethiopia	Somali invasion begins.
March	Zaire	French and Moroccan rescue operation, Kolwezi.
July	Libya	Egyptian punitive expedition.
August	Mozambique	Rhodesian forces commit Nyadzonia massacre.
September	Ethiopia	Somali forces occupy Jijiga.
November	Mozambique	Rhodesian forces commit Chimoio massacre.

1978

January	Ethiopia	Soviet, Cuban and Ethiopian forces open counter-offensive against Somalia.
March	Ethiopia	Defeat of Somalis in Ogaden War.
May	Zaire	French rescue operation, Kolwezi.
October	Tanzania	Ugandan army invades Tanzania; war opens, to continue until April 1979.

1979

January	Western Sahara	Polisario opens major offensive.
April	Uganda	Tanzanian troops enter Kampala.

1980

April	Zimbabwe	Independence.
August	Zimbabwe	Violence opens in Ndebele rural areas.

1981

February	Uganda	Museveni opens conflict against President Obote.
September	Western Sahara	Ceasefire implemented.

1982

June	Chad	Habré occupies N'Djamena.

1983

January	Sudan	Refusal of the 105th Battalion to redeploy to the north.
July	Sudan	Formation of Sudan Peoples Liberation Army.
August	Chad	Major Libyan incursion defeated.

1984

December	South Africa	Campaign of rioting and civil unrest opens.

1985

August	South Africa	Clashes between Inkatha and opponents in Durban and Pietermaritzburg.
December	Burkina Faso and Mali	Five-day border war.

1986

January	Uganda	Museveni enters Kampala.
April	Libya	United States aircraft bomb targets in Tripoli and Benghazi.

1987

January	Somalia	Northern SNM opens attacks on government forces.
October	Angola	Battle of Cuito Cuanavale opens.
December	Eritrea	Major EPLF offensive opens.

1988

July	Angola	Ceasefire agreed.
November	Chad	Deby displaces Habré in Chad.

1989

December	Liberia	NPFL entry into Liberia opens civil war.

1990

February	South Africa	Effective ending of apartheid. Inkatha begins attacks on hostels in Transvaal.
	Eritrea	EPLF occupies Massawa.
March	Namibia	Independence.
August	Liberia	ECOMOG force arrives in Liberia. Death of Doe.
October	Rwanda	First RPF assault mounted from Uganda.
December	Somalia	Aideed's USC takes control of part of Mogadishu.

1991

May	Ethiopia	EPRDF enters Addis Ababa. EPLF enter Asmara.
July	Sierra Leone	RUF insurgency opens.

1992

February	Algeria	Fundamentalist campaign opens.
June	Algeria	Assassination of Boudiaf.
October	Mozambique	Ceasefire agreed and implemented.
December	Somalia	US Marines of UNITAF land at Mogadishu.

1993

April	Eritrea	Referendum votes for independence.
October	Burundi	Ethnic violence follows murder of President Ndadye.

1994

February	Somalia	Final withdrawal of UN forces.
April	South Africa	Elections on universal franchise.
	Rwanda and Burundi	Presidents killed in aircraft crash following rocket attack.
	Rwanda	Hutu massacre of Tutsi opens. RPF begins invasion.
July	Rwanda	RPF enters Kigali.

1995

August	Liberia	Abuja agreement for ceasefire.

1996

May	Central African Republic	French military intervention following army mutiny.
August	Somalia	Death of Aideed.
November	Sierra Leone	Ceasefire agreed.

1997

May	Sierra Leone	Officers' coup opens conflict with ECOMOG forces.
	Zaire (Congo)	Kabila and ADFL army enter Kinshasa.
June	Congo (Brazzaville)	Faction warfare opens.

Selected reading

Note: This bibliography has been selected for the relevance to the operational aspects of warfare rather than any overall political analysis.

Abi-Saab, G. *The United Nations operation in the Congo, 1960–64* (Oxford, 1978).

Abshire, D. M. & Samuels, N. A. *Portuguese Africa, a handbook* (London, 1969).

Africa south of the Sahara (London, 1996).

Ageron, C. R. *Modern Algeria, a history from 1830 to the present.* Translated by M. Brett (London, 1991).

Aloa, A. [Article in] *Jane's intelligence review yearbook: the world in conflict 1994/95.*

Amadi, E. *Sunset in Biafra* (London, 1973).

Arnold, G. *Wars in the Third World since 1945* (London, 1995).

Barbier, M. *Le Conflit du Sahara Occidental.* French text (Paris, 1971).

Baynham, S. *Military power and politics in Black Africa* (London, 1986).

Beckett, I & Pimlott, J. *Armed forces and modern counter-insurgency* (London, 1985).

Bekker, S (ed.). *Capturing the event: conflict trends in the Natal region, 1986–92* (Durban, 1992).

Berdal, G. J. *Angola under the Portuguese: the myth and the reality* (London, 1978).

Bender, M. "The resumption of civil war in Angola", *Jane's Intelligence Review*, June 1993.

Berman, E. *Managing arms in peace processes: Mozambique* (Geneva, 1996).

Bhebe, N. & Ranger, T. *Soldiers in Zimbabwe's liberation war* (London, 1995).

Blaxland, G. *The regiments depart* (London, 1971).

Blaxland, J. M. & Collins, R. O. *Requiem for the Sudan: war, drought and disaster relief on the Nile* (Boulder, CO, 1995).

Bridgland, F. *The war for Africa* (Gibraltar, 1990).

Clayton, A. *Communication for new loyalties: African soldiers songs* (Athens, OH, 1978).

Clayton, A. *Counter-insurgency in Kenya, 1952–60* (Manhattan, KS, 1984).

Clayton, A. *Factions, foreigners and fantasies: the civil war in Liberia* (Camberley, England, 1995).

Clayton, A. *The wars of French decolonization* (London, 1994).

Clayton, A. *The Zanzibar revolution and its aftermath* (London, 1981).

Copson, R. W. *Africa's wars and prospects for peace* (Armonk, NY, 1994).

Cornwall, B. *The bush rebels: a personal account of Black revolt in Africa* (London, 1973).

Daly, M. W. & Sikainga, A. A. *Civil war in the Sudan* (London, 1993).

Davidson, B. *The guerillas cause: a history of guerillas in Africa* (London, 1981).

Ejoor, D. A. *Reminiscences* (Lagos, 1989).

Erlich, H. *The struggle over Eritrea 1962–78: war and revolution in the Horn of Africa* (Stanford, CA, 1983).

Erulin, P. *Zaire: sauver Kolwezi*. French text (Paris, 1980).

Fauvet, P. "Roots of counter-revolution: the Mozambique National Resistance", *Review of African Political Economy* **29**, 1984.

Flower, K. *Serving secretly: Rhodesia into Zimbabwe 1964–1981* (London, 1987).

Geffray, C. *La Cause des armes de Mozambique: anthropologie d'une guerre civile*. French text (Paris, 1990).

Godwin, P. *Mukiwa, a white boy in Africa* (London, 1996).

Goodwin-Gill, G. & Cohn, I. *Child soldiers: the role of children in armed conflicts* (Oxford, 1994).

Hastings, A. *Wiriyamu* (London, 1974).

Heitman, H.-R. *War in Angola: the final South African phase* (Gibraltar, 1990).

Heggoy, A. A. *Insurgency and counter-insurgency in Algeria* (Bloomington, IN, 1972).

Henderson, I. & Goodhart, P. *The hunt for Kimathi* (London, 1958).

Hodges, T. *Western Sahara: the roots of a desert war* (Westport, CN, 1983).

Horne, A. *A savage war of peace: Algeria 1954–62* (London, 1985).

Hoskyns, C. *The Congo since independence, January 1960–December 1961* (Oxford, 1969).

Human Rights Watch/Africa. *Mauritania's campaign of terror* (New York, 1994).

Illiffe, J. *Africans: the history of a continent* (Cambridge, 1995).

Ingham, K. *Obote, a political biography* (London, 1994).

Innes, D., Kentridge, M. & Perold, H. *Power and profit: politics, labour and business in South Africa* (Cape Town, 1992).

Iyob, R. *The Eritrean struggle for independence: domination, resistance, nationalism 1941–1993* (Cambridge, 1995).

Jorré, J. de St J. *The Nigerian civil war* (London, 1972).

Kane-Berman, J. *Political violence in South Africa* (Johannesburg, 1993).

Keegan, J. (ed.). *World armies* (London, 1983).

Kentridge, M. *An unofficial war: inside the conflict in Pietermaritzburg* (Cape Town, 1990).

Lan, D. *Guns and rain: guerrillas and spirit mediums in Zimbabwe* (London, 1983).

Lee, J. M. *African armies and civil order* (London, 1969).

Lefèvre, E. *Tchad 1983: Opération Manta*. French text (Paris, 1984).

Leys, C. & Saul, J. S. *Namibia's liberation struggle: the two-edged sword* (London, 1995).

McKenzie Smith, J. *Breaking with the past? A consideration of Yoweri Museveni's National Resistance Movement, and of social and political action in Uganda during its government* (Edinburgh, 1993).

Magyar, K. P. & Danopoulos, C. P. (eds). *Prolonged wars: a post-nuclear challenge* (Washington, 1994).

Maloba, W. O. *Mau Mau and Kenya: analysis of a peasant revolt* (Bloomington, IN, 1993).

Marcum, J. A. *The Angolan revolution: the anatomy of an explosion* [2 vols] (Cambridge, MA, 1969).

Martin, D. & Johnson, P. *The struggle for Zimbabwe: the Chimurenga war* (London, 1981).

Mazrui, A. A. (ed.). *The warrior tradition in modern Africa* (Leiden, Holland, 1977).

Mmbando, S. M. *The Tanzania–Uganda war in pictures* (Dar es Salaam, 1980).

Mondlane, E. *The struggle for Mozambique* (London, 1969).

Moorcraft, P. & McLaughlin, P. *Chimurenga! The war in Rhodesia, 1965–1980* (Marshalltown, IA, 1982).

Munslow, B. *Mozambique: the revolution and its origins* (London, 1983).

Murray, M. J. *The revolution deferred: the painful birth of post-apartheid South Africa* (London and New York, 1994).

Museveni, Y. K. *Sowing the mustard seed* (London, 1997).

O'Ballance, E. *The secret war in the Sudan, 1955–72* (London, 1977).

Obasanjo, O. *My command, an account of the Nigerian civil war, 1967–70* (Ibadan, 1980).

Odom, T. P. *Dragon operations: hostage rescue in the Congo 1964–65* (Washington, DC, n. d.).

Omara-Otunnu, A. *Politics and the military in Uganda 1890–1985* (Oxford, 1987).

Oyewole, F. *Reluctant rebel* (London, 1975).

Portheu de la Morandière, F. (ed.). *Soldats du Djebel.* French text (Paris, 1979).

Prunier, G. *The Rwanda crisis 1959–1994: history of a genocide* (London, 1995).

Ranger, T. *Peasant consciousness and guerilla war in Zimbabwe* (London, 1983).

Reed, D. *111 days in Stanleyville* (London, 1966).

Rotberg, R. & Mazrui, A. A. (eds). *Protest and power in Black Africa* (New York, 1970).

Spikes, D. *Angola and the politics of intervention* (Jefferson, NC, 1993).

Steenkamp, W. *South Africa's border war* (Gibraltar, 1989).

Urban, M. "Soviet intervention and the Ogaden counter-offensive of 1978", *Journal of the Royal United Service Institution for Defence Studies* **128**(2), June 1983.

van der Waals, W. S. *Portugal's war in Angola* (Rivonia, 1993).

Ventner, A. J. *Report on Portugal's war in Guiné-Bissau*, Munger African Library Notes No. 19 (Pasadena, CA, 1973).

Vines, A. *Renamo: terrorism in Mozambique* (York, 1991).

von Horn, C. *Soldiering for peace* (London, 1966).

Welch, C. E. *No farewell to arms?* (New York, 1987).

Index